North Atlantic Civilization at WAR

North Atlantic Civilization at WAR

The World War II Battles of Sky, Sand, Snow, Sea, and Shore

As Experienced by
a Soldier,
a Ship
and some Spirits

Through the Battles of
Britain
El Alamein
Stalingrad
the Atlantic
and Normandy

Patrick Lloyd Hatcher

An East Gate Book

M.E. Sharpe
Armonk, New York
London, England

An East Gate Book

Copyright © 1998 by M. E. Sharpe, Inc.

Library of Congress Cataloging-in-Publication Data

Hatcher, Patrick Lloyd.
North Atlantic civilization at war : the World War II battles of sky, sand, snow, sea, and shore / Patrick Lloyd Hatcher.
p.   cm.
"An East gate book."
Includes bibliographical references and index.
ISBN 0-7656-0135-4 (alk. paper)
1. World War, 1939–1945—Campaigns.   2. Battles—History—20th century.   I. Title.
D743.H38   1997
940.54′2—dc21   97-14509
CIP
Printed in the United States of America

MV (c)   10   9   8   7   6   5   4   3   2   1

For Robert, Ted, Michele, Brandon, and Nicole Hatcher

Civilizations, vast or otherwise, can always be located on a map. An essential part of their character depends on the constraints or advantages of their geographical situation. . . . To discuss civilization is to discuss space, land and its contours, climate, vegetation, animal species and natural or other advantages. It is also to discuss what humanity has made of these basic conditions: agriculture, stock-breeding, food, shelter, clothing, communications, industry and so on. . . . Much of the West and its dependencies today, in fact, are grouped around [the Atlantic Ocean], rather as the Roman world of former times was grouped around the Mediterranean.

—Fernand Braudel, *A History of Civilizations*
(Allen Lane, The Penguin Press, 1994, pp. 9–10).

Contents

Acknowledgments

One of the perks of teaching is an occasional invitation to lead a tour. If the lectures cover anything that happened in living memory, such as World War II, the teacher has three audiences. Members of the first lived through the events, often correcting, or adding to, the lecture based on what happened to them. Their's is an "I was there" tradition. Members of the second, born right after the events, inherit the received wisdom of their family and friends who were there. Their's is an oral tradition. The third audience, at least two generations removed, fold the events—if they are ahistorical Americans—into ancient history, encountered, if at all, in a novel or, more likely, at the movies.[1] Their's is a visual tradition; their experience of war, if any, involves computers, lasers, and satellites.

I am a historian. As such, I was trained to make a little sense out of the past. In 1994, I gave a series of lectures on two tours of Europe, the occasion being the fiftieth anniversary of the allied landings in Normandy. Like those historic landings, my groups came to the beaches in waves. I experimented on the first wave, which started from Paris in May. The next crossed over from London in June; they received a corrected version. To both I owe a debt of gratitude for suffering through my rehearsals for this book.

In giving the lectures, I tried to reach all three audiences simultaneously, especially since I wanted a book to come out of the effort.

Tired of the traditional approach, which emphasized the grand strategy and battle plans of generals, I incorporated work from social historians who had looked at the home front and the efforts of ordinary citizens. I decided to include the impact of popular culture—the motion pictures and music of the war years. Every time my London group boarded our bus, they were bombarded by the songs of Vera Lynn singing the odes of WW II Britain. Or they had to listen to the plots of Humphrey Bogart's war movies and the lyrics of Irving Berlin's war-inspired songs. During the several weeks we spent together, I had time to test and retest my arguments. (Beware a tour led by a historian contemplating a new book!)

When I organized the lectures, I already possessed one of the ordinary objects that I planned to use in illustrating the haphazard nature of war. The object, a bottle of rum, came from a liquor horde that reportedly once belonged to the British Army, then the German Army, and finally the American Army. In 1982, my friends Bill and Billie Haynes gave me the bottle of rum along with its printed history while I was in Germany visiting them. I have them to thank for starting me on its trail.

In the process of telling my first group the history of the rum, I made a discovery. One member who had been born after the war, hence part of the transition-to-ancient school of history, showed me a photograph of her father with a similar bottle of rum, the photograph taken in occupied Austria in 1945. She and her sister had also inherited a collection of their father's wartime letters. Upon closer examination of the photograph and letters, I had unexpectedly found my typical soldier. In lieu of a professional or college graduate, I wanted a kid, an eighteen year old. Here he was. My thanks to Elizabeth Crocker O'Neill and Katherine H. Crocker for allowing me to quote from their father's letters.[2]

I repeated the rum story with my second group, adding the history of rum in the British and American navies. A few days later, we were in Portsmouth, and among the many sleek vessels set to restage the Channel crossing, including the royal yacht, was the American "ugly duckling," the Liberty ship SS *Jeremiah O'Brien*. I recognized the *O'Brien* as the third ordinary object that I wanted for my new history. When the *O'Brien* and I returned from Channel waters to the San Francisco Bay area, I visited the ship, the ship's office at Fort Mason,

San Francisco, and, through the help of Marci Hooper and Gene Anderson, was able to incorporate the *O'Brien* into my history. Both Marci and Gene made this part of the history a reality, and I thank both of them for their time and support.

Possessing three ordinary players, I searched for a larger theme. I had decided not to include the Pacific operations because my emphasis was on the ideological impetus behind WW II, which I saw as one clash in a trio of political wars that dominated the twentieth century. Japan's attempt at empire was an old-fashioned land grab; Tokyo had no political ideology to export. Once I had decided to stay within the larger Eurocentered world, I chose to think of it in terms of the North Atlantic basin. And I wanted geography and climate to be the major determinates of the thrusts and turns that the war took. In that way I hoped to add another dimension for historians to use as they continue trying to make sense of that war.

I am a great believer in visiting the scene of the evidence. In a series of trips, I visited southern England, northern France, southern Italy, northern Africa, and southern Russia. By ship I crossed the North Atlantic twice, once from Bermuda to Liverpool on a British freighter, the *Santander,* and once from New York City to Bremerhaven on a troop ship, the USS *Rose.* I have steamed up the Rhine, Elbe, Oder, and Vistula Rivers, as well as down the Danube and across the Black Sea. I have walked along stretches of North African coast and spent time in Africa's inferno, the Sahara. Moscow and St. Petersburg have welcomed me to a Russian winter. I have crossed the English Channel in all seasons, from Dunkirk to Dover, from Dover to Calais, from Portsmouth to Cherbourg. I even invaded the Burbank, California, backlot at Warner Brothers where most of Bogart's wartime films were shot. To all my hosts and hostesses, a debt of gratitude is owed.

Sheila and Chalmers Johnson read first drafts and made suggestions for improvements. Massimo Franco guided me through Italian sources. Stephen McKae taught me about wartime rationing, especially of rubber. Everyone has a favorite librarian. Mine is Berkeley's Marc A. Levin. My map makers are two gifted Berkeley women—Cherie Semans and Jennie Freeman. No book makes it to publication without good editors and their staff. Mine were at M.E. Sharpe. The results are this book, my attempt to make a little bit of sense out of a big bit of history.

Notes

1. Anne Cronin, "America's Grade on 20th Century European Wars: F," *New York Times,* December 3, 1995, E5. See also Mark C. Carnes, ed., *Past Imperfect: History According to the Movies* (New York: Henry Holt, 1995).

2. Elizabeth Crocker O'Neill and Katherine H. Crocker own the copyright to these letters. Ruel Richard Crocker, Jr.'s personal letter © 1943–45 Ruel Richard Crocker, Jr.

North Atlantic Civilization at WAR

Prologue

The twentieth century's second Great War roared into action on September 1, 1939; it sputtered to a halt on May 8, 1945. During those six years came the killing, fifty million more or less, almost a million a month. Amid three titanic struggles, World War II is the midway war, preceded by World War I (1914–1918) and followed by the Cold War (1947–1989). A threesome, they dominated a cruel century, a latter-day version of the Hundred Years' War. Like that earlier Anglo–French fighting, periods of peace interrupted the strife, a holiday from hating. In the case of World War I, Robert Graves's farewell to arms reminds a reader of the American, Ernest Hemingway, who bade goodbye to all that the first Great War had meant. Even the defeated of 1918 sighed for Erich Maria Remarque's quiet, on all fronts.[1]

Neither the farewells and goodbyes nor the quiet had finality. Robert Graves, who barely escaped death in WW I but lived to see his eldest son die in WW II, discovered that the years from 1919 to 1938 marked only an interlude, a long weekend. Both Albert Einstein and Sigmund Freud, to name but two, tried to elongate this interregnum of peace, but to no avail.[2] The physicist and the psychoanalyst could not postpone the century's propensity for megamurder. Into the woods of war humanity again streamed, this time many motoring toward death as war revved up its machinery in 1939. In like manner, George Kennan, present at the postwar creation of Soviet–American enmity, captured the short intermission following the end of hot combat in 1945 and the frigid contest starting in 1947.

Classified one way, the three upheavals were one extended crucifixion, a political war of the North Atlantic people.[3] True, the wars ranged globally, but, in the main, the core actors and debates remained in those states that either fronted on or had nearby sea access to the North Atlantic basin. An extended warrior tribe inhabited the periphery of this ocean. Many things divided them; many things they shared, especially the tendency to fierce warfare. In the seventeenth century, they fought their religious wars; in the eighteenth century, commercial wars; in the nineteenth century, imperial wars. For the twentieth century, their leaders composed a deadly dirge in which political dervishes whirled whole populations into a dance of death: choreographed demonology.[4]

Two qualities exemplify this era of total warfare: mass bereavement and the mobilization of the imagination. Death occurred in such numbers that no citizens escaped a sense of loss of kindred and friends. To fortify the hatred, states employed artists to mobilize the imagination of citizens. From motion pictures to popular music, all joined in the battle for their ocean basin.

More that any other geographer, Fernand Braudel introduced modern historians to water-basin studies, their geography and climates as cradles for human endeavors of all kinds, including wars. Braudel's basin was the Mediterranean Sea, his century the sixteenth, his leading combatants the Spanish Hapsburg king, Philip II, with allies, versus the Ottoman Turkish sultan, Selim II, with vassals.

With an Austrian, Don Juan, in command of the last crusading fleet, the culminating sea victory, the Battle of Lepanto of October 1571, did not break Ottoman power. Instead, it checked it, leaving this last Mohammedan caliphate to decline over the next three centuries, the withered sultanate on the Golden Horn.[5] Of greater importance, checking meant a strategic shift that reversed nine hundred years of forward thrust by the Islamic East toward the Christian West.

The West absorbed what Islam—the "intermediate civilization" between the Orient and the Occident, between antiquity and modernity—had preserved.[6] With a quickened pace brought on by the industrial revolution that occurred first in the West, the North Atlantic people globalized their civilization by the end of the nineteenth century. Yet internal contradictions abounded, enough to bring on the blood bashings to follow. Whereas Islam gave the eastern Mediterranean an encompassing world view, the West had rocketed from low to high renaissance, from reformation to its counter, from enlightenment to its reaction.

At the end of the nineteenth century, proponents for a democratic society hoped that their vision would triumph. When in power, they wanted a balance between a representative democracy that protected the individual as guaranteed by private property and a social democracy that promoted the community as guaranteed by public goods. As secularists, they rendered what was due to Caesar, leaving religious rendering a private matter. They offered a compromise between conflicting national impulses that Alexis de Tocqueville described as individualism versus communitarianism.[7]

Imperfect in early execution, democracy as a political system complemented the scientific world view, which based its primacy on the advance of Western rationalism, a force that had placed North Atlantic civilization in the vanguard of social, political, and economic progress.[8] This progress was centered mainly in France, Britain, and the United States, which had progressed in their transformations from medieval to modern, but whose progress was marred by corrosive civil–religious wars and political–social revolutions. Severed heads of kings served as talismanic busts for the dethronement transition: in the case of pitiless France, the head of the queen also, whereas the United States settled for a political decapitation from King George III.[9]

Workers from the industrializing democracies also paid the early, and very high, price of the industrial revolution. This added economic and social turmoil to the political struggle. Notwithstanding the fact that they had miles yet to travel in search for a just society, the politicians of franchise democracy—socialists in France, liberals in Britain, and progressives in the United States—began to smell victory at the close of the nineteenth century.[10] Mass enfranchisement set them apart from their ocean neighbors. In fact, democracy confronted strong pockets of resistance among several North Atlantic states.

A class analysis reveals the contradictions prevalent in the West in 1900. In the years leading up to the First World War, democratic forces faced a substantial holdover of the old order, the aristocracy, remnants of divine absolutism. As a group they blocked social progress. Having suffered a withering blow from the French Revolution, three truncated versions of absolutism, most especially the Russian variant, failed in the great transformation from authoritarianism to republicanism. Vested interests centered in Berlin, Vienna, and St. Petersburg refused to abolish the privileges of birth within their respective North Atlantic empires. Inside their borders, the upper classes found new allies in that last refuge of scoundrels, virulent nationalism, a type of triumphant tribalism.[11]

Tribe against tribe, the North Atlantic went to war. Against monarchial despotism stood the three representative democracies capitaled in Paris, London, and Washington. Holding their imperial noses, Russian aristocrats allied their Slavic empire with the ordurous Franks and Anglo-Saxons as the lesser evil. Together they fought the Teutonic tribes that Berlin and Vienna herded toward the slaughterhouse.

Democracy's alliance with Russian despotism did not survive the war; in 1917 a coup brought a new Soviet state whose revolutionary impulses thundered down the rest of the century, until all the noise it could muster in 1989 was its death rattle. Even with Lenin capitulating to Berlin's terms, by the eleventh hour on the eleventh day of the eleventh month of 1918, royal absolutism died in the western trenches of France and Flanders.

Victorious in this first epic phase of political strife, the North Atlantic democracies, weakened by the Great Depression of the 1930s, soon found themselves facing fascism, which, in the countries where it routed weaker democratic forces, had attracted a frightened middle class to its fashionable banner. This middle group, especially the petite bourgeoisie, blocked political progress. Again war, again victory, this time over fascist felons.

In a repeat performance, the Soviet Union, after a flirtation with Nazi Germany lasting from 1939 to 1941, found itself in league with democratic republics against Hitler. Forced into a war that none of them wanted, the three allies—the United States, the United Kingdom, and USSR—differed in their internal politics and fought for differing national interests. The United States, a constitutional republic, fought for opening the world to American influence; the United Kingdom, a constitutional monarchy, fought for preserving the British Empire; and the USSR, a constitutional dictatorship, fought for securing its extended borders: to open, to preserve, to secure.[12]

Unconditional German surrender led to another shaky peace; then, without decent interval, war came again, the 1945 victors-of-convenience splitting into two camps. On this occasion, what the German philosopher Karl Jaspers called the new fact—nuclear weapons—kept the last phase of civil strife cold, but a war nonetheless.[13]

In its third struggle, democracy faced communism, whose leaders located their class base in the laboring strata, the proletariat. Unfortunately for its unchained adherents, this alliance between state bureaucrats and socialist toilers blocked economic progress. Making almost everyone equally poor seemed its biggest achievement. That failure, more than any other, brought it down, as cold combat consumed a national fortune.[14] By 1989, a still-imperfect representative democracy survived as a North Atlantic model, while the core of communism—evildoing on a grand scale—went the way of absolutism and fascism before it.

From 1914 to 1989, the North Atlantic population suffered from an infection that mimicked a hemorrhagic virus in which millions died of an acquired immunity against peace. No one was more surprised than the combatants themselves. At the dawn of the twentieth century, many citizens of the North Atlantic world thought themselves safe from the warring disease. Even pessimists had hoped that their region had established a peaceful order within, while living in a state of delicate balance with the battle-driven world of terror that existed outside the Atlantic core. Only later did they understand that a social virus could mutate inside a polity and return twice as strong, immune to philosophic remedies the way that new strains of syphilis were immune to pharmaceutical prescriptions.

Three segments of one century-long war, the totality of destruction by this trio reached further than the physical presence of rubble piles. War corrupts, and total wars corrupt totally. Here corruption was both visible and invisible. Befouling the air, bloated corpses littered the battle areas, as millions did not even receive the decency of burial. Of greater importance than their stench, the odorless decomposition of the human spirit was the chief victim of twentieth-century warfare.

The overture war, World War I, set the tone. Its great battle, Verdun, lit the ice-blue fire for the cremation of the nineteenth-century ideal of progress. Germany crawled out of Verdun's immolation, its immature political culture castrated, leaving for its predecessor at Weimar mainly sun-starved Nordic nihilism, a trivial hedonism.[15] Spain played the blazing intermezzo, its civil war forever captured in Pablo Picasso's antiwar masterpiece, *Guernica*. The lightning-fast movements were reserved for World War II, badly conducted by banal troglodytes bunkered beneath Berlin, a Nazism the color of dried, blackish-red vomit.

For encores came glum-grey peripheral wars, a spate of Asian and Middle Eastern combats, played from major to minor. Some long— Vietnam and Afghanistan—some short—Six-Day and Yom Kippur— American and Soviet ushers tried to act as mob-control agents at unfinished symphonies banged out mainly by local yokels.[16] During these Cold War tempi changes, many causes marched to their own drum. This trio of wars needed a Goya to paint them, a Wagner to score them.

All three military stages of this century-long civil combat deserve their telling within this analytical framework. This volume, however, concerns itself with the second stage, and only that part that deals with the greater North Atlantic basin.

Overview

Like Braudel's Mediterranean basin, the North Atlantic has a shore-line, a strip of fertile land reaching inland, and the beginnings of hills that lead to mountains. Beyond lay rich hinterlands, plateaus and plains that form the continental backdrop. Adjacent seas and gulfs invite deep penetrations; for Braudel's model these include the Black and Red Seas, for the North Atlantic basin they include the eastern Mediterra-nean and Baltic Seas, in addition to the Gulf of Mexico and the Gulf of St. Lawrence.[17]

Rivers flow down to the North Atlantic basin; they also offer gate-ways to the interior. Peninsulas—some large, some small—punctuate the coast. Cities appear near rivers or bays; a coastal and riverine civilization flourishes.[18] Climates fluctuate; the farther from water, the warmer or colder, depending on how the continent adjusts to the sea-sons. Facing an ocean, not a sea, each of these North Atlantic features measures larger than Braudel's model. Moreover, differences exist.

The North Atlantic washes east–west, from Europe to North Amer-ica, whereas Braudel's basin runs north–south, Europe to Africa. In diet, North Atlantic people generally favor animal fats to olive oil, beef to lamb, dairy to goat products. Because of climatic conditions, North Atlantic people prefer the warmth of wool to the sheen of silk. Atlantic rainfall suffices for a greater variety of crops, a richer soil rewards agriculture, and abundant mineral resources enriches mining. Deeper forests predominate, offering a larger diversity of timber. More remains, but let it suffice that the settling of the North Atlantic basin gave each settlement some similarities as well as obvious differences.[19]

When this basin erupted into war, combatants faced the constraints of their geography and climate, especially when they fought at the periphery of their core. Never was this more the case than in World War II, in which the geography and climate of five military thrusts heavily influenced the outcome. Chronologically, the five propel this tale from the outbreak of war to its conclusion. As nature's quintet, they include the battles of the sky, sand, snow, sea, and shore. More precisely, they are the air battle of Britain, the desert battle of El Alamein, the winter battle of Stalingrad, the logistical battle of the North Atlantic, and the invasion battle for the Norman shore of France.

In retelling these five turning points, little attention need be paid to war leaders and their traits: a courageous Churchill, a defiant de Gaulle, a horrific Hitler, a resolute Roosevelt, a satanic Stalin, to name but a few. In this reiteration, the analysis needs the touch of the ordinary; for our purposes, three subjects taken from everyday life—a soldier, a ship, and some spirits—suffice to illustrate the experience of the millions who did the dying.

More than any other biographer, Jonathan Spence introduced modern historians to small events, commonplace objects, and insignificant individuals as examples of human endeavors of all kinds.[20] His research methods are the opposite of Braudel's. The smaller the detail, the better. Spence looks for the DNA of history. His microprocessor fuses the nitty gritty of history into wholeness. Spence's methodology is microscopic, whereas Braudel's is telescopic. Combining both methodologies favors completeness, the tapestry of a time and place.

Three Ordinary Subjects

Wars begin as exceptional events; extraordinary egotists begin them, even more egotistical exceptionalists win them. Between the beginning and the end, ordinary folk fight them. In meeting the demands of combat, that which is commonplace pins together the fabric of fighting, its tactics and strategies. Concentrating on one soldier, one ship, and one supply of spirits simplifies this saga.

Allowing age precedence, we start with the oldest member of our trio. Out of Missouri he came. Ruel Richard Crocker, Jr., or Red as he signed himself, hailed from Iron county in the southeast Ozark hills of Missouri, on the far periphery of the North Atlantic basin. Born on October 28, 1924, in the village of Middlebrook, so small a place that his mother estimated the population as one hundred souls counting the chickens, Red came of age as the Great Depression of the 1930s tore into working-class aspirations.

When the army inducted him on April 27, 1943, Red was eighteen, still a kid. Red's father was working the docks in St. Louis, and his mother was managing a St. Louis boarding house. Seeking better economic opportunities, Red's family, minus the new inductee, headed for golden California's war industries. Red's parents settled in Alameda, working in shipyards that launched the ships that transported the soldiers and supplies to battle. Even his mother worked, not as a ship's riveter as in the case of the thousands of liberated-by-necessity "Rosy the Riveters," but as a shipyard guard. All around her women filled the vacant jobs, some as lady brakemen on the railroads, some as pilots for the airlines.[21]

Initially, Red-the-GI trained in the United States: Wyoming, Arkansas, Alabama, and New York. Next, Red-the-liberator soldiered in Europe: Britain, France, Germany, and Austria. On every stop along his North Atlantic journey, he wrote his "Dear Folks." Luckily these letters survived the war, neatly bundled by his mother. While training on the home-front, he reported on his military experiences from state-to-state:

> September 10, 1943: My Daddy: I'll bet you are enjoying meeting fellows from all over the States and listening to the stories that they have to tell. I know I do.

Once in Europe he wrote as frequently:

> December 20, 1944: Dear Folks: Was standing guard the other night and heard some school children singing Christmas carols down in the village. . . . This England inspires me to read up on my history. That's funny because I always did hate history.

Red and his buddies had popular figures to lend credence to what they felt they had to do, namely, kill and, in some instances, be killed. Both visual and audio icons abounded. Of the many, we examine two:

Humphrey Bogart in motion pictures and Irving Berlin in musical comedies—Hollywood and Broadway. They represent popular culture's support of the war effort; their movies and melodies campaigned alongside Red.

Critics might object to evidence obtained from such mundane items as cinema and song. One should remember that, at the time of creation, most creations rank as mundane; later, intellectuals lift certain pieces to the high altar of art. The Dutch historian Johan Huizinga, who wrote as the twentieth century started its warring, ably described the Burgundian Netherlands of the fourteenth and fifteenth centuries through ordinary paintings and ballads.[22] Huizinga possessed a storyteller's acumen. In his day he shared his tale via a masterful book; today's history might receive its telling in a master's film.

When the world was half a thousand years older than Huizinga's 1440s, all events had a much sharper focus. How? The camera replaced the brush, film replaced canvas, the piano replaced the mandolin. Music broadened its scope—opera, symphony, musical comedies. Static paintings became motion paintings; in both they reflected their times. These new pictures could sing and speak their stories, the collective myths of memory. As for songs, for all we know the sandal-shod Homer sang portions of his epic poetry of Western civilization's first great war. By such means the Greek tribe knew its legends. Storytelling and singing crystalize the emotions; they tell us who we were, who we are, and who we might become. That, at least, is what they told Red, a man "of twists and turns, driven time and again off course."[23]

The second eldest of our ordinary threesome, the spirits date from 1927, day and month no longer available. To a North Atlantic warrior, especially to the millions of civilian conscripts, spirits meant alcoholic beverages. These ocean-bred patriots demanded an occasional drink; in fact, as occasional as possible. Drink relieved the long hours of boredom that marked most of war's waste; Evelyn Waugh required a trilogy, *Sword of Honor,* to explain how his WW II hero spent 99 percent of his time waiting for something to happen. Drink also helped blur the memory of the 1 percent of the time devoted to killing.

Among the first to act with alcoholic libation specifically in mind, the British military instituted regular doses of spirits. If Napoleon's Grande Armée marched via its cuisine (at a minimum, bread and wine), the British Royal Navy sailed via its drink (at a minimum, two gulps of rum). The juice of the colonies, rum came from the Americas, more specifically the West Indies.[24]

Here, on the periphery of the North Atlantic basin, most of the sugar islands conveniently belonged to a group of core North Atlantic empires. Rum derives its name from the Latin *saccharum,* meaning sugar. After extracting the bulk of sugar from the cane, Caribbean colonialists distilled their liquid-brown spirits, which joined the gins, scotches, cognacs, beers, and vodkas that originated in the imperial homelands.

Vice-admiral Edward Vernon, a Nelson-in-miniature who took the Spanish colonial town of Porto Bello in November 1739 with six men-of-war, had much to do with the manner in which the British Navy issued rum. By Vernon's time, rum had replaced beer in those squadrons operating in the West Indies. Vernon insisted that the purser mix the rum ration with sugar and lime to make it more palatable. This mixture needed a name; the British seamen christened it after Admiral Vernon's waterproof boat cloak, his old Grogram. Thereby, grog entered the sailor's vocabulary.

By the time Queen Victoria began her reign, rum had triumphed throughout the fleet as the seagoing drink of choice. Officers tended to stay with wine, for which they received an alarmingly liberal ceiling: an admiral, not to exceed six tons (1,260 gallons) per annum; for a captain first/second rates, three tons; for a lieutenant, a half ton! The British Army followed the rum trail. For example, in the subzero weather of the Crimean War of 1853–1856, the British Army issued soldiers a rum ration in the morning and evening.[25]

Before they rebelled, sailors from the thirteen English-speaking colonies in North America enjoyed the rum tradition. More than three thousand of them served with Admiral Vernon in the campaign against the Spanish Main, called the War of Jenkin's Ear. Among their ranks, Lawrence Washington, older brother of George, upon returning to Virginia at the close of hostilities, built the plantation, which he named Mount Vernon after the admiral. Later, having won independence under the leadership of Lawrence's brother, these rustic rebels found it easier to give up George III than old devil rum. In fact, the American Navy has never given up its fondness for this tradition.[26]

Unlike the eastern slope of the North Atlantic, the western side lost the battle with the temperance movement. In April 1914, Josephus Daniels, secretary of the Navy under President Woodrow Wilson, liquidated the drinking of alcoholic beverages on U.S. Navy ships as well as within any navy yard or station. A teetotaler from rural North Carolina, Daniels presented a target the press could not refuse. One cartoon depicted him as admiral of the USS *Grapejuice Pinafore*. But his order stuck.[27] This meant that American sailors had to compete for their drinks ashore, and compete they did.

With the coming of prohibition, 1920 to 1934, rum moved from legal to illegal status. In fact, the United States fought an undeclared rum war at sea. Rum-runners tried to smuggle their liquid loot to rum-thirsty citizens. From the Caribbean they came. They steamed up the Atlantic coast along a sea path known as Rum Row. Large mother ships remained beyond the three-mile limit. They offloaded onto small swift craft, speedboats being the favorite. Then the cat-and-mouse game began. On shore duty, the U.S. Treasury Department, the Customs Service, and the Bureau of Internal Revenue blocked delivery. On sea duty, the first line of defense, the Coast Guard blocked landings. All to little avail. Americans simply refused to stop drinking, even with the severe penalties under the Volstead Act. For fourteen years, they thumbed their noses at the law when thirsty for liquor.[28]

The history of our World War II rum reads like a travelogue. Distilled in 1927 at the height of American prohibition, during World War II this Jamaican product traveled in the company of English gin, Scotch whiskey, and French cognac. Its first war mission came when it was shipped from Britain intended for the British forces' messes and clubs in North Africa. Approximately 500,000 gallons went to Tobruk; on June 20, 1942, General Erwin Rommel's Afrika Korps captured Tobruk and the immense booty stored there. The British had even bought Munich-bottled Löwenbrau beer in Lisbon and conveyed it onto the sands of Tobruk. Surprised by British largess, the Germans drank.[29]

Burdened by an oversupply of spirits, Rommel's staff shipped the excess to Italy. Contemporaries "report that about 1.9 million liters of liquor in casks left North Africa for the Italian port of Anzio." Carried by German supply ships, they managed to dodge the British blockade. "The cargo was stored in the warehouse of a local brewery in Nettuno, a small town near Anzio."[30] Former Chief Petty Officer Peter Zentis, recalled the journey when he was later interviewed about the crossing.[31] For fifteen months the liquor stock remained a captive in Nettuno, losing only about 20 percent to Il Duce's local supporters. The day of liberation came on January 22, 1944, when the allies included Nettuno in their Anzio beachhead.

As the barometer of blood rose up the leg of the Italian peninsula, U.S. authorities decided that their captured casks proved impractical and unwieldy. They ordered that what remained of the stock, after several celebrations, be bottled. The archives of the Rome Chamber of Commerce show that in 1945 the authorities chose the Delva Company to do the bottling.[32] Owing to wartime conditions, 1,420,000 bottles of all sizes, colors, and shapes soon swallowed what remained of the liquor. An official Italian document, Tax Control No. UTF 213, not only authenticates the bottling but also cites the designer and printer of the labels, the P. Casette Company in Rome. (The label designer printed the Italian spelling of rum—*Rhun.*)

Going into occupation duty in the former Third Reich, military units in possession of the "Nettuno Secret" wanted their liquid treasure to follow. Hence, they decided to ship the stock to Linz, Austria. Judging by the dates on the old Italian newspapers used as packaging material, the rail shipments must have started in late 1945 and ended by August 1946. The forwarding company of Chierichetti & Torniani in Milan substantiated the shipment to Linz, as did Dr. Mando Zanchi, a former executive of the Delva Company.[33]

Not all the liquor arrived in Linz. In 1946 one shipment of bottled joy made its way by rail across the Soviet zone of occupation in Austria. On its journey, one freight car caught fire. The train stopped, and Soviet troops soon found the liquor. Not a bottle from this shipment reached Linz. But bottles from others did. Upon arrival, the bottles went underground, cool wine caves a hundred feet below the surface of Kapuzinerstrasse. And depletion continued.

In 1946 and 1947, large-scale sales through the U.S. Army's Post Exchanges took the greatest toll. During this time, Red met his Rommel in the form of a bottle of this "Rhum." Having arrived in Austria on occupation duty, Red had himself photographed with his half-empty booty of "Rhum" in the foreground. Easily read in the surviving print is the Italian "Rhum" markings to include the prominent name of the Delva Company on the label.[34]

To complete the story, in 1947 the local U.S. Army commander in Linz, Colonel Inman, alerted that his office would close, presented the remaining stock to the Austrian state. Vienna entrusted the Customs Office at Linz with its supervision. A document from the Austrian Federal Ministry of Finance indicates that, from 1947 to 1976, Austria had charge of the liquor.[35] In 1963 the Austrian government sold about

600,000 bottles to a firm in Liechtenstein. After that sale, about 250,000 bottles remained sleeping in the Linz cave.

In 1974 the Austrian authorities sent about 50,000 bottles to various customers after having it tested to ensure that it remained fit for human consumption.[36] At that time Headquarters United States Army Europe became interested and had their Alcohol Procurement Office in Heidelberg buy 169,000 bottles, which they sold through their Class VI stores throughout Europe.[37] On May 7, 1979, a German firm in Frankfurt auctioned the remaining 40,296 bottles, advertising it as "Rommel Liquor."[38]

The youngest of our threesome saw more combat action than the other two. On June 19, 1943, at South Portland, Maine, the United States launched our junior member. Built in fifty-six days and christened the SS *Jeremiah O'Brien,* this Liberty ship took part in the Battle of the North Atlantic and the Battle of the Norman shore, before joining the war in the Pacific. With Liberty ships American naval architects modified an earlier British hull into an economical and simple-to-build workhorse of the sea.

The real miracle came with the manufacturing process; full speed ahead and damn the costs. Never before had so many sailors needed so many ships. Elegance mattered little; President Roosevelt, an "old salt" of some renown, christened Liberty ships "ugly ducklings." Ugly or not, three modifications to shipbuilding made all the difference for these ducklings.

First, line production meant that ships came down shipways the way automobiles came down assembly lines. Admiral Emory S. Land, chairman of the U.S. Maritime Commission, preferred it that way: "We are more nearly approximating the automobile industry than anything else." Second, prefabrication and preassembly added more speed; of the 250,000 separate parts, most arrived shaped and fitted together before reaching the shipway. Third, these seahorses could be almost entirely welded rather than riveted, an easier task to teach to the people like Red's father and hundreds like him who had never before seen the sea or a ship.

The United States had tried all this before. In the World War I phase, America needed ships instantly as it also went into that combat late. But ships ordered in 1917 never reached the war zone; peace came before they could. In the World War II phase, shipbuilders had to try to beat the calendar again. This time they won. In the fall of 1942,

Henry Kaiser's Oregon Shipyard launched a Liberty ship just ten days after keel laying; his Richmond, California, yard did even better. It assembled a launchable vessel in just four days. These feats proved exceptions, good for publicity. On average a shipyard took twenty days from start to launch. Nevertheless, even twenty days was a manufacturing miracle.

Employment opportunities drew thousands. In 1939 the San Francisco Bay area offered work to about 6,000 shipbuilders. By 1944 the number topped 244,000, amounting to one-sixth of all wartime ship construction workers. Five billion dollars in wartime contracts had made the Bay area the largest shipbuilding center in the world.[39] Southern California's aircraft industries, also the largest in the world, competed for the limited supply of labor. In the case of ships, not all yards faced the Pacific. Gulf coast and Eastern seaboard yards joined the race. In all, eighteen U.S. shipyards took up the task, finally producing ships faster than the Germans could sink them. Among them, the SS *Jeremiah O'Brien* went to war in both the Atlantic and Pacific basins.

From July 1943 to October 1944 the *O'Brien,* traveling as part of a convoy, made four trips between the United States and the United Kingdom. On her fourth voyage the allied high command diverted her for eleven shuttle runs between English ports and the beachheads in Normandy. Strafed, bombed, and torpedoed, she survived. One of the two troop ships that carried Red's unit to France did not have the same luck. Two troop ships crossed to Normandy on December 24, 1944. A German submarine sank one, the *Léopoldville,* resulting in a large loss of life.[40] By chance, Red embarked on the vessel that made it safely across what, at that late date in the war, remained a dangerous crossing. By coincidence of war, in late 1944 both the *O'Brien* and Red docked in Cherbourg; the *O'Brien* in October and Red in December.

The *O'Brien*'s fifth ocean crossing carried her to South America and back to New Orleans; the sixth to the Philippines with a return to San Francisco. On her last wartime voyage she steamed to Sydney, Calcutta, Shanghai, Manila, and back under the Golden Gate Bridge, whose waters still harbor her to this day. Now she is a ceremonial ship, saved to help salvage the past.[41]

So, what is the story we are about to tell? The impact of weather and geography on five World War II campaigns aside, this book is about boys and battles, Bogart and ballads, boats and basins, booze and barometers, bombs and babes. With this cast of characters in place, our story can now commence.

Notes

1. On the literary impact of WW I, see Paul Fussell, *The Great War and Modern Memory* (New York: Oxford University Press, 1975). Literature of WW II relies less on despair, more on resignation. Note Norman Mailer: Strewn across his battlefield are the naked and the dead. See Mordecai Richler, ed., *Writers on WW II: An Anthology* (New York: Knopf, 1991). In contrast, the Cold War novel focused mainly on espionage, good for motion picture scripts, less so for human insights. Critically acclaimed novels set in the war years continue to be published. For WW I, there is Sebastian Faulks, *Birdsong* (New York: Random House, 1996); for WW II, we have Michael Ondaatje, *The English Patient* (London: Bloomsbury, 1992).

2. In the 1930s Einstein and Freud exchanged a number of letters on what "could be done to protect mankind from the curse of war." Sigmund Freud, "Why War? 1932," in *Princeton Readings in Political Thought,* ed. Mitchell Cohen & Nicole Fermon (Princeton: Princeton University Press, 1996): 556–65.

3. Eric Hobsbawm in *The Age of Extremes: A History of the World, 1914–1991* (New York: Pantheon, 1994) uses another means to make a similar point. Also see Gabriel Kolko, *Century of War: Politics, Conflicts, and Society Since 1914* (New York: New Press, 1994), and John Lukacs, *The End of the 20th Century and the End of the Modern Era* (New York: Ticknor and Fields, 1993).

4. Giovanni Arrighi argues that economics motivated most of the long, durable conflict in the twentieth century. Surely it has much to do with it; however, I emphasize what I consider the dominant element, politics. See Arrighi, *The Long 20th Century* (London: Verso, 1994). Each of the centuries I describe had a dominant conflictual theme, but this does not exclude other factors. For example, the religious wars of the seventeenth century had many causes—dynastic, social, ideological, and class conflict, in addition to resource shortages and a Little Ice Age—but religion remained the soul of the matter. See David R. Gress, "Is the 'West' Religious or Secular," *Orbis* (Summer 1996): 415–27.

5. Fernand Braudel, *The Mediterranean and the Mediterranean World in the Age of Philip II* (New York: HarperCollins, 1972). Don Juan of Austria, perhaps the last crusader, commanded the Western forces at the battle of Lepanto. Samuel Huntington predicts that the twenty-first century's great chasm will again be the division between the West and Islam. See his "Clash of Civilizations?" *Foreign Affairs* (Summer 1993): 22–49. Huntington is a Eurocentric scholar, most at home in the North Atlantic basin. Pacific Basin scholars suggest that the clash of civilizations might more likely occur between the West and Asia's Pacific Rim nations where wealth is rapidly accumulating. See Richard Madsen, "After Liberalism: What If Confucianism Becomes the Hegemonic Ethic of the Twenty-first Century?" Japanese Policy Research Institute, Working Paper No. 14, November 1995.

6. The debt owed by North Atlantic civilization to the Islamic world is highlighted by Bernard Lewis, *The Middle East: A Brief History of the Last 2,000 Years* (New York: Scribner, 1996). A German-born writer also told the history of East and West via the Mediterranean. See Emil Ludwig, *The Mediterranean: Saga of a Sea* (New York: Whittlesey House, 1942).

7. Political scientists sometimes equate American democracy with pluralism. See Robert A. Dahl, *Pluralist Democracy in the United States: Conflict and Consent* (Chicago: Rand-McNally, 1967) and his *Dilemmas of Pluralist Democracy: Autonomy Versus Control* (New Haven: Yale University Press, 1982), and Ralf Dahrendorf, *Class and Class Conflict in Industrial Society* (Stanford: Stanford University Press, 1959). On representation see Hanna Pitkin, *The Concept of Representation* (Berkeley: University of California Press, 1967), and Joseph Tussman, *Obligation and the Body Politic* (New York: Oxford University Press, 1960). For current arguments about community versus individuals, see Robert N. Bellah et al., *Habits of the Heart: Individualism and Commitment in American Life* (Berkeley: University of California Press, 1985), and Amitai Etzioni, *Spirit of Community: The Reinvention of American Society* (New York: Simon & Schuster, 1993).

8. Wolfgang Schluchter, *The Rise of Western Rationalism: Max Weber's Developmental History* (Berkeley: University of California Press, 1981). For an overview see William H. McNeill's *The Rise of the West: A History of the Human Community* (Chicago: University of Chicago Press, 1963). Also see J.B. Bury, *The Idea of Progress: An Inquiry into Its Origin and Growth* (New York: Macmillan, 1932); Reinhard Bendix, *Kings or People: Power and the Mandate to Rule* (Berkeley: University of California Press, 1978); and Orlando Patterson, *Freedom: Freedom in the Making of Western Culture* (New York: Basic Books, 1991).

9. R.R. Palmer, *The Age of the Democratic Revolutions* (Princeton: Princeton University Press, 1959). Also see Michael Walzer, ed., *Regicide and Revolution: Speeches at the Trial of Louis XVI* (London: Cambridge University Press, 1974). On the democratic tradition in France, see Daniel Halévy, *The End of the Notables* (Paris: Editions Bernard Grasset, 1930); and David Thomson, *Democracy in France Since 1870* (London: Oxford University Press, 1969); on Britain, Robert Livingston Schuyler, ed., *Frederic William Maitland, Historian: Selections from His Writings* (Berkeley: University of California Press, 1960); and William H. McNeill, ed., *Lord Acton: Essays in the Liberal Interpretation of History* (Chicago: University of Chicago Press, 1967); on the United States see Richard Hofstadter, *The Age of Reform: From Bryan to F.D.R.* (New York: Knopf, 1959); and James Willard Hurst, *Law and Markets in U.S. History: Different Modes of Bargaining Among Interests* (Madison: University of Wisconsin Press, 1982). Pockets outside France, Britain, and the United States made a partial transformation toward democracy. For example, see Robert D. Putnam, *Making Democracy Work: Civic Traditions in Modern Italy* (Princeton: Princeton University Press, 1994).

10. As an example of the price paid by industrial workers, see E.P. Thompson, *The Making of the English Working Class* (New York: Random House, 1963). The term *franchise democracy* is the most descriptive because the task after the revolutions of 1688, 1775, and 1789 was to wait for the volcanic political activity to subside and then to turn subjects into citizens. The critical instrument for citizenry was the ballot, granted first to white Christian males who owned property, then spreading to all adults. Also see Sydney Verba, Kay Lehman Schlozman, and Henry Brady, *Voice and Equality: Civic Voluntarism in American Politics* (Cambridge: Harvard University Press, 1995). On page 12: "Many of the

basic writings in democratic theory consider equality to be simply that each person has one vote, and the vote is equally weighted."

11. On nationalism, see Ernest Gellner, *Nations and Nationalism* (Ithaca: Cornell University Press, 1983); Liah Greenfield, *Nationalism: Five Roads to Modernity* (Cambridge: Harvard University Press, 1993); and William Pfaff, *The Wrath of Nations: Civilization and the Furies of Nationalism* (New York: Simon & Schuster, 1993).

12. Gaddis Smith, *American Diplomacy During the Second World War, 1939–1945* (New York: Knopf, 1985).

13. Karl Jaspers, *The Future of Mankind* (Chicago: University of Chicago Press, 1958), 1–9.

14. The cost for the United States alone totaled nearly $12 trillion. See Patrick Lloyd Hatcher, *Economic Earthquakes: Converting Defense Cuts to Economic Opportunites* (Berkeley: Institute of Governmental Studies Press, 1994), 30.

15. In fiction, the French arguably tell the Verdun story best. For example, Jules Romains, *Verdun* (New York: Knopf, 1939). In British nonfiction, see Alistair Horne, *The Price of Glory: Verdun 1916* (London: MacMillan, 1962). Also see Peter Gay, *Weimar Culture* (New York: Harper & Row, 1968), 163–64.

16. Patrick Lloyd Hatcher, *The Suicide of an Elite: American Internationalists in Vietnam* (Stanford: Stanford University Press, 1990).

17. The following are two examples of waterborne penetrations at the periphery of the North Atlantic world: (1) As merchant-mariners, the Scandinavian Vikings crossed the Baltic Sea to the Gulf of Finland, went up the Neva River to Lake Ladoga, down the Volkhov River to Novgorod, up the river Lovat to a point where they dragged their vessels on log rollers a short distance overland, reaching the source of either the Dnieper River winding 1,400 miles to the Black Sea and contact with the Byzantine Empire at Constantinople or the Volga River flowing some 2,400 miles to the Caspian Sea and contact with the Abbasid Caliphate at Baghdad. On these journeys there exists the manuscript of Ibn Fadlan from A.D. 922 and the entertaining tale Michael Crichton made of it in his *Eaters of the Dead: The Extraordinary Adventures of an Arab Courtier Among the Fierce 10th-Century Vikings* (New York: Ballantine Books, 1976), and the *De Administrando Imperio* of Byzantine Emperor Constantine VII Porphyrogenitus (A.D. 905–959). (2) As merchant settlers, the New England Puritans traveled, in war and peace, from Deerfield, Massachusetts, up the Connecticut River, through passes in the Green Mountains, then up Lake George to Lake Champlain, then via the St. Lawrence River to Montreal in French Canada. Colonists in New York used the easier Hudson River for the same northward thrust. A constant, colorful, and complicated exchange of cultural traffic between native Indian, Protestant English, and Catholic French. See John Demos, *The Unredeemed Captive: A Family Story from Early America* (New York: Knopf, 1994), 25–26. France made the earliest, deepest penetrations, using the St. Lawrence River, the Great Lakes, and the Mississippi River, hence St. Louis and New Orleans. See Francis Parkman, *Pioneers of France in the New World* (Lincoln: University of Nebraska Press, 1996).

18. Jackson Turner Main uses the rivers and bays of the United States to

explain who did and who did not vote for the U.S. Constitution. Those connected to water transportation generally did; those disconnected to it generally did not. "This is a socio-economic division based on a geographical location and sustains a class as well as a sectional interpretation of the struggle over the Constitution" (*The Antifederalists: Critics of the Constitution, 1781–1788* [New York: W.W. Norton, 1961], 270–71). Democracy also infiltrated along these same waterways, carried by four variants of Anglo-Saxon settlement. David Hackett Fischer calls them "freedom ways" in his *Albion's Seed: Four British Folkways in America* (New York: Oxford University Press, 1989), 8, 11, 815.

19. As an example of the interdisciplinary approach of Braudel and the French Annalists, see Anthony Reid, *Southwest Asia in the Age of Commerce,* vols. 1 & 2 (New Haven: Yale University Press, 1988 and 1993). Reid shows how a region's culture can permeate outward from elite to mass, from core to periphery. To judge the impact of this regional approach, see Victor Lieberman, "An Age of Commerce in Southeast Asia? Problems of Regional Coherence," *Journal of Asian Studies* 54, no. 3 (August 1995): 796–807.

20. Consult two miniatures by Jonathan D. Spence: *The Death of Woman Wang* (New York: Viking Press, 1978) and *The Question of Hu* (New York: Knopf, 1988).

21. Claudia D. Golden, "The Role of World War II in the Rise of Women's Employment," *American Economic Review* (September 1991): 741–56; Jocelyn W. Knowles, "The Lady Brakemen: Women Working on Railroads During WW II," *American Heritage* (July–August 1995): 62–74; John Barlow, "Remembering the Women Air Force Service Pilots of WW II," *Saturday Evening Post* (May–June 1995): 58–63.

22. Johan Huizinga, *The Waning of the Middle Ages* (New York: St. Martin's Press, 1924), 193, 214, 216, 222–96. Jacob Burckhardt and Jules Michelet also used pictorial sources, according to Lionel Gossman, "Before Huizinga," *New York Times Book Review,* September 8, 1996, 4. Two recent books from Princeton University Press indicate how young scholars use films to explain historical experiences: Janet Staiger, *Interpreting Films: Studies in the Historical Reception of American Cinema* (1992) and Antonia Lant, *Blackout: Reinventing Women for Wartime British Cinema* (1991).

23. With "Sing to me of the man, Muse, the man of twists and turns," Robert Fagles starts his translation of Homer's *Odyssey* (New York: Viking, 1996). Red is our Odysseus, albeit a poor youth and a citizen of twentieth-century democracy.

24. Rum—first distilled in Barbados in the 1600s—remains an important product of the Caribbean, with each island producing its own distinctive flavor (Frank J. Prial, "Rum's Punch," *New York Times Magazine,* June 13, 1993, 56).

25. J.J. Pack, *Nelson's Blood: The Story of Naval Rum* (Hampshire, U.K.: Kenneth Mason, 1982), 20–29, 73.

26. As late as 1996, the U.S. Navy Memorial Foundation had kept an arrangement with the British distiller who, with the Admiralty's blessing, blended the six West Indian rums that went into traditional "Pusser's Rum." In exchange for that blessing, the Royal Navy Sailor's Fund, a naval charity more commonly called the "Tot Fund," receives a substantial donation from the sale of each bottle of British Navy Pusser's Rum. Not to be outdrunk, the American deal with London was for the U.S. Navy Foundation to sell a John Paul Jones decanter—a ceramic

copy of a Royal Navy ship's decanter—along with a bottle of the Pusser's Ltd. rum. The U.S. Navy Memorial Foundation receives a significant donation for the sale of each decanter. Fate decreed that I receive such a decanter. My "new" Pusser's rum, with decanter, sits near the "old" bottle of WW II Rommel's rum. See note 34 below.

27. Pack, *Nelson's Blood,* 131, 138.

28. Malcolm F. Willoughby, *Rum War at Sea* (Washington, DC, Government Printing Office, 1964), 11–19.

29. David Irving, *The Trail of the Fox: The Life of Field-Marshal Erwin Rommel* (London: Weidenfeld and Nicolson, 1977), 171.

30. Document, "The Story of 'Rommel Liquor,'" "prepared for Class VI Operations at Headquarters U.S. Army Europe, Heidelberg, West Germany. I obtained this document from Harold D. Simpson in June 1995 when I interviewed him in Vierheim, Germany. Simpson, a U.S. citizen now retired in Germany, had been the director of the Class VI operation that sold liquor through government stores in Europe. He held that job in 1974 when the U.S. military authorized the purchase of the "Rommel Liquor" from Austrian authorities.

31. Ibid.

32. Letter from Rome, Camera di Commercio Industria Artigianato e Agricolto, February 24, 1977, subject: Delva Company Authorized to Bottle Nettuno Liquor in 1945.

33. Letter from Rome, Dr. Mando Zanchi, former executive Delva Company, subject: Shipping of Delva bottles from Nettuno to Austria. The Milan company forwarded the shipment to Austria under number 24430.

34. During a visit to Giessen, Germany, in May 1981, the author stayed with Lt. Col. and Mrs. William Haynes. Lt. Col. Haynes had retired from active duty and then served in the Class VI depot at Giessen. He gave the author a bottle of "Rommel's Rhum," a bottle that matched the one in the 1946 photograph of Red.

35. Letter from Vienna, Bundesministerium für Finanzen, March 17, 1976, subject: Liquor under its control from 1947 to 1976.

36. Letter from Vienna, Versucusstation für das Garungsgewerbe in Vienna, to Firma F.u.G. Mertl, Vienna, May 22, 1974, stating the results of tests on whiskey, cognac, gin, and "in taste, a pure and matured Rhum with alcoholic contents at 38.87% vol."

37. Around the neck of the bottle of rum given to the author by Lt. Col. Haynes (see note 34 above) hung a small brochure giving a short synopsis (in English and German) of the rum's historical pedigree. After a nationwide search for the individual whose name appeared on the brochure, the author located Jack Gaustad and interviewed him on December 27, 1996. As a retired U.S. Army lieutenant colonel residing in Germany in 1975, he was asked by another U.S. Army colonel on active duty in Heidelberg to work with the group that wrote the brochure. While the brochure labeled its story as a "legend," it quickly attracted attackers and defenders. Some claimed that it was a scheme to help a liquor company sell its wares, while others claimed to have known soldiers who came across the liquor in Linz in 1945.

38. George Eberl, "Rommel Rum," *Stars amd Stripes,* January 11, 1977, 10; auction announcement in the *Frankfurter Neue Presse,* May 2, 1979, for 19,200 *flaschen* whiskey, 17,340 *flaschen* rum, and 3,043 *flaschen* cognac from the

Weltkrieges (Rommel-Spirituosen); "Touted Africa Korps Liquor: The Story of 'Rommel Liquor,'" *Shoppers Bi-Weekly News* (free to the U.S. military personnel in Germany). The ad gave a price of $98 for each bottle; the ad was placed by the German firm Wilhelm Philipp GmbH, Glauber/Stockheim.

39. Charles Wollenberg, *Marinship at War: Shipbuilding and Social Change in Wartime Sausalito* (Berkeley: Western Heritage Press, 1990), 2–3, 28–29. Also see James W. Hamilton and William J. Bolce, Jr., *Gateway to Victory: The Wartime Story of the San Francisco Port of Embarkation* (Stanford: Stanford University Press, 1946). How much the war changed California is debatable. The August 1994 issue of the *Pacific Historical Review* was dedicated to this debate, much of it occasioned by the publication of Gerald Nash's "Fortress California at War," *Pacific Historical Review* 63, 3 (August 1994): 289–421.

40. Jacquin Sanders, *A Night Before Christmas* (New York: G.P. Putnam's Sons, 1963).

41. Carl Nolte, "Jeremiah O'Brien Weighs Anchor Again," *San Francisco Chronicle,* June 24, 1996, A13. This trip combined visits to six ports in the Pacific Northwest with a television miniseries.

The Sky

British weather? Think wet and windy, cold and cloudy. Pundits once proclaimed that the sun never set on the earth-girdling British Empire. (They failed to note that at home it shone with less frequency.) As the sun was to the empire, rain is to this island: moisture in some form drips down on part of Britain almost every day. This sceptered isle— 84,400 square miles—does not have wet and dry seasons; rain falls in all four. Unlike the bygone British Raj in India where monsoons followed droughts, Britain never dries out, hence the dampness. It is not an accident that woolens are one of Britain's major manufactures.

Green pastures fodder cattle. They in turn furnish food: the weekend meal of choice, roast beef and yorkshire pudding.[1] Swirling seas and an organic-rich ocean serve up the weekday repasts of fish and chips. Britain's poets echo the sea: Water, water everywhere, but not a drop to drink. And British rain gear, while often a fashion statement abroad, is a practical necessity at home. Shakespeare has Portia speak of "gentle rain," but she never says how much. Surely it must be at least a pound per person per annum.

Take London. On average, in January rain falls 17 days out of 31; in April, 14 days out of 30; in July, 13 out of 31; and in October, 14 out of 31. This does not include the heavy mist or pea-soup fog. Soup became the air metaphor. Luckily, radar helped in turning thick soup into clear bouillon. Before aircraft and radar, the high-tech introduction of the compass guided British mariners through misty fogs and rain squalls. In no other far-flung corner of the world did Albion plant so hearty a seed as along the eastern seaboard of North America, using its gulfs, bays, and rivers to penetrate the continent's hinterland.[2] One seed in particular, political democracy, later tied the Anglo-Americans together through all three phases of twentieth-century war. At a less magisterial level, they also shared North Atlantic weather patterns.

Did the climate matter to combatants? After the war Dwight Eisenhower wrote *Crusade in Europe*. In his index he has a longer entry for weather, especially British, than he does for either Rommel or tanks. While planning the Normandy operation, Eisenhower met with the Meteorologic Committee twice daily, once at nine-thirty in the evening and once at four in the morning. German records also reflect practical problems. In 1940, when the German squadrons arrived at their airfields near Calais, they found the fields planted in grain. Messerschmitts were parked beneath trees where available and under camouflaged netting when not. By fall the makeshift landing fields had become so sodden from the incessant rain that aircraft had to be supported by planks and logs. In frustration, the squadrons moved to higher ground farther inland, adding additional flying time to their targets.

Britain's slice of wild blue yonder was more wild than blue. Year-round flying posed hazards, especially for early combat pilots. Alone in a fighter at 20,000 feet, unable to see most of the ground and little of the airspace, carrying rudimentary navigational equipment, fired on by enemy aircraft, and running out of fuel, there were better places to fly. But in 1940 the enemy was here, in an otherworldly environment. And he was in airplanes, one of the key weapons that had undergone improvements in the years of the long armistice—1918 to 1939.

During the 1914–1918 phase of North Atlantic civil strife, three weapons revolutionized warfare, all designs courtesy of Leonardo da Vinci. On land, the tank, first seen seriously in 1917 on the battlefield at Cambrai, pounded across Flanders. From beneath the sea, the submarine—submerged as early as the American Civil War, but only a miniature of what followed—surfaced. And in the sky, the airplane, which had its combat initiation in 1911 during the Italian campaign for Libya, spit fire.

Libya's desert creatures heard the sand-echoed thunder of Field Marshal Erwin Rommel's tanks thirty years after Italy's Libyan sky show. The ranks of Rome and Rommel had air cover thanks to an

American duo, the Wright brothers. In December 1903, the brother-experimenters flew—for twelve seconds—the first powered aircraft, the "Flyer," taking off from a spit of land stretching out into the Atlantic Ocean. Near Kitty Hawk, North Carolina, the Wrights flew their flying machine into the Atlantic-swept sky near the Carolina outerbanks, hunting waters that, after 1941, Germany's Grand Admiral Karl Donitz sometimes favored with his submarines.

Initially, early combat aircraft performed missions similar to those Napoleon had assigned to balloons—the observation of enemy movements. When the kaiser's forces pushed toward Paris in those critical autumn days of 1914, Gallic pilots, circling in their airborne platforms high above the advancing enemy front, spotted the First German Army's exposed flank. Upon landing, they informed General Joseph Galliéni, the military governor of Paris. Based on that intelligence, Galliéni speedily mobilized what forces he could rouse, including the taxis of Paris, for the counterattack that led to the first battle of the Marne, thus halting the German advance and giving the allied armies a chance to regroup.

In 1915 a Dutch airplane designer, Anthony H.G. Fokker, synchronized the gears in order for a machine gun to fire through a revolving propeller without striking it. Once successfully tested, the knights of the sky added aerial combat and crude bombing runs to their intelligence-gathering missions.[3]. "Dog fights" above made heros below. To name three: Germany's Red Baron, Manfred von Richthofen, eighty aircraft downed, killed in action; the American (who lived to write his memoirs) Eddie Rickenbacker, only twenty-six aircraft downed, but in the sky for less than one year before peace, and an ace only because of the intercession of then Colonel Billy Mitchell, whom Rickenbacker initially served as driver; and the Russian ace, Major Alexander de Seversky, who, following the Communist coup of 1917, immigrated to America, and, as a citizen of the United States, designed and manufactured many of the airframes and much of the equipment that later helped defeat Nazi Germany in the sky and on the ground.[4]

Another crack pilot from the Great War of 1914 carried a German name into the Great War of 1939. In early 1917, Herman Goering took command of the fabled Richthofen Jagdgeschwader. With this squadron he won the Second Reich's highest award for air bravery, the Blue Max. That medal, established by Frederick the Great, rested on Oberleutnant Goering's chest in a Berlin ceremony attended by his kaiser, William II. Two decades later Goering received the command of the Third Reich's air arm from his führer, Adolf Hitler, who also awarded him medals, in addition to the title of Reichsmarschall.

Goering soon discovered that along with the medals and titles came major tasks, each more difficult once fighting started in September 1939. First came Poland, an easy air victory. Next came France, less easy. Then, in the summer of 1940, came Britain. Goering faced a career killer. His air fleet had to dominate the sky over the English Channel in order for Operation Sea Lion to succeed. Sea Lion was Hitler's Normandy invasion in reverse; he planned to go the other way, following the example of William the Conqueror. But in 1066 that Norman duke did not have to face fire-spitting, Anglo-Saxon air mounts.

Following the French defeat in May 1940, Britain was the last of Europe's democratic societies. Eliminating democracy there meant overcoming a geographical obstacle of no mean dimensions. Unlike France's vaunted manmade Maginot line, Britain had a valuable nature-made big ditch, the Channel. Deep and dangerous, tanks could not roll around it, using a forest as cover as they had the Ardennes. For the German Army to threaten London as it had threatened Paris meant that the German Navy must ferry it across the water barrier. For Germany to control the Channel long enough for a crossing in force meant that the German Air Force, the Luftwaffe, would have to dominate the air over the channel during the passage. Performing that air miracle entailed defeating Britain's Royal Air Force. Goering said he could do it.

Goering could not and did not. Why? America's own golden boy of the air, Charles Lindbergh, impressed on prewar visits to Hitler's Reich by what he saw of German aviation, told influential people in Britain and the United States how invincible he thought this air armada. In retrospect, Lindbergh, aviation's golden boy, like Goering, the ace of yesteryear, was also wrong. What explains their error? A multitude of factors, including a paucity of funds, poor targeting, and pathetic leadership—all on the German side.

As to a paucity of funds, the Germans had limited marks to spend. Inasmuch as German war planners gave precedence to the army with its panzers, then the navy with its surface raiders and underwater wolf packs, this left the air force the runt of the litter. To make matters worse, by 1939 great powers faced several air missions—air superiority, close air support, and strategic bombing—each of which necessitated expensive, specialized aircraft.

Air superiority required that a state control the air above its homeland, then the air over the battlefield, and finally the air over the enemy homeland. This mission called for aircraft that could fight other aircraft. Close air support required that the air arm fly as an adjunct above the advancing army, acting as an offensive and defensive umbrella. This mission called for short-range aircraft that could land on unimproved runways, refuel, and race forward with tanks, at the same time engaging enemy armor, artillery, or other tactical assets on the ground. Strategic bombing required that bombers accurately drop tons of munitions onto industrial, transportation, and communication centers deep in the enemy rear. This mission called for long-range bombers that long-range fighters could escort over their targets. After the war, when the American air general Carl Spaatz asked Goering at what moment he realized that Germany had lost the war, Goering replied: "When I saw your bombers over Berlin protected by your long-range fighters."[5]

Affording all this required capital, more capital than either the United Kingdom or the United States possessed alone. Therefore, to finance their air war, the two Anglo-Saxon allies reduced the financial hurdle by dividing the work. The United Kingdom concentrated on fighters and associated small aircraft, the United States on bombers and associated large aircraft. Also, following Hitler's takeover of Austria, the U.S. government, itself not at war yet, allowed Britain to purchase American aircraft, in the process turning Lockheed Corporation and Douglas Aircraft Company in particular, and southern California in general, into the war's aircraft manufacturing center. Lockheed engineers redesigned their latest airplane, the *Super-Electra,* into a bomber that London christened the *Hudson.* By the end of 1941 Britain had ordered 1,700 *Hudsons.*[6]

In the case of fighter aircraft, Britain, under the manufacturing blitz commanded by Lord Beaverbrook, the minister of aircraft production, doubled production. For the year 1940, Britain produced 4,283 fighters compared to Germany's production of just over 3,000. After the American entry into the war, Germany fared even worse when one compares bomber production figures. Albert Speer, Hitler's armaments minister, visited the Junkers plant in Dessau in the fall of 1941. While there the plant manager took Speer into a locked room where he showed Speer a graph comparing German and American bomber production estimates for the future. This future looked so bad for the German side that Speer reports the manager "broke into uncontrollable tears," particular after he told Speer that the German leaders he had briefed refused to believe the statistics.[7]

As allies, the United States and the United Kingdom had combined their manufacturing talents. Germany had no such ally; the burden fell to it alone. Hence, the German Air Force had to fly a limited number of aircraft, suitably designed for one mission but ill suited for another, as best it could juggle the missions against available air assets. This best proved insufficient, a second place, an airborne defeat.

As to poor targeting, Berlin erred grievously when it switched targets from Royal Air Force (RAF) airfields and their radar control systems to the British capital and its citizens. Royal London presented a terror target with limited strategic significance; Royal Air Force radars and landing strips presented strategic sites of the utmost importance. Effective targeting meant destroying that part of Britain's defenses that kept the Royal Air Force in the sky. Since the British had dispersed their air assets, some form of command and control, acting on rather precise intelligence, had to order separated British squadrons to meet approaching Luftwaffe formations at designated coordinates. Here lay the key to British air supremacy, the destruction of which the Germans initially seemed to understand when, on August 13, they targeted the RAF for destruction under the code name Adlerangriff (Eagle Attack).

Once Hitler realized that Britain would not come to terms with him as master of continental Europe, he set August 15, 1940, as the invasion date. The Luftwaffe launched their offensive on July 10, first targeting the channel ports and shipping. In August German pilots went after the radar stations, seemingly having discovered the key for victory. To the radar targets they added the fighter airfields of the southeast, next to the radar stations Britain's most critical link in her chain of air defense.

Then on September 7 Berlin changed targeting priorities. Real estate belonging to the Church of England such as St. Paul's Cathedral in London ranked higher then RAF real estate such as Fighter Command's headquarters at Bentley Priory in Middlesex. The landlord in charge of the former, the Archbishop of Canterbury, now took the beating that the landlord of the latter, Air Chief Marshal Sir Hugh Dowding, should have suffered.

On that fateful day, Goering stood with his entourage at Cap Blanc Nez. Passing overhead were nearly one thousand warcraft headed for

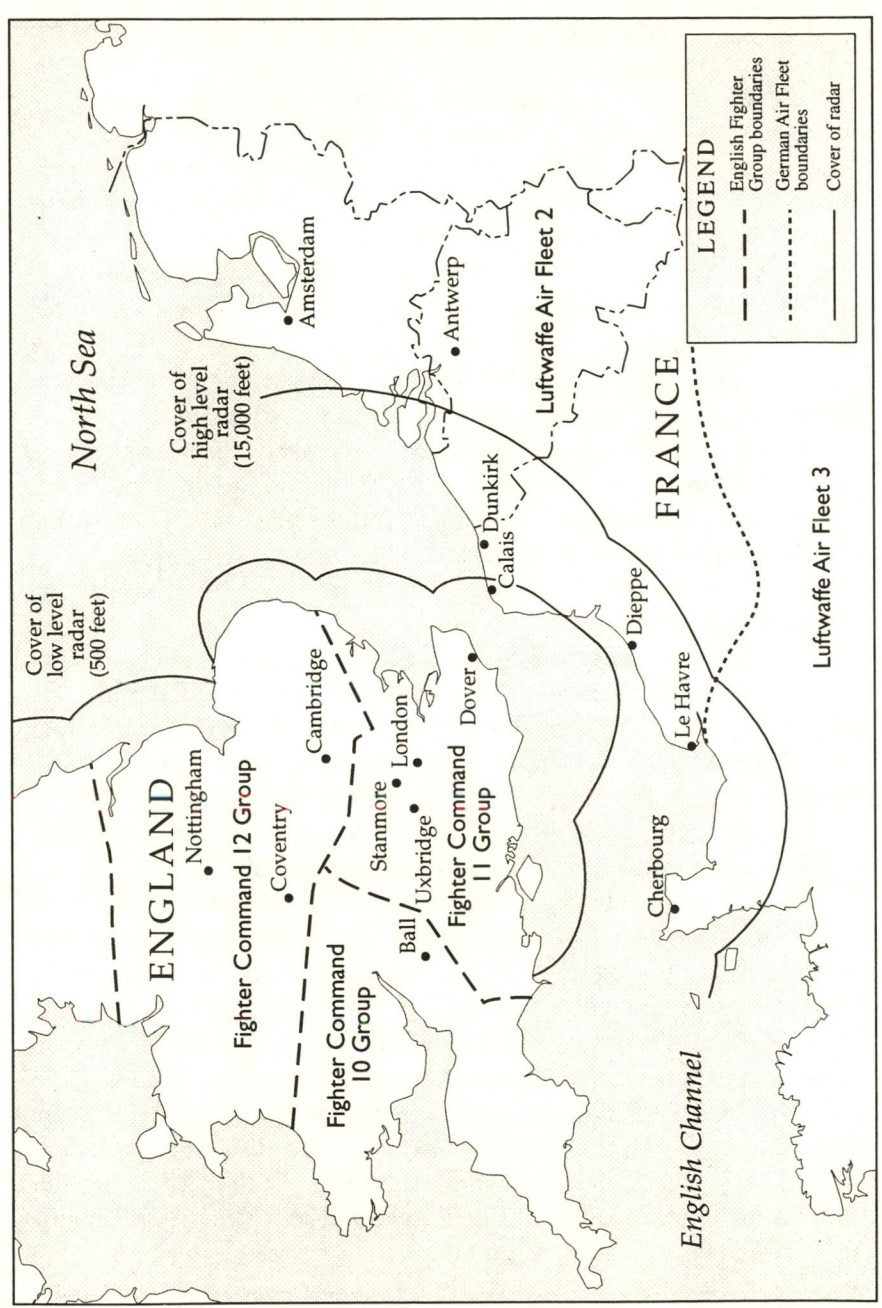

North Sea

Cover of
high level
radar
(15,000 feet)

Cover of
low level
radar
(500 feet)

● Amsterdam

● Antwerp

Luftwaffe Air Fleet 2

FRANCE

● Dunkirk
● Calais

● Dieppe

● Le Havre

● Cherbourg

Luftwaffe Air Fleet 3

ENGLAND

● Nottingham

Fighter Command 12 Group

● Cambridge

● Coventry

Stanmore

London ●

Ball
Uxbridge ●

Fighter Command
10 Group

Fighter Command
11 Group

● Dover

English Channel

LEGEND

– – – English Fighter
Group boundaries

········· German Air Fleet
boundaries

———— Cover of radar

the Thames Estuary. Stepped from 14,000 to 23,000 feet, they covered 800 square miles.

Revenge and fury had replaced tactics and strategy. It made no sense. R.V. Jones, who from 1939 to 1946 headed Scientific Intelligence on Britain's air staff, understood that the German scientific community knew of the technical possibility of radar at about the same time as the British. Jones suggests two German failings: first, Germany wanted radar for the offense, Britain for the defense; second, because of circumstances and cultures, the Germans looked for perfection, the British for practicality.[8]

Jones could have added that British military leaders, aware that danger lay ahead, had a pragmatic organization for air defense in place by 1936 when the RAF set up separate commands, each responsible for specific functions—Bomber, Fighter, Coastal, and Training. Britain also had in Sir Henry Tizard a modern Merlin who forecasted the value of radar. Thanks to his efforts, Britain had five radar stations on its east coast by December 1935. In August 1937 the government authorized fifteen additional stations.

As for pathetic leadership, Hitler's own armaments minister, Albert Speer, blames the führer for "his confused planning of the air war against England." In his position near the top, Speer discovered that Hitler had started an air campaign, refusing to acknowledge that he did not have enough fighters, the only aircraft that could destroy British *Spitfire* and *Hurricane* defenders. In 1939 Germany possessed only 771 fighter aircraft. During the last phase of the war, Speer's ministry delivered 12,720, but by then it was too late to influence the outcome.[9]

The characteristics of German aircraft held equal importance to their numbers. When the Battle of Britain began in earnest in August 1940, the Germans committed two air fleets (Luftflotten 2 and 3) consisting of 875 high-level bombers and 316 dive-bombers. The latter proved so vulnerable to British fighters that the high command withdrew them after August 18. Of fighters, the Germans had 929 available, mostly single-engine Messerschmitt 109s. Its problem? Its radius of action, out and back, was slightly more than 100 miles. With that range, from the occupied coasts of France and Belgium, the Me-109 could just reach London, then have scant time for fighting before fleeing back to refuel at its base.[10]

Many a Messerschmitt fighter fell from the sky above Britain. To raise morale on the home front, the American military shipped a few downed Messerschmitts back to the United States. Red saw his first such enemy aircraft in distant Wyoming.

> September 1, 1943, Wyoming: Dear Folks: I took a piece of fabric from a German Messerschmitt. The plane was shot down in Europe and is over here on exhibition. The cowboy who was guarding it when I tore the little piece off wanted to whip me but I talked him out of it.

Needing a weapon that would down allied fighter aircraft, Hitler assigned the wrong mission to what could have been Germany's most effective secret weapon, the jet airplane. Instead of consulting professionals such as Professor Ernst Heinkel, who correctly saw a great advantage in jet fighters, Hitler ordered his aviation specialists first to stop production and then, when started again, to waste their talent on jet bombers. All this occurred late in the war, with Germany under agonizing bomber attack—bombers escorted by fighters, both of which represented ideal targets for jet fighters.[11]

Hitler did not act without selective advice. Wrongheaded as usual when it came to grand strategy, Goering and Field Marshal Albert Kesselring had acquiesced in the switch to daylight raids against London, thus sharing in Hitler's blunder. In Goering's case, his interest had turned to raiding art treasures from conquered Europe. Obesity and drug use already marked his ruin, later consummated in suicide in his Nuremberg cell.[12] Subordinate to Goering, Field Marshal Erhard Milch and others had to toil to save what they could.

The British military historian B.H. Liddell Hart suggests that the bombing of the two capitals, London and Berlin, accidently started on the night of August 24, 1941, when ten Luftwaffe bombers, lost on a night raid aimed at Rochester and Thameshaven, instead dropped their bombs on London. That mistake led to an immediate reprisal raid on Berlin, which London repeated to ensure that Berlin understood the message. Tit-for-tat soon led to devastation from the air. Bitterness, the mark of a civil blood-letting, replaced hardheadedness. Cain versus Abel, not David against Goliath. This was not war as the continuation of politics by other means; this was war as the elimination of one political order by another. A family feud; death had occurred for which no last will and testament existed, so the relatives tore each other apart over the inheritance.

In Berlin, Hans-Georg von Studnitz served in the information and press section of the Foreign Ministry from 1939 to 1945. From February 1943 to April 1945 he kept a journal. He observed bombs in the streets and at the opera. On February 5, 1945, he wrote that the preceding Saturday's attack on the center of Berlin was "the ultimate apocalypse." That raid began at 10:45 A.M. and left most shelters a foot deep in water, with no lights, cracking under the punishment of massive explosions. Later he saw "the Foreign Minister (Ribbentrop) and the Japanese Ambassador (Oshima) wandering among the ruins." Unexploded bombs made the streets impassable: "Never had the city looked so devastated . . . water bespatters its ruins with muck, and streams of filthy water runs through the streets."

In an earlier trip to Italy, Studnitz had already experienced the fear of bombing. Determined to hear the best Italian singing, on March 1, 1943, he stopped in Milan and went to La Scala to enjoy *Rheingold.* But the "Rhine daughters floating about above the stage swayed violently all over the place . . . this was a real danger . . . as an air raid precaution, the dress-circle was underpinned by wooden beams . . . the chorus and stage-hands were so frightened of a possible air raid that they refused to work in the evenings in the Scala."

The next year Studnitz went to Vienna for his music vacation. Before dinner on February 17, 1944, he found himself walking in the woods with Herbert von Karajan, who was full of bitter complaints against Gustav Furtwangler, Germany's greatest living conductor. The latter, he said, "is doing all he can to injure his career" and "has closed the doors of the Philharmonic to Karajan and refuses to allow him to conduct in Vienna—whose citizens are quite sure they will not be bombed."

By the next month both he and Karajan were back in Berlin, where Studnitz went to the State Opera to hear Karajan's concert. "The bombed-out interior, which is said to have been restored in accordance with the original design, is much more like a Sarotti bonbonniére."[13] With bombs falling, the Germans marched off to hear their Bach, Beethoven, Brahms, and Bruckner. In October 1944, Furtwangler recorded Bruckner's Ninth Symphony with the Philharmonic in Berlin even though elements of the Third White Russian Front had penetrated East Prussia on August 17 and began a devastating rape of country and citizens.[14] An atavistic vengeance swept forward, marked by savagery and frenzy. But on played the orchestras!

In London, Britain's most published diplomat recorded a macabre view of destruction there. During the week, Harold Nicolson would watch the air raids against London from his office at the Ministry of Information, where he slept when the blitz turned really bad. On weekends, Nicolson and his wife, Vita Sackville-West, would watch fighter duels above their gardens at Sissinghurst:

> Diplomat's Diary entry September 12, 1941
> (In London) Dine with Guy Burgess at the Reform and have the best-cooked grouse that I have ever eaten. The bombardment begins again at 9:15pm. I have to walk back to the Ministry through a deserted London. I have no tin hat and do not enjoy it. When things get very hot, I crouch in a doorway. In one of them I find a prostitute. "I have been drinking," she says: "I am frightened. Please take care of me." Poor little trull.

> Diplomat's Diary entry September 15, 1941
> (At Sissinghurst) A slack morning with the usual raid going on overhead. After luncheon there is a terrific dog-fight above us. Two 'planes come down near Sissinghurst village and one crashes in flames at Frittenden. We see a parachute descending slowly with the man below it wriggling as if on a pendulum. They take four German prisoners.[15]

One of Nicolson's favorite composers, Benjamin Britten, gave a lifetime of service to the cause of pacifism. Britten waited until after the war to compose his masterpiece, the *War Requiem*. Part of his inspiration came via Wilfred Owen's antiwar poems from the 1914 phase of North Atlantic political strife. At the second Atlantic war's conclusion, Britten, in the company of Yehudi Menuhin, made a concert tour of concentration camps. In July 1945 they played at Bergen-Belsen; their audience, skeletons dressed in blanket material. Britten characterized the concert as a "terrifying experience." Upon his return he had to borrow the words of John Donne, ending with "death be not proud," in order to find expression for his work of terror, *The Holy Sonnets of John Donne.*

Britten fared better in his use of music than did German and Russian composers; their respective dictatorships commissioned compositions for propaganda. In fact, wartime composers on both sides discovered that commissions for new works often came from the motion picture industry, which needed patriotic melodies to underscore patriotic pictures.[16]

While the British took the blows, many Americans experienced the blitz vicariously through motion pictures, an example of the popular culture instructing ordinary folk. When MGM released the film *Mrs. Miniver* in 1941, the people of Great Britain received a propaganda boost to supplement lend-lease supplies. Churchill declared the Greer Garson–Walter Pidgeon film worth a fleet of destroyers; President Roosevelt ordered the film's final speech copied and dropped by the thousand over occupied Europe. In 1942 the film garnered five Academy Awards, including Best Picture and Best Actress. When it came time to give the Best Director award to *Miniver*'s director, William Wyler, he, a volunteer for the Army Air Corps, was busy dropping bombs over Germany. Press praise further ensured lines at the box office.

> Bosley Crowther in the *New York Times:*
> The film tells most eloquently of the humor and courage of these people under fire. And the climax is a shattering revelation that it is they, as well as the soldiers, who fight this war.

> Howard Barnes in the *New York Herald Tribune:*
> A stirring celebration of the people's part in a people's war. It is a film which you will not forget for a long time after you have seen it. A few works of art succeed in impinging on a time of crisis with stunning force and meaning. "Mrs. Miniver" is one of these.[17]

After half a dozen raids over Germany, Wyler filmed a documentary about his experiences and those of an American bomber crew. The War Activities Commission released *Memphis Belle* in 1943. Strikingly original, it provided a lot of library footage for later movies. Wyler's daughter Catherine co-produced a sequel, which Warner released in 1990. Both docudramas indicated that the war had not stamped out romance.

In or out of uniform, teenagers had raging hormones, which rose up each day looking for release. Flyboys were no exception; no war was going to ration their sex drive. It curtailed it; in the rush of war Americans learned to do it quicker. Cole Porter's lyrics enjoined them to do it; birds do it, bees do it, so let's do it. Straight and gay Americans, draftees and volunteers, came out for Uncle Sam, proud service cum private sex. Even a parked flying fortress could prove a mating bed for love-starved air Romeos and their willing land-based Juliets. Pleasure push-ups for lovers rated higher than training sit-ups for sergeants, in addition to using more muscle groups. From *Miniver* to *Memphis* the Wylers captured the hydraulics of wartime romance.

As if to match the *Miniver–Memphis* lend-lease, Britain sent America a celluloid success. Noel Coward represented a one-man industry—composer, lyricist, playwright, actor, singer. His songs, at once sentimental and satirical, kept Britain singing: "London Pride," "Mad Dogs and Englishmen," "Don't Let's Be Beastly to the Germans," "The Stately Homes of Britain." These and other ditties ventilated British life; they gave it a sense of confidence and coherence. Coward had a talent to amuse, and he amused both sides of the Atlantic.[18]

There seemed nothing Coward could not do. So he did it, it being to write, score, produce, and co-direct (with David Lean) a big patriotic film. The American premiere of *In Which We Serve* occurred on December 23, 1942, and Bosley Crowther wrote in the *New York Times* that "one of the most eloquent motion pictures of these or any other times had its American premiere last night." The film stared a ship, the HMS *Torrin*. Much like our ship, the SS *Jeremiah O'Brien*, the *Torrin* met the challenges of the war. Hastily commissioned for service in the summer of 1939, this destroyer saw duty when the war was going against Britain. Its filmed history matched the impact of *Mrs. Miniver*. Crowther again: "This observer does not expect ever to see anything more moving on the screen than the look of the oil-smeared sailors in this film as they watch their loved ship sink."[19] The film won Coward a special Academy Award in 1943.

A prolific writer before, during, and after round two of the North Atlantic wars, Compton Mackenzie created one of the jewels of British cinema. First as a novel, second as a film, nothing quite had the whimsy of *Whisky Galore*. Released in 1947, Compton wrote both the novel and screenplay. Told on a small scale, filmed in black and white, minus stars, *Whiskey Galore* captures the day-to-day struggle of ordinary people making do until the conflict ends.

Set on a small Hebridean island a hundred miles north of Scotland, disaster strikes when the island runs dry, that is, dry of whiskey. Prepared to defend the island against invading Germans, the minuscule force of locals drills and builds road blocks. As the Home Guard they will sacrifice but not give up their liquid habit. When a freighter carrying 50,000 gallons of whiskey goes on the rocks near their harbor, they salvage this fluid manna—finders keepers. They help London beat Berlin, but they do not return the whiskey to London authorities. They keep their gift from the sea.

Motion pictures offered wartime Americans a family outing that was not limited by government rationing. Since the military devoured huge amounts of rubber and gasoline, both fell to the rationing program.[20] And even if you had a few gallons and tires, the government outlawed the use of private autos for leisure pursuits, thereby eliminating the family car for short hauls. In order to go to a picture show, one walked or took the trolley. Arriving at the local cinema, the audience often gazed at the face of a damaged-dude, the detective Sam Spade from the classic filme noir, *The Maltese Falcon*. Sometimes a detective, sometimes a gangster, Bogart worked both sides of a shady street for a total of thirty-two gangster-related movies in a career of seventy-nine feature films.[21]

For the war, Warner Brothers transformed Humphrey Bogart into the man with a past who fought for a better future. From 1942 to 1945 Bogart starred in seven celluloid combat releases in which he struck at the Axis powers; armchair strategists sat in the dark traveling with Bogart to exotic places to even the score with the Axis thugs.[22] Often the locale came with a French accent; in the 1940s that indicated exotica. Of all his war films, only *Casablanca* became a classic.[23]

In the 1944 *Passage to Marseilles* Bogart escapes from Devils Island, makes his way across the Atlantic Ocean to Great Britain, and, as a freed Frenchman, joins a Free French squadron that flies alongside the RAF against the Nazis. As a Gallic hero he did not convince; as a movie star playing the reformed loner, he could make audiences suspend belief. Corny or not, like a Paris-bound Dickens character who also thought that what he did was a far better thing than he had ever done before, Bogart carried the American moviegoer, millions of them, to a moment of self-sacrifice. Again, film opened the imagination to fantasy and made an indelible imprint on collective memory.[24] (Warners, which had released *Casablanca* to coincide with the allied landings in North Africa, wanted to release this Bogart yarn for the liberation of France. But the war did not keep to Warner's schedule.)

Bogart held a very low opinion of *Passage to Marseilles*. In a wire to Jack Warner, Bogart described his role as a "very bad one which could have been played by anyone."[25] In his own war with Warner, Bogart reacted negatively when Warner told him that it was his patri-

otic duty to star in such vehicles, political pictures for a political pugi-
list. Democracy versus fascism Bogart understood, but bad scripts
bothered him. Nevertheless, to show Warner he could wave the flag as
well as the next star, Bogart went the extra mile.

So popular was Bogie that he toured overseas entertaining combat
troops by reciting from his war movies. Hardened veterans heard lines
like "Play it, Sam," to "Here's looking at you, kid" in the magic of the
night. While Red saw Bogart only on the silver screen, he and his
comrades craved combat movies, especially those that involved liberating France or saving Britain.

These films, and the newsreels that preceded them, were a public
relations coup for British Commonwealth and Free French leaders. The
more the cinema showed the allies bombing Germany, the surer the
home front was of securing victory. Even Red was convinced that the
war would soon end, bombing having defeated the enemy:

> June 29, 1943: Dear Folks: . . . It wouldn't surprise me if Germany and
> Italy folded up soon in the near future. The way we are bombing them
> something is bound to pop.

The battle of the sky even influenced Red's civilian plans. He considered volunteering for postwar sky service.

> August 31, 1945: Dear Folks: Thinking of joining the Air Corps. Air
> transportation is going to be a big thing after the war.

Before Red and millions of GIs could engage in the fracas, Britain
had to win its sky battle. With France out of the fray, British leaders
hoped that, bleak as it seemed, in the fog of war it still held the
brightest lamp. Like a laser beam, the tolerance of a democratic society, however imperfect, cut through the rhetoric of intolerance. British
high-mindedness allowed Britain to add to its stock of native leaders
those nonnationals who either volunteered against tyranny or escaped
from it.

First, from the empire they volunteered—men like Air Marshal
Keith Park, a New Zealander, who commanded Fighter Group 11 at
Uxbridge. Park had flown in round one, 1914; in 1939, he had returned
for round two. On the morning of September 15, 1940, Park had one of
many unscheduled visits by Winston Churchill, this time escorting his

wife, Clementine. Churchill protested that he did not want to disturb anyone; he just wondered if anything interesting might happen. If not, he said, "I'll just sit in the car and do my homework." Feisty Clementine, a year older that day, told Winston that a good bag of German fighters would make a fine present. As if by royal edict, the alarm sounded. Dutifully escorting the couple, it fell to Park to explain tactfully to the prime minister—and not for the first time—that the air conditioning in the bomb-proof operations room, fifty feet below ground, could not cope with cigar smoke.[26]

With an unignited Cuban missile clinched between his teeth, Winston and Clementine Churchill watched as the Uxbridge team commanded *Hurricanes* and *Spitfires* into combat against two massive Luftwaffe raids over London. The boundary for Park's group ran from the bulge on the Suffolk coast, inland across the north of London, down to the Hampshire–Dorset border and along the south and southeast coast: in other words, the critical and closest approaches from the continent. Outnumbered, Park inspired his team of men and women. As tension mounted, Churchill had to speak, Park to answer. A conversation at Uxbridge, September 17, 1940, went as follows:

> *Churchill:* There appear to be many aircraft coming in.
> *Park:* There'll be someone there to meet them.
> Noticing Park's anxiety as the battle reached a fierce pitch:
> *Churchill:* What other reserves have we?
> *Park:* There are none.[27]

Reserves or not, Uxbridge won the day, and on September 17 Hitler postponed the invasion. Officially the Battle of Britain ended on October 31, 1940, while the blitz over London continued to the last stages of the war, with V1 and V2 rockets hitting the capital. The Nazis, using inaccurate rockets against civilians and knowing that they had already lost the war, reemphasized that this political war had turned to revenge.

By the time large numbers of Americans poured into Britain, Red among them, a fearfully damaged British capital awaited them. Red wrote home about his furlough in London where he eyed the sights and the local ladies.[28] The British public jokingly referred to these young Yanks as "overpaid, oversexed, and over here." Here or there, paid or broke, from the GI perspective nothing as little as a war was going to get in the way of something as big as sex. Wartime American Hamlets, princes of democracy, knew the answer to the question, to love or not to love? Yes, yes, and yes again.

Perhaps Park and his Commonwealth colleagues caroused less than the Yanks, nevertheless Park did find himself a British wife. Even New Zealanders got lonely. Park also had qualities that made Dwight Eisenhower and other Americans both like and respect him. Park's great trick was to conjure up a bottle of gin prior to his meetings with squadron commanders. He titled these warm-up sessions "Father's Prayers." The gin dispelled inhibitions, and the officers opened up with their boss. From the sky battle over Britain, he went to block supplies reaching the sand battle in Africa. On July 14, 1942, Park assumed command of RAF Malta.

Perched on the permanently anchored aircraft carrier that was the Maltese rock, Park shared his limited supply of port with his flyboys. When visitors began to visit this Maltese falcon, they began to drink the Officers' Mess dry. Park blocked that liquid leak. Unfortunately for the thirsty Maltese garrison, Park arrived one month too late to try to recapture the rum Rommel's staff sent by ship from Tobruk to Italy. If anyone could have re-requisitioned it, Park was the man, as he proved to the dismay of his staff and superiors.

Park broke all his own flying rules. Often overdue in his own *Spitfire,* in January 1943 he diverted a lone, twin-engine *Beaufighter,* in which he, a passenger en route to Cairo from Malta, ordered an attack on five German bombers. Surprised, the Germans fired back and knocked out the *Beaufighter*'s port engine, leaving it to return over 160 miles of dangerous sea dependent on one engine. Park organized a sweepstakes with the other two men abroad as to whether they would make it, and, if not, how short would they fall! Upon his safe landing, his steaming boss gave him a royal ass chewing, while King George VI awarded him the KBE, or Knight Commander of the Most Excellent Order of the British Empire. And the king steamed to Malta on the cruiser *Aurora* for the ceremony.

For these and other reasons, Park had his detractors. But he lived long enough to see himself played favorably by Trevor Howard in the film *The Battle of Britain.* Park also found himself hero worshiped by Peter Townsend, one of the Battle of Britain's most famous pilots, in addition to being the love interest of the young Princess Margaret. (Even the stiff-upper-lip British did not give up romance during the war.) And Park won accolades from various allied pilots like Ben Fisz of the Polish Air Force.[29]

While Townsend and Fisz were becoming air aces, Red practiced his own marksmanship. Not yet graduated from high school, Red spent his free time hunting, a right of passage for many rural American males. With the Great Depression, hunger returned to the working class. To obtain the meat for their table, Red reduced the number of Ozark squirrels and rabbits. He even sold their fur. But until America sent its squirrel-gun–trained youth to join the fighting, Britain had to look elsewhere.

It was from places like Poland that Britain found more assistance. Polish pilots escaped from occupied Europe to fight another day. While British and British colonials predominated in the ranks of the RAF, Polish-accented English sometimes came from a *Hurricane* cockpit. Crushed between two liars, Hitler and Stalin, Poland fell in 1939. Before defeat, the Polish Air Force ordered all pilots to make their way to Romania. From there they crossed Yugoslavia, northern Italy, and into France, helped along the way by British and American military attachés.

In France, those who could speak some English, especially fighter pilots, went to Britain to fly with the RAF. But many Polish bomber pilots flew for France, whose proud tradition in aviation Antoine de Saint Exupéry celebrated in his award-winning air memoir, *Air, Sand, and Stars*. Those who piloted over France, the Mediterranean Sea, and North Africa's Sahara were well advised to read his air-map marking danger spots.[30]

Once France fell, flight beckoned again. Having lost pilots in the battle of France, and losing more in the Battle of Britain, RAF leaders were overjoyed to inherit trained pilots itching to fight. First inter-mixed with British squadrons, once enough Poles had mastered rudimentary English, they had squadrons of their own, the famous 302 and 303 Polish RAF fighter squadrons, and the 300 and 301 Polish RAF bomber squadrons were only four of many.

Jerzy Solak typifies the feisty Polish flyboys. Immensely proud of their record, they soon beat British pilots in the number of Luftwaffe kills. And they had their aces like General Witold Urbanowicz. During the Battle of Britain, Solak flew *Hurricanes* in the 11th Group under Park. He liked the New Zealander at once.[31] Park, like Solak, never forgot his own country. What Solak saw was a man proud of his uniform, ratty though it had become. Allowed to wear their own dark blue New Zealand uniforms until they were no longer serviceable, at which time RAF uniforms would be issued, men like Park hung onto their native threads with a passion.

Augmented by the Polish air crews escaping from France, the number of Polish squadrons doubled, then tripled. Via early stealth methods, other East European flyers arrived. The 310 and 311 RAF squadrons spoke a Czech-accented English. What Britain built was an Allied Air Force, a year before America's entry into combat. And they flew tirelessly. For example, Solak did back-to-back tours, defending London early in the war, followed by an assignment in the Shetland Islands giving air cover to attacks on Norway, reassigned to Cambridge as a test pilot for the new *Typhoon* aircraft, and later attacking Channel shipping from his *Spitfire.*

Bored with a short ground assignment at Oxbridge, Solak wangled himself a job as adjutant to General Ujejski and flew off with him to Cairo, Tunis, and Naples. Unhappy as an adjutant, he returned to Britain, where he became a liaison officer to the newly arrived American Ninth Air Force, a group he characterized as "green, green, green."[32]

Did these Poles matter? Air Chief Marshal Lord Dowding thought they did.

> The other Commands, the Commonwealth countries and four allies contributed unstintingly to meet the emergency, but if it has not been for the magnificent material contributed by the Polish contingent and their unsurpassed gallantry, I hesitate to say that the outcome of the battle (of Britain) would have been the same.[33]

High praise indeed.

And what of those green Americans that Solak advised? They came by the thousands until they outnumbered any single allied nationality. But they came late and so played no role in the defensive Battle over Britain. But they couldn't wait to get into the offensive battle over Germany. And get into it they did. Among them came film stars like Jimmy Stewart, cinema's all-American boy, fresh from two 1939 hits. In the first, *Destry Rides Again,* Stewart, a mild-mannered sheriff cleans up a corrupt western town and saves Marlene Dietrich from a ruinous life serving the boys in the back room. In the second, *Mister Smith Goes to Washington,* Senator Stewart cleans up Congress's back rooms with a little bit of ordinary kindness, fighting the corrupt politicos in democracy's name. With a war on, Mister Stewart flew bombers to help clean up the North Atlantic world to make it safe for ordinary people.[34]

Some ordinary people wanted to fly democracy's banner. Fighting extraordinary odds, the first black American pilots came forward. After much agitation Washington compromised and created an Air Training Center in Tuskegee, Alabama, exclusively for black air crews, who were itching to show their patriotic fervor. These "Afro-Saxons" affirmed their excellence by their own actions, often equalling the standards set up by Anglo-Saxons, sometimes besting them.[35] A wartime meritocracy, it wasn't integration, but it would do until the real thing came. One of the chinks in the armor of franchise democracy, it lacked the civic rewards for pockets of the citizenry, a lack determined in the United States by race.[36]

Nevertheless, by late 1942 the Tuskegee center had graduated forty-three black pursuit pilots, who formed the Ninty-ninth Fighter Squadron. First bloodied over Sicily, they next flew air missions for the British Eighth Army in Italy. And with these flights came the honors due brave men, all volunteers for a democracy they were yet to know in its fullest meaning.[37] Like the Polish pilots, they proved by doing: their deeds spoke for them. Black women also refused to be excluded from the war effort, be it as a civilian defense worker or a lady in uniform. Charity Adams Early, the first black woman commissioned in what was then the Women's Auxiliary Army Corps, rose to the rank of lieutenant colonel and commanded the only unit of black women to serve overseas in World War II.[38] But before the Americans came the Poles.

In 1940, Poles, like crocuses, kept popping up all over Britain, even in British gardens. Virginia and Leonard Woolf kept a country place in Rodmell, one hour south of London by train. From their rooms there, the Woolfs could hear the German bombers headed toward London, where German bombs destroyed one of the Woolfs' achievements, the Hogarth Press. An unending succession of regiments on troop marches passed by Rodmell. They often camped in the nearby fields, land belonging to the Woolfs. Patriotic but antiwar—Leonard considered it a great bore—they would put up the officers in the spare bedroom and the garden room.

One afternoon, balanced high on a ladder picking figs, Leonard was greeted by a Polish lieutenant stationed with a nearby Lancashire regiment. Fresh from the Polish embassy staff in Washington, the Pole had volunteered to join Britain in its war against Germany. He had come to the house to borrow something; once he saw the library, he stayed for forty-eight hours to read and talk.

Different in birth, nationality, education, and experience, the Pole and Leonard had their meals in the kitchen "discussing love and life and death and politics and literature." He went as he came—suddenly. (Polish ground units grew large enough for them to form the Polish First Armored Division, which went into the Normandy campaign under the control of the Canadian First Army. The Polish First Armored Division played an important role at the battle of the Falaise Gap.) Two years after the war ended, the Polish lieutenant reappeared at Rodmell, returning to the garden and library to thank its owner.[39]

On another occasion, Leonard put up officers from a Kent regiment camping in his field. When he went to see if there was anything else he could do, one of the lieutenants had discovered that Virginia's novels were translated into his native language. There he sat reading *Flush* in Czech.[40]

For those refugees too old to fight, other duties awaited. Polish physicists like Joseph Rotblat escaped Nazi-occupied Poland to settle in Britain, where he joined in work on the atom bomb. During the Cold War he turned his attention to disarmament issues, winning the Nobel Peace Prize in 1995. Like a fellow Polish Nobel laureate, Madame Marie Curie, he sought the atmosphere of scientific openness in the western tip of Europe when their native land fell to tyranny.

Some older Americans insisted that they were not too old to fight, even if famous in their professions. One of these, Glenn Miller, a composer and big band leader, volunteered for aerial combat. In no other land except America would a national asset like Miller be allowed to go into harm's way. But there he was. And he paid the greatest price. Glenn Miller died on December 16, 1944, a casualty of the air war against Germany. But his legacy plays on, proof again of what Immanuel Kant said of music—that it speaks without concepts through nothing but feelings. And the first notes of the war's trumpets heralded the air battle of 1940 over Britain.

Why choose the Battle of Britain in lieu of other air campaigns? Because it saved the island from invasion, the plans for which Hitler and his staff made very clear. Without an unconquered Britain on the allied side, no war against Germany from the West could succeed. With no safe haven on the eastern edge of the North Atlantic, the United States could not wage an offensive war from the western edge of its own coastline. The battle for the sky over Britain was the first of five tide-turning victories and had to be won before the battles of sand, snow, sea, and shore brought the allies into the German homeland.

Notes

1. In an amusing essay, Simon Schama captures the British love affair with beef. Citing a manuscript recipe of 1763, he offers the reader Baked Buttock of British Beef. For visual proof of the pudding, he offers William Hogarth's 1748 painting, *The Gates of Calais, or the Roast Beef of Old England.* Now hanging in London's Tate Gallery, it confirms the belief of the earlier Tudor historian Holinshed, who boasted that "the English cookes, in comparison with other Nations, are most commended for roast meates." The greatest British scandal of the 1990s was not the divorce of Princess Diana and Prince Charles, but the outbreak of mad-cow disease attacking "the four-legged symbol of essential Britishness" (Schama, "Mad Cows & Englishmen," *The New Yorker*, April 8, 1996, 61–62).

2. David Hackett Fischer, *Albion's Seed: Four British Folkways in America* (New York: Oxford University Press, 1989).

3. Bernard and Fawn M. Brodie, *From Crossbow to H-Bomb: The Evolution of the Weapons and Tactics of Warfare* (Bloomington: Indiana University Press, 1973), 178.

4. Stanley M. Ulanoff, ed., *The Red Baron: The Autobiography of Manfred Von Richthofen* (New York: Barnes & Noble Books, 1969); Edward V. Rickenbacker, *Fighting the Flying Circus* (New York: Frederick A. Stoker, 1919); and Alexander P. Seversky, *Victory Through Air Power* (Garden City, NY: Garden City Publishing Company, 1943).

5. Quoted in Russell F. Weigley, *The American Way of War: A History of US Military Strategy and Policy* (New York: Macmillan, 1973), 343. The long-range fighters to which Goering refers were the P-51 *Mustangs.*

6. Anthony Sampson, *The Arms Bazaar: From Lebanon to Lockheed* (New York: Viking Press, 1977), 94.

7. Figures comparing British fighter production in 1941 to German production are in B.H. Liddell Hart, *History of the Second World War* (Boston: G.P. Putnam's Sons, 1970), 92. Speer's story is in Albert Speer, *Inside the Third Reich: Memoirs* (New York: Macmillan, 1970), 220.

8. R.V. Jones, *The Wizard War: British Scientific Intelligence, 1939–1945* (New York: Coward, McCann & Geoghegan, 1978), 198–99.

9. Speer, *Inside the Third Reich,* 274, 482–83.

10. Liddell Hart, *History of the Second World War,* 90–92.

11. Speer, *Inside the Third Reich*, 431–432, 504. A British engineer, Sir Frank Whittle, first patented the idea of a jet engine in 1930. Working independently of Whittle, Han J.P. von Ohain designed a German jet engine. The first German jet flew in 1939 (four days before the outbreak of war); the first British jet did not fly until 1941. By 1944 both countries had a small number of jet aircraft in action.

12. Inasmuch as biography sometimes fails to capture an individual, a carefully constructed historical novel can illuminate better than other means. The work of Ella Laffland attests to this in her treatment of Goering, *The Knight, Death and the Devil* (New York: William Morrow, 1990). Another sketch of Goering emerges in Simon Schama's *Landscape and Memory* (New York: Knopf, 1995), 67–70, 73, 118–19.

13. Hans-Georg von Studnitz, *While Berlin Burns: The Diary of Hans-Georg von Studnitz, 1943–1945* (London: Weidenfeld and Nicolson, 1964), 36, 167–68, 173–74, 241–42.

14. The reputations of both Bruckner and Furtwangler suffered because of the use made of them by the Nazis. Luckily, Bruckner was long dead, but even after Furtwangler's death he was the subject of Ronald Harwood's successful Broadway play *Taking Sides,* which delved into Furtwangler's Nazi connections and the American attempt to denazify him (Bryan Gilliam, "For Bruckner, a Vague Nazi Aura Persists," *New York Times,* October 6, 1996, H33; Vincent Canby, "Shining a Light on the Mind of a Genius," *New York Times,* October 27, 1996, H5).

15. Harold Nicolson, *The Diaries & Letters of the War Years: 1939–1945,* vol. 2, ed. Nigel Nicolson (New York: Atheneum, 1967), 112–13.

16. Alex Ross, "In Music, Though, There Were No Victories," *New York Times,* August 20, 1995, H25. Also see Humphrey Carpenter, *Benjamin Britten: A Biography* (New York: Charles Scribner's Sons, 1992), 226–28.

17. Joe Morella et al., *The Films of World War II* (Secaucus, NJ: Citadel Press, 1973), 72–73.

18. Philip Hoare, *Noel Coward* (New York: Simon & Schuster, 1995), 306–55. He and his friend Marlene Dietrich spent part of the war visiting the wounded and performing for the troops—an audacious Anglo–German alliance. She had a thing for the boys; so did he.

19. George Amberg, *The New York Times Film Reviews, 1913–1970* (New York: Quadrangle Books, 1970), 204–5. Also see Anthony Aldgate and Jeffrey Richards, *Britain Can Take It: The British Cinema in the Second World War* (Edinburgh: Edinburgh University Press, 1994).

20. John Morton Blum, *V Was for Victory: Politics and American Culture During World War II* (New York: Harcourt, Brace, Jovanovich, 1976), 95–96.

21. Bogart came from an upper-middle-class family that hoped he was headed for Yale. Instead, he was expelled from prep school and joined the U.S. Navy in time for WW I. While serving, he received the scar on his upper lip that caused the distinctive lisp, his screen trademark (John McCarty, *Hollywood Gangland: The Movies' Love Affair with the Mob* (New York: St. Martin's Press, 1993), 83–84, 101–11).

22. Pauline Kael captures the nature of Bogart's success. See her *I Lost It at the Movies: Film Writings 1954–1965* (Boston: Little, Brown, 1965), 214. Warner Brothers has created its own museum in Burbank, California, where a researcher can now obtain important film facts. Most of Warner's film documents are housed at the University of Southern California.

23. On November 12, 1996, an original poster for *Casablanca* sold at Christie's, the British auction house, for $38,000. The film opened in 1942, only three weeks after the allies landed at Casablanca ("'Casablanca' Poster Sold for $38,000," *San Francisco Chronicle,* November 14, 1996, C10).

24. As late as 1987, Berlitz published a travel guide to Morocco in which the following image of the Moroccan town of Taroudant (225 kilometers southwest from Marrakesh) appeared: "Within them (high tawny walls) dusty squares and market-places, almost unaltered, could provide the backdrop for a Humphrey Bogart film." (*Morocco* [Bienne, Switzerland; Berlitz, 1987], 67).

25. Humphrey Bogart to Jack Warner, Western Union Wire, May 26, 1944, Warner Brothers' Museum, on loan from the Warner Brothers Archives, School of Cinema-Television, University of Southern California.

26. Winston Churchill, *The Second World War: Their Finest Hour* (Boston: Houghton Mifflin, 1949), 333–37. In June 1994 the author visited the underground operations room at Uxbridge as part of a fiftieth anniversary tour commemorating the Normandy landings. RAF personnel gave a briefing; the room remained as it looked in the last days of the war—operation maps, squadron positions, special telephones, all the accoutrements of the Battle of Britain.

27. Vincent Orange, *A Biography of Air Marshal Sir Keith Park* (London: Methuen, 1984), 110.

28. Letter, posted from France and dated January 16, 1945. Red mentioned that some local London ladies—prostitutes—were after GIs who had the money to pay for a good time.

29. Orange, *A Biography of Air Marshal Sir Keith Park,* 147–49, 167, 181. Also see Peter Townsend, *Duel of Angels* (London: Corgi, 1972).

30. Antoine de Saint Exupéry, *Wind, Sand and Stars* (New York: Reynal and Hitchcock, 1940). In the 1920s he flew for Aéropostale between Toulouse in southwestern France and Dakar in French West Africa. In the 1930s he tried to fly from Paris to Saigon but crashed in the Libyan desert. He then flew in the Spanish Civil War, the 1940 Battle for France, escaped to the United States after France fell, flew against the Germans again in North Africa in 1943, was shot down in the desert, and lived to tell his story in the 1952 *The Wisdom of the Sands.*

31. Jerzy Solak, "War Diary," unpublished. The author interviewed Solak in his California home.

32. Interview with Solak on February 8, 1996.

33. Air Marshal Lord Dowding, letter, "Polish Airmen in the Battle of Britain," *Wings* (London: Polish Air Force Association, May 1993), 51–52.

34. Donald Dewey, *James Stewart* (Atlanta: Turner, 1996), 228–57. See David Freeman, "Mr. Stewart Goes to Hollywood," *New York Times Book Review,* September 15, 1996, 20.

35. I borrow the term *Afro-Saxon* from the courageous Plummer Professor of Christian Morals at Harvard, Peter Gomes.

36. Half a century after the fact, seven black soldiers received Medals of Honor for their daring deeds of WW II, the first black servicemen to receive that highest accolade in that bloodiest of wars. One of the seven, Staff Sergeant Ruben Rivers, had a white army commander, Captain David Williams, who had fought since the war for River's recognition (Kevin Fagan, "Medals Awarded 50 Years After: WW II Heroism of 7 Black Soldiers Finally Recognized," *San Francisco Chronicle,* January 14, 1997, A1).

37. Alan L. Gropman, "Tuskegee Airmen," *Air Force Magazine,* March 1996, 52–56.

38. Charity Adams Early, *One Woman's Army* (College Station, TX: Texas A&M University Press, 1989). Also see Gretchen Lemke-Santangelo, *Abiding Courage: African American Migrant Women and the East Bay Community* (Chapel Hill, NC: University of North Carolina Press, 1966).

39. Leonard Woolf, *The Journey Not the Arrival Matters* (New York: Harcourt, Brace, Jovanovich, 1969), 66–68. On the Polish Armored Division at Falaise, see Carlo D'Este, "Falaise: The Trap Not Sprung," *MHQ: The Quarterly Journal of Military History* (Spring 1994), 58–68.

40. Woolf, *The Journey*, 68.

The Sand

North Africa has one dominant geographical feature, the Sahara. The largest tropical and climatic desert on earth, it covers an area of 3,320,000 square miles (8,600,00 square kilometers). As large as the United States, this queen of deserts holds eleven countries within its sun-scorched boundaries. With a 3,200–mile coastline, the Sahara constitutes the eastern end of the Afro–Asian desert. The name is derived from the Arab word for desert, *sahra:* a petrified ocean. It is opposed to the Mediterranean as a camel is to a horse or a date is to an olive. In a word, different. It is assumed to be mostly sand, but in fact sand makes up only 20 percent, the remainder being small stones and smooth rocks. Libya, which is 99 percent arid, and Egypt, which is 98 percent, are true Saharan states.

The Sahara has the highest evaporation rate in the world. Some areas receive no precipitation for years at a stretch. It also has the lowest relative humidity, with some areas falling to the life-endangering low of 2.5 percent. Along the North African coast from Tunisia to Egypt, rain is rare. Ten inches (250 millimeters) per year would be considered flood stage. And the Mediterranean basin is a mixing bowl for strong winds. Funneling in from the north is the mistral, a cold, dry river of air. Around Saharan Africa flies the warm, dusty *ghibli* or *khamsin* (Arabic for "fifty"). And out of Africa storms the sirocco, dry and hot.

Sandstorms take regional names; in southern Morocco the fellahin defend themselves against the *aajej* with knives. But the harmattan dies offshore in the Atlantic, carrying with it a red powder that ferments a wine-stained sea. When lucky, Egypt suffers only three months of the khamsin. Tunisia has the dry, heated dust of the ghibli. The *datoo* brings fragrances from Gilbraltar while the Sudanese *haboob* is a high, butter-yellow wall. Sandy storms shape themselves into circles, columns, or cliffs. They come hot and dry from Arabia, the *nafhat,* or violent and cold in the Berber Valleys, the *mezzarifoullousen.* Standing still, you are pillared like Lot's wife, sculptured of sand, not salt. Such storms can peel paint, uproot polls, unseat riders, decapitate statues, transport stones, and kill. A climate of white-hot heat and bone-chilling cold.

Then why fight in North Africa? Partly because the remnants of Atlantic empires stretched from French interests east of the Moroccan coast to British interests west of the Egyptian canal, with Italian interests squeezed between in Libya. And Italy's axial dictator hungered for glory. Senior in dictatorship to Hitler, no one ever accused Benito Mussolini of having mastered the military art. Mediocre and mendacious, Mussolini was destined to hold a rendezvous with disaster. Dreaming of again making the Mediterranean a Roman lake—mere nostrum—Italy's Duce skulked around until he saw France fail in May 1940.[1] Impatient to grab those spoils his Axis ally Hitler would tolerate, Mussolini could not wait for the invasion of Britain. Instead, on June 10, 1940, he, lusting after Egypt, an old Roman curse, precipitously declared war on Britian.

Mussolini made two classic blunders: He mistook Malta as meaningless, and he failed to see that, closer to Italy, only Tunisia offered ports modern enough from which to unload the logistics needed for his North African war. (Libyan ports and their infrastructures could not compare with Bizerte in Tunisia or Alexandria in Egypt.) First, he should have stormed minute Malta, simultaneously joining Germany at the outset of the campaign against France in 1940. Second, with the fall of France, he could have demanded French Tunisia as a zone of occupation the way Germany demanded northern France. A greedhead of the first water, he was out of his shallows in his Mediterranean strategy. Without Malta and ports in Tunisia, his war waxed and waned, but he could never win it. Minus Malta, Mussolini's misfortunes mounted.[2] In the end, he lost everything.

Inasmuch as Italy forced Britain to fight in the desert periphery of

North Atlantic power, Italy also dragged Germany into this sandtrap when Britain reversed Italian gains and invaded Libya. To meet the new German–Italian push toward the Nile Delta and the manmade seaway at Suez, Britain had to station its largest field army in the desert.

Once Britain had regained the initiative, British leaders wanted U.S. assistance in North Africa and the Mediterranean for two purposes: to drive the Axis allies away and to secure this southern sealane for Anglo–American shipping. As British leaders saw it, this would commit the Americans to the European theater while keeping casualties low, at the same time allowing time to prepare for a landing on the continent. Once successful in North Africa, British leaders hoped that Italy, only a short jump away, would offer the allies a back door into Hitler's Reich. With all his eloquence and stubbornness, Churchill persuaded an irresolute Roosevelt to fight a Mediterranean-first overture to invasion.[3]

Steaming in Moscow, an always suspicious Stalin felt betrayed by this Mediterranean side-stepping. He demanded a leap onto the European continent, a second front, to draw German forces away from an imperiled Soviet Union. (In June 1941, Hitler, unable to invade Britain, had instead invaded the Soviet Union, his co-conspirator in the 1939 Polish campaign.) Some influential Americans agreed with Stalin. Disgruntled in Washington, senior American military leaders such as General George Marshall felt obligated to support President Roosevelt's Europe-first strategy, but less so a Mediterranean-first overture. (Commanders in the Pacific theater of war, especially General Douglas MacArthur and Admiral Chester Nimitz, reminded Washington staffers that Japan, not Germany or Italy, had attacked Pearl Harbor. Hence, they wanted the first counterblow to fall on Japan.) After the dust settled on the debate, British views prevailed.[4] The battle of the sand took precedence.

The Great War of 1914 had also jumped the Mediterranean to the African continent, arriving three days after the outbreak of European fighting. French African colonies fought German African colonies; the British did the same when their colonial ambitions saw an opportunity at Germany's expense. German Togoland fell first; the French spearing in from Senegal and the British from the Gold Coast. White European officers and noncommissioned officers led African colonials into miniature versions of World War I battles.

Later films and novels captured those martial moments; in the French case, the Academy Award–winning best foreign film *Black and White in Color;* in the British case, the C.S. Forester novel-turned-film, *The African Queen,* for which Humphrey Bogart won an Academy Award.[5] In 1914, when colonial contretemps combusted, they did so in sub-Saharan Africa. In the second global war, north Saharan Africa substituted its sand for the soil of the tropical south.

When Mussolini trumpeted war in June 1940, he had troops in four parts of Africa: Ethiopia, Eritrea, Somaliland, and Libya. Reinforcements for the first three colonies had to pass through the Suez Canal into the Red Sea, a passage to India that Britain easily blocked. With British warships at Gibraltar, that Mediterranean outlet did not entice Italian ships either. Libya presented another challenge. Only the British garrison on molecule-sized Malta harassed crossings of the Mediterranean narrows between Italy and North Africa. Mussolini had stationed 200,000 troops in Libya, contrasted to 63,000 British imperial troops in Egypt. Italy also had more aircraft in North Africa than did Britain, and so could focus its fleet on the mid-Mediterranean. In contrast, Britain, given the danger from German air and sea power, had to concentrate the Royal Air Force and the Royal Navy on the defense of the British Isles.

Operating on the maxim that the best defense is a good offense, the outnumbered British troops in Egypt attacked. Their orders had instructed them that, immediately upon the outbreak of war, they should strike the Italian frontier posts. Unwarned that war had indeed broken out, these forward positions fell. In those first three months of war, Italian casualties amounted to nearly thirty-five hundred, while the Brits counted only one hundred and fifty. At that rate the odds would soon change in Britain's favor.

Chastised by this early defeat, Mussolini scored a victory when his garrison in Somaliland overran the British colony of the same name. Crestfallen by that defeat, Churchill, determined to meet the Italian main-force units moving to the Egyptian border, ordered an armored brigade to Egypt. Its supply caravan, including its spirits, traveled with it.

Churchill wanted the Admiralty to send at least the tanks via the shortest route, the Mediterranean. But not even the prime minister could induce such a risk on the part of admiral of the fleet, First Sea Lord, Sir Dudley Pound, who sent them round the Cape, adding three weeks to the journey. (Churchill later gloated that the Admiralty did ferry tanks to Egypt through the Mediterranean in the worst days of 1941, when the Luftwaffe was establishing itself in Sicily.)

Along with tanks came aircraft. The aircraft for Egypt initially came ashore from carriers off the coast of West Africa; pilots then flew them via Khartoum to Cairo. Ordinary supplies, including a goodly ration of rum, made the dicey journey via the Mediterranean.

Many ships found themselves vessels without countries. Such was the case for the Belgian ship the *Léopoldville*. The prewar owners of the craft, commissioned in 1929, assigned it to the Congo run, carrying passengers and cargo between Antwerp and Matadi. At the time of the German attack on Belgium, the *Léopoldville* was homeward bound from Africa. The ship's captain changed course for the French port of La Pallice, latter a key U-boat base for the German underwater fleet. Fearing confiscation by the French at the time the Belgian king Leopold III ordered his subjects to surrender, the vessel set course back to the Congo. The next trip took the ship to New York, where she came under British control. The cargo hold underwent a change; the ship, once able to carry three hundred passengers, could now carry twenty-three hundred troops.

The *Léopoldville,* with her Belgian crew still in service, saw duty carrying soldiers to Egypt, Algeria, Sicily, Italy, and finally Normandy. In this manner, the ship was a Belgian addition to democracy's fleet. On Christmas Eve, 1944, along with the SS *Cheshire,* she helped to transport two regiments of the U.S. Sixty-sixth Infantry Division, in which Red served, to Normandy. But in the early years of the war, the *Léopoldville*'s first task involved getting soldiers to the sea of sand.[6]

On September 13, 1940, as British tank and air reinforcements continued to arrive in Egypt, the long-awaited Italian invasion commenced. Marshal Rodolfo Graziani led troops of the Italian Tenth Army sixty miles inside Egypt. On December 9 the forces of Field Marshal Sir Archibald Wavell counterattacked, driving Graziani's army back four hundred miles into Libya, a pell-mell retreat along the single coastal road. Wavell's haul of prisoners exceeded 130,000.

Worse yet, the Italian fleet, umbilical guardian of the supply cord to the mother country, suffered two defeats by the British: On July 8–9 Force H of the Royal Navy (based in Gibraltar) and the Mediterranean Fleet (based in Alexandria) caught the Italian fleet between Sardinia and Calabria and shellacked it. Then on November 11 an air group operating from the deck of HM Carrier *Illustrious* surprised the Italian battleships moored in the harbor at Taranto; a mini Pearl Harbor ensued. This destruction of Italian sea assets assured General Wavell that the Italian fleet could not sever British supply lines.

Among the four major battles of Wavell's campaign—Sidi Barrani, Bardia, Tobruk, Beda Fomm—Tobruk received the most notice. Chester Wilmot, a war correspondent accredited by the Australian Broadcasting Commission's Field Unit in the Middle East, followed the Sixth Australian Division into Tobruk. With speed and stealth on Wavell's side, twenty-nine hours after the first Australian troops broke through the Italian perimeter, Tobruk surrendered on January 22, 1941.

Coming after the June 1940 evacuation from Dunkirk, the fall of Tobruk stiffened British spines like a shot of rum. While the Italians had destroyed much equipment, they left intact one area of strategic, and one of sipping, importance. Of strategic import, the water-supply plant remained intact, along with two water distilleries delivering twenty thousand gallons a day and the sub-artisan wells, which could provide a further twenty thousand. Of spirit import, they had refused to destroy the Chianti supplies.

Chester Wilmot reported that the Italians "had left substantial stores of Chianti, cognac, aniseed brandy and a mineral water named Recoaro." The journalist and the troops liked the Chianti, but found the brandy fiery and the aniseed worse. The Recoaro "was excellent and the Italians had shipped hundreds of thousands of cases of it from Italy." Apparently, their officers would only drink this water; on hardly any occasions did ordinary soldiers partake of this refreshment. The Anglo liberators found "one huge iron shed packed with cases of it and almost every mess in General O'Connor's forces was soon well supplied."[7]

Along with liquid refreshment came food. The Italians took Napoleon literally when it came to an army traveling on its stomach. They had stocked Tobruk with enough tinned food for a garrison of 25,000 to survive for two months. There were "vast supplies of tinned cherries, strawberries, pears, apricots, beans, peas, carrots, pulped tomatoes, great boxes of spaghetti, and several hundred tons of flour which went straight into British bakeries."[8]

With Wavell on the threshold of victory in North Africa, two decisions—one in London, one in Berlin—derailed his final push. First, Churchill decided to reinforce British forces in Greece; second, Hitler decided to rescue German forces in Libya. British regulars needed in

54

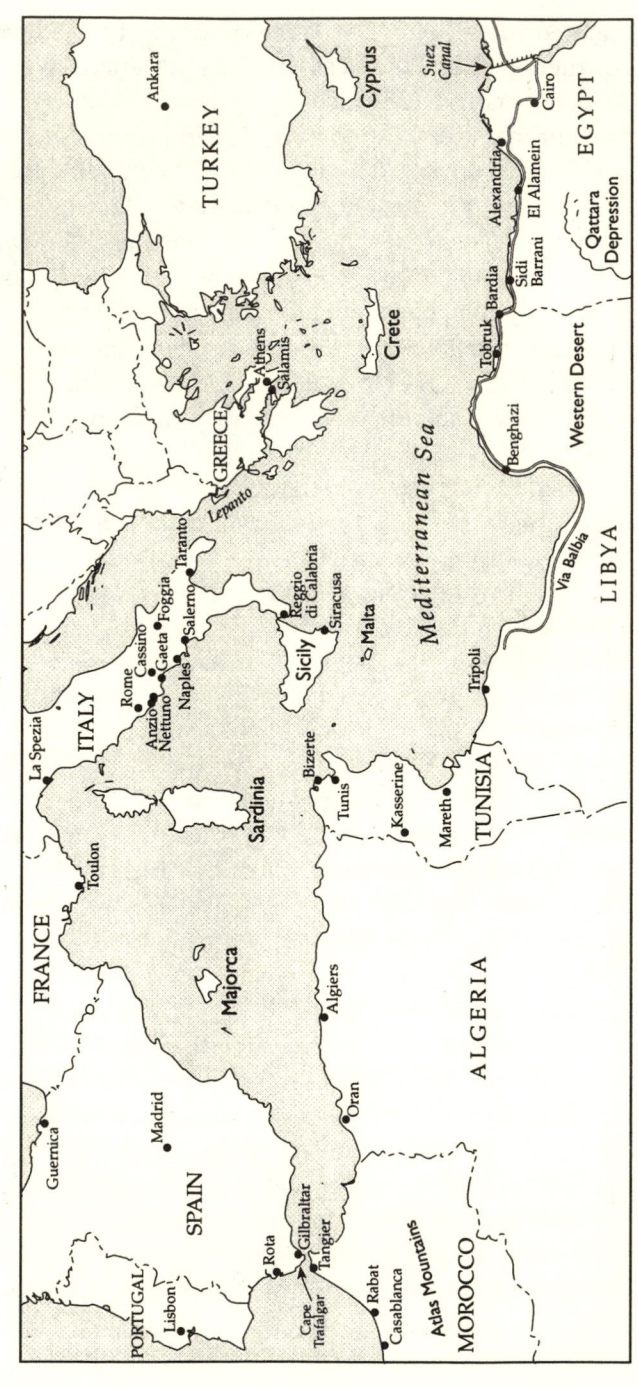

North Africa went to Athens; German rescuers needed for the upcoming Russian campaign went to Tripoli. A senior rescuer carried a name: (Johannes) Erwin Eugen Rommel.

Briefed on February 6, 1941, by Hitler himself, Rommel stopped in Rome before flying to Libya. Under defeatist conditions, Rommel reorganized the Tripolitanian forces. Ever the fox, to fool the British he ordered dummy tanks made and mounted on old Volkswagen chassis. Not one to waste time, Rommel counterattacked forty days after his advance guard arrived in Tripoli. Now the British retreated back along their coastal road of victory, a withdrawal that took them eastward toward Egypt.

Rommel made his reputation in North Africa—a trailblazing general of quality, of his type they made legends, and films. (Decades after WW II, many imagined Rommel looking like James Mason, his stand-in when Hollywood filmed the *The Desert Fox.*)[9] The force Rommel favored, the Afrika Korps, initially consisted of the Fifth Light and Fifteenth Panzer Divisions. With their tanks he hoped to capture the land of the pharaohs (a place his prewar doctor had prescribed to cure Rommel's rheumatism).[10]

Even though Germany produced the better tank, their tanks gulped huge amounts of fuel. The farther one advanced, the longer grew the supply lines; a logistical nightmare, as the tankers that transported the fuel used almost as much in getting to their destinations as they carried with them. In the North African campaign, two fluids determined victory, fuel for vehicles and water for humans. And always the sand.

Did the sand bother Rommel? To read his diary and letters home, one could mistake him for the senior meteorologist assigned to German forces in Africa.[11] In his first encounter with an African sandstorm (*ghibli*), he wrote in his diary that he flew into one and tried to abuse the pilot into continuing the flight. Even in the face of the Desert Fox's anger, the pilot refused and landed, which forced Rommel to continue his inspection of the front by car.

Quickly, Rommel realized "what little idea we had of the tremendous force of such a storm." He couldn't see. "Immense clouds of reddish dust obscured all visibility and forced the car's speed down to a crawl." And he had not experienced such winds. "Often the wind was so strong that it was impossible to drive along the Via Balbia . . . sand streamed down the windscreen like water." He thought he would choke. "We gasped in breath painfully through handkerchiefs held over our faces and sweat poured off our bodies in the unbearable heat ... so this was the Ghibli."[12] (Rommel wasn't the only general who tried to fly in sandstorms. His opposite on the British side, General Wavell, foolishly flew from the sandy airstrip in Tobruk in his two-engine Lockheed *Lodestar* straight into what the British call a sandstorm by another Arab name, a *khamsin*. He crashed, lived, and never flew into one again.)

The Via Balbia mentioned in Rommel's correspondence was not simply any road; it was the only road. Its builders had followed the coastline for more than 1,000 miles, never suspecting that Italian, British, and German armies would use it to advance and retreat along. Sometimes it was covered by sand; at other times it was a hot ribbon twisting around the sea's indentations.

Rommel's letter to his wife, Lu, on May 6, 1941, complained of the heat, relieved only when night came. He told her he had never been so thirsty. By July 3 he wrote that the atrocious heat no longer lifted at night; all one could do was lie in bed tossing and turning while dripping with sweat. In October he wrote his son Manfred about sandstorms with dust-clouds so thick that one could only see two to three yards in any direction.[13] As if to spite these dry storms, Rommel continued to push forward.

The sand met the shore at Tobruk, a fortified position held by the British. It had a new tenant, the Ninth Australian Division. These Aussies harassed Rommel's dash along the coastal plain and around British positions. He could not leave such a strong garrison in his rear during his thrust into Egypt; supply lines were fragile enough without allowing the Aussies to cut his at will. Besides, he, like the British, needed small ports like Tobruk, unimpressive as they looked, for re-supply.

To reach Alexandria and its vital dock facilities, Rommel had to travel 1,200 miles from Tripoli. For both combatants, seesawing across the desert meant dashing from one miniature maritime haven to another, whether you advanced or retreated, which both did several times. Usually, the force retreating abandoned the harbor in question. Senior British officials, aware that the Aussies were full of piss and vinegar, chose to let them stand and fight. As owners by conquest, they refused to go quietly.

Tobruk, commanded by a slight Australian, a former head of a department in a Sydney shipping firm, withstood an eight-month siege. While most Australian generals were citizen soldiers, this one, Major

General Leslie J. Morshead, earned the name "Ming the Merciless." Not only the enemy but any perceived British slight to Australia brought down his ire.

Once, in the middle of a German attack, Morshead's superior, an officer of His Britannic Majesty, wrote to this unpolished opal from the South Seas: "I must bring to your attention that there have been further instances of Australian drunkenness in Benghazi. An inebriated Australian soldier even came into my own HQ . . . words fail to express my disgust . . . your division will not become a useful instrument of war until you improve discipline."[14] Morshead wrote back that he would not put up with this anti-Australian attitude! Later, assigned to take charge of Tobruk's defenses, it was Morshead's turn to face a raging sandstorm. Morshead raged back and held the town.

Australians of different callings served Britain in its lonely war. Even intellectuals put aside their stinging rebuke of human folly and came to the colors. Patrick White, later Nobel laureate in literature, raised the Australian pen against totalitarianism. White served alongside Graham Greene in British intelligence services in Africa and the Middle East.

Failing to capture Tobruk in April, Rommel had to face a new danger. The Royal Navy, implementing code Tiger, now chanced a resupply of tanks via the Mediterranean. Once the tanks arrived, Wavell, who still commanded the Western Desert Force (its name changed to Eighth Army in September 1941), went over to the offensive. Inventive as always, Rommel sandbagged British tank formations with his 88–mm guns, excellent antiarmor weapons. Undermined by this setback, London transferred Wavell to India in exchange for Claude Auchinleck. As the new commander, Auchinleck made it his task to raise the siege of Tobruk and the British–Polish force that had replaced the Australians.

The Polish contingent had come by sea, wading ashore as German aircraft attempted to stop their unloading. Initially based in Syria, Lebanon, and then Palestine, the Polish Army in the Middle East was made up of Poles either who escaped Europe or whom Stalin un-imprisoned under allied pressure. The Poles came to fight with the allies once the British wrestled the Arab lands in the Levant away from Vichy French control, as was the case in Syria and Lebanon, or fought off local rebels, as was the case in Iraq.[15]

Among the wet and weary replacements at Tobruk was George

Lenczowski, one of the lucky Poles who had avoided capture by either the Nazis or the Soviets. Awash in the Middle East, he served as a young soldier, then diplomat. In his memoirs, he captures the downside of Tobruk, the constant artillery pounding from big German guns, and the upside, the excellent cognac available to ordinary soldiers like himself.[16] Auchinleck's relief of Tobruk on December 10, 1941, interrupted the cognac break.

Rommel now retreated, resting from the fatigue of "supply overstretch," which then began plaguing the British. Sensing this, Rommel counterattacked on January 21, 1942, driving the British forces back once again. Along the way he learned to scavenge equipment from the retreating enemy. On January 27, 1942, Rommel wrote his "Dear Lu" that he was busy clearing up the battlefield, collecting abandoned enemy guns, armored cars, tanks, rations, and ammunition for his own forces. His blindingly speedy advance had gained him much booty. But he still hated the weather, which had turned chilly and rainy. The only good thing about the rain, according to Rommel, was that it kept the British from getting planes off the ground from airfields in their sector of Libya.[17]

Then on January 28, Benghazi capitulated to Rommel, again rewarding him. "Vast quantities of vehicles, arms and material which fell into our hands served to equip and motorize many of our own units."[18] Unfortunately, British imperial troops had drunk the rum-well dry in Benghazi. The commander of the Indian division in the town had set his demolition squads a task—destroy supplies. "Seven million cigarettes went up in flame. Countless barrels of rum were destroyed."[19] With or without the rum, Rommel had the worrisome weather.

Rommel wrote his wife about a change in March, a change for the good, he hoped. "It's pleasantly warm at sea level, but there is a lot of wind and it's downright cold up here where we are, 2,500 feet up." Then the spring sun came out, and Rommel wrote that he "got thoroughly sunburnt yesterday, but we have the right ointment." Rommel enjoyed the British sense of humor. When they hastily evacuated his quarters, the British wrote on the door, "Keep clean, we'll be back soon."

Because he prided himself on his front-line generalship, in April Rommel fell victim to a shell splinter, which "came through the window recently and landed in my stomach after going through my overcoat and jacket." It left a multicolored bruise the size of a plate. Finally stopped by his trousers, Rommel remarked: "The luck of the devil."

His luck did not hold with the weather. On April 25 he wrote his wife that the temperature was around zero. But he was fascinated with the land, calling it "a real moon landscape. Dawn has a fantastic beauty in this country of flat-topped mountains."[20]

Warm or cold, Auchinleck prepared to counter Rommel's counter, but the German fox countered first. He hit the British forces on May 27. This time Auchinleck ordered his command back to Alam Halfa, near El Alamein and the natural obstacle of the Qattara Depression, a gigantic desert sandtrap some 436 feet below sea level.

Behind the German front, but still in British hands, lay Tobruk. But not for long. Toughened, Rommel turned on this thorn. Out he plucked it after a week of siege, when, on June 21, 1942, the Second South African Division surrendered. Coming four months after the fall of Singapore—the Asian fortress built to last a thousand years—this defeat caused British morale to fall as German morale soared.

The British war correspondent Alan Moorehead wondered if, with the captured equipment and supplies, "the richest treasure the desert had ever yielded," Rommel would soon be on the Nile. In empire terms he phrased the question as follows: "Would his officers realize their ancient dream of drinking whisky and soda in the bar of Shepheard's Hotel?"[21] That hotel served as the Cairo watering hole for the British establishment in Egypt.

Whiskey and soda not withstanding, Hitler elevated Rommel to field marshal, news of the promotion reaching Rommel by wireless. (In Prussia, field marshals never retired, nor could anyone dismiss them. They retained the rank for life and were entitled to a car with driver, a private secretary, and other perquisites. They were Wotan's immortals.)

A field marshal's baton notwithstanding, the greater award consisted of the huge amount of supplies captured with Tobruk's garrison. The vast booty that had befallen him, including ammunition, petrol, food, and war material of all kinds surprised even the unflappable Rommel. His men had other concerns. One German writer reports that while the rank and file took their decorations in their own inimitable way, they "descended upon the loot. The men of the 200th Panzer Reconnaissance Unit were as happy as sandboys when Karl Dorn returned with a crate of real German blood sausage." The British had captured it a year before from a German unit. Now it had returned to its rightful owners.[22]

Among the captured stores laid a treasure's worth of spirits; mainly

English gin, scotch, and rum. Ali Baba and the forty thieves would have seen it as booty, a liquid horde of diamond gin, topaz scotch, and amber rum. The Germans simply drank it, some of it.

Wherever the British military standard had flown, so had its spirits run. A pleasure to capture in bulk, a drink for everyone, and everyone for a drink. Not as cooling as Bavarian beer, but even Berlin under the Nazis had taken to gin-and-tonics in the summertime. The scotch whiskey one drank neat, not with ice as the Americans demanded. For the rum, it did go nicely with Coca-Cola, but as yet no Yank supply dumps lay in the path of conquest. With so much liquid treasure about, for storage the German staff sent the excess to Italy in the empty holds of Axis transports.

German euphoria did not last because replacement supplies did not arrive. As he entered Egypt, Rommel knew that captured stores had tided him over the crisis in his supply situation after the fall of Tobruk, but now he needed replenishment. He ruminates in his diary that in modern warfare supplies decide the battle; therefore, "it is easy to see how the clouds of disaster were gathering for my army." By the time Rommel reached Egypt, up to 85 percent of his transport still consisted of captured enemy vehicles. Nevertheless, during the month of July, Rommel tried to break the El Alamein line. He failed. On July 3, 1942, he wrote to "Dear Lu" about the struggle for the last position before Alexandria. He had been up on the front for days, living in his command car or a hole in the ground, while suffering attacks by the Royal Air Force. The letter's tone had the sound of resignation about it.[23]

Rommel's depression originated with the stalemate in the Egyptian desert; so did Churchill's. The prime minister, desperate for a victory after having to defend himself against a motion of censure in the House of Commons on July 1, flew to Egypt in August. He came to purge, and purge he did. Auchinleck went, and Harold Alexander came. Under Alexander's command barked a regular British bulldog, Bernard Montgomery. Montgomery-the-meticulous took command of the British Eighth Army. Risk-averse, he wanted no part of playing Rommel's desert game of maneuver. For him a crushing defeat of the German forces in a set-piece battle would do. While Monty prepared his battlefield, Rommel, never all that robust, flew home on sick leave in September—stomach trouble.

From the Russian front came General Ritter von Thoma, who reluctantly replaced Rommel. He saw the need to withdraw in the face of growing British strength. Hitler refused with a hold-each-grain-of-sand policy. Thoma would still have had to retreat if it had not been for the damnable supplies captured at Tobruk, now an albatross around the German neck. In a postwar interview, Thoma explained: "We would have had to retreat in spite of Hitler's order but for the fact that we were able to feed our troops with the supplies which we had captured from your (British) stores at Tobruk." These supplies "kept us going," avoiding a dangerous setback at El Alamein but ensuring a disastrous set-to in North Africa![24]

Two events occurred that fall. First, the Americans had come on board, figuratively and factually. To shore up British morale for El Alamein, the American military generously offered to divert supplies of its new Sherman tanks, a weapon that could match the Panzer *Mark IV*. Quickly accepting this needed assistance, 300 Sherman tanks and 100 self-propelled guns came to Egypt in September via the Cape since the Americans were not willing to risk the Mediterranean route.

Second, the Royal Navy suffered a disastrous setback in the Mediterranean. To supply Malta, the British had to risk convoys to the island garrison. In the ill-fated Pedestal convoy of August, the Royal Navy, desperate to bring food and fuel to the defenders, lost one aircraft carrier and two cruisers along with eleven out of sixteen merchant ships. But Malta, Mussolini's mistake, survived, even though the Luftwaffe's Fliegerkorps X and II dropped twice as many bombs on it in two months of 1942 as fell on London in the year-long blitz. And Malta continued to serve in the war's aftermath. (Published in 1943, C.S. Forester's *The Ship* gave British and American readers a shipful of shivers. It was the story of convoy duty to Malta.[25])

Meanwhile, the British Desert Air Force inflicted major damage on three out of every four Italian convoys steaming from Italy to Tripoli, convoy smashing on a massive scale. Joining the battle of supply interdiction, Britain kept fifteen submarines of Malta's Tenth Flotilla operating from the island without the safety of submarine pens. Suffering 50 percent losses, they stayed for the battle and sank 75 enemy ships in sixteen months of duty. Joining these sea raiders, stripped-down British subs acted as cargo carriers known as the magic-carpet service to Malta. Unfortunately for the Axis powers, they could not avoid the air, sea, and underwater dangers. Neither the Germans nor the Italians had a safer, longer route around the Cape. Every Axis ship had to steam the gauntlet of the Mediterranean shooting gallery.

The Axis powers did have one early trump, the submarine. German U-boats entered the Mediterranean in force in 1941. They shared the Italian base at La Spezia and had their own base at Salamis in occupied Greece. Salamis carried a magical name from antiquity; here the classic Athenians had defeated an invading Persian fleet, thus ending the Persian danger. Initially, German U-boats shared this magic. Within weeks of their arrival, they sank two British warships near Alexandria, the battleship *Barham* and the cruiser *Galatea*. But their greatest success came when Lieutenant Commander Friedrich Guggenberger took U-81 past the Rock of Gibraltar on the night of November 12, 1941.

Boldly speeding on the surface with an eastward tide, dodging destroyers while caught in the beam of a Spanish lighthouse, U-81 cleared the British bastion guarding the narrow Atlantic entrance to the Mediterranean. The next day Guggenberger caught his prey, the British carrier the HMS *Ark Royal*. With a spread of torpedoes he struck. It took the great carrier twenty-four hours to die, but sink it did.[26] That was 1941; by late 1942 the Mediterranean naval tide turned in Britain's favor. And Malta never surrendered.

After the war, Malta helped to keep the rum flowing. In 1946 Supernumary J. Harwood served on the HMS *Phoenicia* out of Sliema, Malta. Ordered to Taranto, Italy, that Easter, Harwood noticed a gallon stone jar full of rum near his locker. He packed it carefully in the middle of his kit—Harwood was underage to draw rum—and he and his rum disembarked for the Italian port. Billeted near a U.S. Army supply depot, Harwood noticed a jeep with a busted windscreen but only thirty miles on the speedometer. He asked the American supply sergeant if he liked rum. Yes, came the answer. "The jeep for a gallon of rum," he replied. The sergeant agreed. The next day Harwood drove the jeep to his billets. The Australian officer in charge agreed to Harwood's keeping it if the Australian could borrow it, even assigning Harwood as the driver and furnishing him with petrol. In August 1946 the Royal Navy ordered Harwood back to Malta. He took the jeep with him and drove it all over the island. In January 1948 he returned to the United Kingdom and was demobilized. He never knew what happened to his first car— the American war-surplus jeep traded for a gallon of rum.[27]

With or without rum, but with a sea controlled by Royal Navy ships, a British land offensive could commence in late 1942. On October 23 of that year, Montgomery launched his pitched battle, a crowbar wedged into the Axis front. On October 24 Hitler phoned Rommel in hospital to ask if he felt well enough to return to a bleak situation. Well or not, Rommel flew back the next day. But by the second battle of El Alamein, the British art of artillery had won. A British commander at the front noted: "We won, but it had been, in Wellington's phrase, 'hard pounding' and the British had the means to pound longest."[28]

Now Rommel, unable to implement Hitler's stand-fast order, challenged himself to save his army—escape westward again. This time the weather helped Rommel; an unseasonal rain fell continuously on November 6 and 7, giving the weary Germans a watery screen for their flight through the open desert. Montgomery cautiously followed, 1,200 miles back to Tripoli, which Rommel reached on January 23, 1943. On his way there he learned of Operation Torch, the Anglo–American landings in Morocco and Algeria on November 8, 1942. Suddenly, he had Eisenhower's First Army in his distant front and Montgomery's Eighth Army close on his rear.

For the North African landings, Ike took up headquarters in dismal settings, damp subterranean passages inside the Rock of Gibraltar. There he waited like Crete's mythological Minotaur, in his case hoping to devour a field marshall. America's entry into the fighting made headlines throughout the United States. Red heard the news while in basic training—"the fighting quartermaster corps"—in Wyoming. He continued to subscribe to the Ozark Record and wrote his folks about items of interest appearing in what had been their outlet to the world.

> July 13, 1943, Wyoming: Dear Folks: Our algebra teacher is in North Africa . . .

One part of North Africa had yet to be invaded—Tunisia. From Tripoli, Rommel raced on, eager to reach a safe haven behind the Mareth Line, France's Maginot line in North Africa. Built before the war to keep the Italians out of Tunisia, Rommel now hoped it would shut the British out. It, like its European cousin, finally proved faulty; the Brits battled by.

Infuriated that the Vichy French commander-in-chief, Admiral Jean François Darlan, on a private visit to Algiers, had double-crossed him and gone over to the allies, Hitler ordered Vichy officials in France to allow the entry of German forces into their Tunisian colony. Vichy acquiesced and German forces arrived, both augmentation divisions from occupied France and the remains of the old Panzer Army Africa, with Rommel at its head. New battles raged, casualties soared, this time including Americans. The American Rommel, George Patton, took command of the U.S. II Corps after its near-disaster at Kasserine pass.[29]

In desperation, Germany brought in improved older models and introduced new experimental ones—the former, the *Tiger* tank, the latter, the MC323 *Gigants* motorized gliders, which could fly petrol to Tunisian fields. All for naught; in the end, Germany lost. Watching the end come, Lieutenant General Sir Francis Tucker approved when "a hearty issue of beer and rum had been sent up for our men, commodities that they had not seen for the past month."[30]

Invalided home on March 6, Rommel lived to fight another day on the Norman shores. What of the remainder? On May 13, 1943, more than 275,000 Axis troops passed into captivity. They looked on this last sand battle as their Tunisgrad, coming so soon after Stalingrad. Unlike the unlucky prisoners from General Paulus's Sixth German Army deep in the Volga snow, a majority of these sand prisoners would survive the war in distant POW camps.

About as far away from North Africa as one could travel, Red met remnants of Rommel's force in remote Arkansas. In April 1944, the Army had reassigned him from Wyoming to Camp Robinson, Arkansas, five miles outside Little Rock, where Red joined the Sixty-sixth Infantry Division. He wrote the following account of his first sighting of the enemy:

> April 10, 1944 (Arkansas): Dear Folks, The other night we went for a little hike from 7 to 10, we went out past the German PW camp. It is in a little valley out in the hills; they call it Peaceful Valley, and with the moon shining down on it, it really looked peaceful. I imagine some of those fellows who were in Africa and Tunis find it a pretty comfortable life. I know they have it a lot easier than we do. They still wear the uniform with that jaunty little Africa Corps hat, and are of course still convinced that Germany will win.[31]

Journalist introduced Red and his buddies to Rommel and Montgomery. Both desert generals graced covers of *Time* magazine; Rommel in 1942 when he was winning, Montgomery in 1943 when he had won. *Time,* and America, loved a winner. The troops these winners led, the desert soldiers of North Africa, were introduced to Red and other soldiers by motion picture producers. Humphrey Bogart, deserting his former gangster and detective roles, became Warner Brothers' favorite lonely American standing up to the Nazi menace. The preferred setting for Bogart-at-war: French colonies. From Morocco (*Casablanca,* 1942) to Martinique (*To Have and Have Not,* 1945), he socked it to them.

Sometimes cast as a civilian-fighter, Bogart donned mufti in his 1943 desert movie, *Sahara.* Hollywood filmed it near Camp Young, California. In the early spring of 1942, General George Patton established his headquarters at Camp Young from where he commanded the California–Arizona Maneuver Area. Almost a million service members received intensive desert training here, a location only one hour east of California's Baghdad-by-the-Desert, Palm Springs. But no resort awaited these fresh recruits. Instead, sand was everywhere. It found its way into food, water, weapons, engines, bedrolls, clothing, tents, and trooper's eyes and mouths. This was great training for North Africa, exactly where Patton and his tank crews were headed. By the time the Yanks arrived, New Zealand soldiers had discovered the most invasive part of desert fighting—sand under the foreskin. Yikes!

For the sand saga *Sahara,* Warner Brothers lent Bogart to Columbia Pictures, and the War Department lent Columbia a cast of thousands from Camp Young. These GIs did some of their training on location with the movie's crew before shipping out for the real McCoy.

Sahara featured Bogart-as-sergeant. Pauline Kael wrote that "the tank keeps rolling, picking up strays along the way until it has a full Hollywood ethnic complement." Bogart commands the crew and strays (British, South African, Sudanese, Free French, and even an Italian who sees the light), finds water at an abandoned oasis, and holds off a battalion of thirsty Germans much needed by Rommel at the Battle of El Alamein. (The writers based the script on an incident from a Soviet film, *The Thirteen.*) Unremarked by Kael, the mulitcultural cast reflected the ethnic diversity of the rapidly expanding American armed forces as Asian-Americans, Mexican-Americans, Native-Americans, and a mix of other hyphenated Americans joined the military.

To repay the War Department, in 1944 Bogart made *A Report from the Front* as a trailer to be shown after other motion pictures. All of three minutes long, it included clips from his tour of allied bases; a filmed version of *Killroy Was Here.* Bogart and his third wife, Mayo Methot, landed in North Africa on December 11, 1943. In a three-month tour, they entertained GIs in camps, hospitals, and field units, both in North Africa and Italy. Shown initially as part of the Motion

Picture Theaters Red Cross Week, *A Report from the Front* raised donations for that cause. According to the French film critic André Bazin, after the war Bogart became the quintessential "actor/myth of the postwar period."[32] His face, lined and leathered; his eyes, sad and sunken; his voice, gravel and grit; his posture, bent but not broken: This was a screen icon the camera loved.

German soldiers did not have a Humphrey Bogart. Wartime motion pictures in the Third Reich meant boring propaganda, whereas in Britain and America propaganda had to entertain. Vive la différence! During the war two historical epics embellished the Teutonic warrior spirit: *Der Grosse Konig* (The Great King) reminded the war-weary Germans of 1942 of the military victories of Frederick the Great, while in 1945 *Kolberg,* three years in the making, recreated a Prussian town's rebellion against Napoleon.

The Nazis also commissioned documentaries. *Battleships on a Voyage* and *Auxiliary Cruiser in All the Seas of the World* presented vivid pictures of shipboard life on, among others, the Scharnhorst, the *Gniesenau,* and the *Kormoran.* In 1940 Berlin released *Feuertaufe* (Baptism by Fire)—ninety minutes of footage of the Luftwaffe bombing Poland. The next year witnessed the release of *Lah im Einsatz* (Operations Now) in which SS front-line cameramen depict the early victorious campaigns in France, Yugoslavia, and Greece. Two decades before the postwar German film industry revived to make *Das Boot* (The Boat), Berlin had commissioned *U-boat am Feind* (Enemy Submarines). It is an original wartime German documentary depicting life on board a submarine during an actual mission. Why, in a time of frugal budgets, spend money on films? Because control of scripts extended Nazi control over popular culture and robbed German filmmakers of any original voice.

Even German high culture withered. Writers immigrated: Among them, Thomas Mann and Bertold Brecht. Woe to a culture that loses its storytellers. Conductors fled, including Bruno Walter and George Szell. More woe for a people who lose their song leaders. Composers prostituted, such as Richard Strauss and Carl Orff. Worst woe for a civilization whose songwriters sell out for a Faustian bargain.

For a time president of the Reich Music Chamber, Strauss's naïveté earned him fascist and antifascist enmity. For a time the Reich's favorite composer, Orff was so unscrupulous as to obtain a commission to write a replacement score for Mendelssohn's verboten "Jewish" score of *A Midsummer Night's Dream*. Thomas Mann did not accidently create a composer as the protagonist in his novel about the Third Reich, *Doktor Faustus*. Nor did the Nazis accidently broadcast the second movement of Beethoven's Fifth Symphony prior to announcing the communiqués of defeats in North Africa.[33]

Did music's charms soothe the savage beast? Lenin admitted to a weakness for music. After a performance of Beethoven's *Appassionata* sonata, he told friends that he could not listen to music too often. "It makes me want to say kind, stupid things, and pat the heads of people. But now you have to beat them on the head, beat them without mercy."[34]

Wehrmacht artillery had shelled Leningrad without mercy; nevertheless, the Germans went down to defeat as the Soviets went up with victory. Leningrad would survive. To celebrate his birthplace, in December 1941 Dimitri Shostakovich completed his Seventh Symphony, the *Leningrad*. The score, sent out of Russia on microfilm, went by air from Kuibyshev—300 miles north of the Caspian Sea to which Soviet officials had evacuated Shostakovich and his family—to Tehran, by automobile across western Iran, Iraq, Jordan, and Palestine to Cairo, by air again to Recife, Brazil, and then by air to New York. There, on July 19, 1942, Italy's greatest maestro, Arturo Toscanini, conducted to a cheering crowd, in which sat many a descendant of German Jewish immigrants. It received sixty-two American performances between the summers of 1942 and 1943. Allied music scored a triumph.

The cheering had not stopped when the citizens of Leningrad heard "their" symphony on August 9, 1942. Wendell Willkie, returning from a Russian visit, summed up the feelings of all: "Shostakovich is a great composer." On July 20, 1942, the composer of the hour appeared on the cover of *Time* magazine wearing a firefighter's helmet while in the background Leningrad's gutted buildings burn and antiaircraft shells burst.[35] By 1945 he had a Russian cover-companion when *Time* honored Sergei Prokofiev. Apparently, as editor-in-chief of *Time,* Henry Luce had decided that field marshals were out and Slavic composers were in.

Once strong sand-soldiers, German troops had only the music of defeat to drum them from the North African desert into scattered Anglo-American stalags. These POW camps reached from South Africa to North America. And tragedy, like a buoy floating in mid-ocean, marked the sea journey to these camps. During the North African fighting, Axis prisoners found themselves locked on board ships waiting to depart. When they departed, the prison ships found themselves in dangerous waters.

On September 12, 1942, the German submarine U-156, commanded by Lieutenant Commander Werner Hartenstein, sighted the 20,000–ton liner the *Laconia*. Both vessels were five hundred miles south of the bulge of Africa headed toward Cape Town. U-156 chased the liner, caught her, surfaced at sunset, and fired. Two torpedoes struck, the liner listed heavily to starboard, her engines failed but her radio worked, thus the crew sent their location, hence the U-boat's location. Closing in for the kill, Hartenstein heard cries from the water—Italian pleas for mercy. The *Laconia* carried 1,800 Italian POWs from North Africa, guarded by 160 Poles (former Soviet prisoners), who had first allowed the 800 British crewman and passengers to board lifeboats.

Hartenstein signaled Admiral Donitz's headquarters in France and commenced a rescue. He took two hundred on his boat, a vessel designed to hold only the crew of fifty. Donitz had ordered the U-156 to join a wolf pack of submarines operating off the approaches to Cape Town, South Africa. He ordered the other U-boats to help the U-156 rescue the Italians. Donitz also requested the Vichy government in unoccupied France to order rescue ships to sea from Dakar, which Vichy did.

Then an American four-engine bomber appeared; Hartenstein ordered his forward gun covered with a tarp that had a large red cross painted on it. In addition he had a rescued British sailor signal that a rescue was in progress. The Americans returned to Ascension Island confused. Their bosses, knowing little but the deadly battle of the North Atlantic, ordered the bomber back, and the bomber bombed the U-156. Badly damaged, the U-156 cut short her rescue and made her way back to the Atlantic coast of France and the safety of a submarine pen.

Admiral Donitz then issued his *Laconia* order, categorically forbidding rescues except to take important POWs. For this he was tried and acquitted at the Nuremberg Trials. Of the ship's company and passengers, 1,091 out of 2,732 survived. The remainder went down with the *Laconia*'s captain.[36] Avoiding death in the afternoon sand, many Axis troops had found death in the evening sea.

But the desert was the real killer. It had claimed other historic victims. In 1187 Saladin, also operating out of Egypt, had allied himself with desert dust and thirst to destroy a Crusader army at the battle of Hattin. Saladin placed 50,000 of his best troops between the Christian knights and their next drink of water. Saladin and the desert won.[37]

Why chose this battle-in-the-sand (El Alamein) over any other desert engagement? A battle that should not have happened in a peripheral region that a strategists would not have chosen.[38] But it happened, someone chose. Why not consult Rommel's opinion? "The battle which began at El Alamein on the 23rd of October 1942 turned the tide of war in Africa against us and, in fact, probably represented the turning point of the whole vast struggle."[39]

El Alamein took on importance because, between 1940 and 1943, North African battles before and after it sucked in the main Anglo–American and German–Italian ground forces committed to fighting on the western front. El Alamein proved that the British had an army that could win, entombed Axis hopes in North Africa, made the Middle East safe at last, secured the Mediterranean route, and, following it, planted American combat feet onto the battle field.[40] The tide turned by accident, but turned nonetheless.

Notes

1. In the decade after the 1939–1945 phase of combat came to a close, the Anglo–Americans made the Mediterranean their lake. During that time, visits between ships occurred. On one such visit to Admiral Lord Louis Mountbaten's flagship, HMS *Glasgow,* a British seaman, J. Hamilton, served as rum bos'n in number five mess. Two visiting American sailors watched in amazement as the mess mustered for their rum tots. Hamilton offered the Americans "gulpers of rum"; after imbibing, their eyes watered, a sure sign that they were tasting Pusser's rum for the first time. One Yank regained his composure in time to exclaim: "Geeze, no wonder you guys fight like pirates, you live like pirates!" See A.J. Pack, *Nelson's Blood: The Story of Naval Rum* (Hampshire, UK: Kenneth Mason, 1982), 139.

2. Through the centuries Malta attracted the attention of many invaders. We have an excellent account of the attack on it by Sultan Suleiman in 1565. That Turkish sultan conquered the island of Rhodes forty three years before he attacked Malta, thus gaining control of the eastern Mediterranean. He needed Malta to control the center of that sea. He almost got it. In 1568 in Barcelona, a Spanish defender at Malta, Francisco Balbi di Correggio, published his account of the battle. See Francisco Correggio, *The Siege of Malta, 1565* (London: Folio Society, 1965). Later, in the time of Napoleon, Malta became a prize fought over by England, France, and Russia. See Georges Lefebvre, *Napoleon from 18 Brumaire to Tilsit, 1799–1807* (New York: Columbia University Press, 1969), 107–14.

3. Michael Howard, *The Mediterranean Strategy in the Second World War* (New York: Frederick A. Praeger, 1968).

4. Samuel Eliot Morison, *Strategy and Compromise* (Boston: Little, Brown, 1958); Forrest C. Pogue, *George C. Marshall: Ordeal and Hope, 1939–1942* (New York: Viking Press, 1965), 348–49.

5. No good biography of Bogart yet exists. He is best captured in a merry piece of enchantment by Katharine Hepburn, *The Making of The African Queen, Or How I Went to Africa with Bogart, Bacall and Huston and Almost Lost My Mind* (New York: Knopf, 1987). Also see A.M. Sperber and Eric Lax, *Bogart* (New York: William Morrow, 1997), and Jeffrey Meyers, *Bogart: A Life in Hollywood* (Boston: Houghton Mifflin, 1997).

6. Jacquin Sanders, *The Night Before Christmas* (New York: G.P. Putnam's Sons, 1963), 30–32.

7. Chester Wilmot, *Tobruk 1941: Capture—Siege—Relief* (Sydney: Angus and Robertson, 1945), 58.

8. Ibid.

9. With the success of Mason's *The Desert Fox* in 1951, Paramount rushed *The Desert Rats* into production. Released in 1953, and starring Richard Burton as a British captain commanding Australians at Tobruk, this motion picture had James Mason giving a reprise of his 1951 impersonation of Rommel. Hollywood notwithstanding, the British Ministry of Information made the best film of the North African campaign. Released in 1943, the documentary format of *Desert Victory* won plaudits on both sides of the Atlantic. *Variety* called it "The greatest battle film of the war" while the *Daily Telegraph* called it "The finest factual film ever made."

10. Some of the harshest postwar criticism of Rommel came from a German author, Wolf Heckmann, in *Rommel's War in Africa* (New York: Doubleday, 1981).

11. In fact, meteorologists did matter in all five of the battles covered in this book. See Patrick Hughes, "Winning the War: Role of Meteorologists During WW II," *Weatherwise* (June–July 1995): 38–42.

12. Erwin Rommel, *The Rommel Papers* (New York: Harcourt Brace, 1953), 105.

13. Ibid., 133, 149, 152.

14. Heckmann, *Rommel's War in Africa*, 53.

15. N.E. Bou-Nacklie, "The 1941 Invasion of Syria and Lebanon: The Role of the Local Paramilitary," *Middle Eastern Studies* (July 1994): 512–30; and Daniel Silverfarb, "Britain and Iraqi Barley During the Second World War," *Middle Eastern Studies* (July 1995): 524–33.

16. George Lenczowski, "Memoirs," vol. 1, unpublished.

17. Rommel, *The Rommel Papers*, 182.

18. Ibid., 183.

19. Paul Carell, *The Foxes of the Desert* (New York: E.P. Dutton, 1961), 138.

20. Rommel, *The Rommel Papers*, 186–87.

21. Carell, *The Foxes of the Desert*, 199.

22. Ibid.

23. Rommel, *The Rommel Papers*, 249.

24. B.H. Liddell Hart, *The German Generals Talk* (New York: William Morrow, 1948), 162–63. General von Thoma did not need to worry about eating again after El Alamein as he was taken prisoner at that battle, and the allies fed him for the remainder of the war.

25. C.S. Forester's *The Ship* (Boston: Little, Brown, 1943) went through six printings in 1943 alone. Interestingly, one can tell that total war had reached its peak; all editions state: "the format of this book is designed to save paper, which is now rationed, as well as other materials." On the bottom of the book's jacket, the publisher encouraged the reader to "Buy war bonds and war stamps. Give books to the victory book campaigns."

26. During WW II, Britain controlled the Mediterranean from its bases at Gibraltar and Alexandria. During the Cold War, the United States controlled the Mediterranean from its central base at Naples. Generally, the Americans kept their strategic submarines out of these waters, using the Spanish facilities at Rota (near enough to Gibraltar, but on the Atlantic side of the entrance) when needed to tender their nuclear underwater fleet on that side of the North Atlantic basin.

27. Pack, *Nelson's Blood,* 141–42.

28. Francis Tucker, *Approach to Battle: A Commentary, Eighth Army, November 1941–1943* (London: Cassell, 1963), 241.

29. Martin Blumenson and James L. Stokesbury, *Masters of the Art of Command* (New York: Houghton Mifflin, 1975), 254–86.

30. Tucker, *Approach to Battle,* 360.

31. The United States imprisoned almost 375,000 German POWs. Within a few months of their arrival in the United States, the Americans put them to work on farms or in factories, paying them minimum wages. See Jack Fincher, "By Convention (Geneva), the Enemy Within Never Did Without," *Smithsonian* (June 1995): 126–43.

32. James Naremore, "American Filme Noir: The History of an Idea," *Film Quarterly* (Winter 1995–96): 12–28.

33. William L. Shirer, *The Rise and Fall of the Third Reich* (New York: Simon and Schuster, 1962), 333–42. Also see Alex Ross, "In Music, Though, There Were No Victories," *New York Times,* August 20, 1995, H25; Paul Jackson, "Maestros of the Storm: How European Conductors Found Refuge at the Met," and David Patrick Stearns, "Between the Lines: Wartime Recordings in Germany," both in *Opera News* (July 1995): 36–39 and 26–30; and David B. Dennis, *Beethoven in German Politics, 1870–1989* (New Haven: Yale University Press, 1996).

34. Orlando Figes, "Censored by His Own Regime," *New York Times Book Review,* October 27, 1996, 32.

35. Elizabeth Wilson, *Shostakovich: A Life Remembered* (Princeton: Princeton University Press, 1994), 149; Ross, "In Music, Though, There Were No Victories," H25.

36. Von der Porten, Edward P. *The German Navy in World War II* (New York: Thomas Y. Crowell, 1969), 188–92.

37. J.F.C. Fuller, *Decisive Battles: Their Influence Upon History and Civilization* (New York: Charles Scribner's Sons, 1940), 240–41. After the war, the Sahara held a strange fascination for a number of American authors, chief among whom was Paul Bowles. Published in 1949, his *Sheltering Sky* (New York: Ecco Press) is set against the silence of this immense sand and gravel pit, in which only those born to it can adjust. Otherwise, it is a killer of all who came from beyond its boundaries. Desert death did not require a war. In 1990, Bernardo Bertolucci filmed the novel; the last fifteen minutes of the film

contain exquisite desert photography, which won him several awards. The North African desert still kills—"Sandstorm Kills 12 in Northern Egypt," *New York Times,* May 3, 1997, 6; "Big Sandstorm Blankets Most of Egypt," *San Francisco Chronicle,* May 3, 1997, A10.

38. For a recent summary of what a strategist thinks was wrong about the German effort in North Africa see Edward N. Luttwak, *Strategy: The Logic of War and Peace* (Cambridge: Harvard University Press, 1987), 210–14.

39. Rommel, *The Rommel Papers,* 302.

40. The influence of geography in war can not be overstated. It is the geostrategy inside the larger debate about geopolitics. See Colin S. Gray, "A Debate on Geopolitics: How Geography Still Shapes Security," *Orbis* (Spring 1996): 247–59. Also see John Keegan, *Fields of Battle* (New York: Knopf, 1996). Keegan demonstrates how North America's mountain chains and river systems have determined where its people fought. Geographical politics has regained influence in Europe, where Lucio Caracciolo and Michel Korinman edit a joint Italian–French journal of geopolitics, *liMes.*

The Snow

Russian snow is unlike ordinary snow, which consists of individual flakes that descend and, sooner rather than later, melt. Rather, Russian snow drops in shovelsful—seemingly unstopping and unmelting. Like swarms of winter locusts, snow squalls swoop down. Forget flurries swirling around Alpine ridges; think blizzards blasting across Soviet steppes. Nothing surpasses a Russian winter for the unprepared invader; it hits like a head-on collision with a roaring Arctic express. Once having crossed onto Russian frost, it is almost impossible to avoid at least one Russian freezing; the short summer makes the massive country too big to conquer in one season. Nor can you add spring to summer to slow down the seasonal clock.

Spring means mush; the snow does melt for a soupy interval, turning the surface of the steppe to swamp, the *rasputitsa,* or internal seas, a mire of mud. Even light wagons sink to their axles. Then a comparatively dry season follows this liquid spring. At best, the dry season lasts from July to September. But soon wetness washes in, the autumn rains moisten the ground again until the first frost repeats the hardening process.

An immense territory of varying climates, most of the Soviet Union lies far from the world's oceans, hence the climate exhibits markedly continental features—warm in summer and cold in winter. How cold? Our chief subject city, Stalingrad, has a mean January temperature of

14 degrees F (–10 degrees C). But the city of Verkhoyansk in the Far East region recorded a temperature of –90 degrees F (–68 degrees C), the lowest temperature ever recorded on the Earth's surface outside Antarctica.

In 1942, what were German soldiers doing freezing before three distant, widely separated Russian cities, along a front that ran from the Gulf of Finland to the Black Sea? In the north, they surrounded Leningrad. In the center, they seesawed against Moscow. In the south, they struggled for Stalingrad. As the blunt implement of Hitler's Operation Barbarossa, the Wehrmacht had broken into the Soviet Union the year before, on the morning of Sunday, June 22.

As in the operation against Britain, Germany initially scored a success only for Hitler to misdirect it. Anti-Slav and anti-Bolshevik posturing did not a strategy make. Nor, in Stalin's case, did fascist bashing. Unfortunately for their soon-to-be canon-fodder people, neither Hitler nor Stalin could master grand strategy. Both tyrants topped a tyrannical time; Hitler far out-tyrannized the kaiser, as Stalin did the tsar.[1] But being top tyrant won no medals for war wisdom.

What did Germany need from the Soviet Eurasian empire? Mainly natural resources, especially the grain of the Ukraine and the oil of the Transcaucasus. How to obtain them? Liberate the Baltic states, Ukraine, and the oil republics of the Caspian region. Terminate collective farms, and do not exterminate collectivized serfs. After capturing Kiev and taking 1,500,000 prisoners, release the prisoners as you hoist the Ukrainian flag, not the swastika. Upon liberating the Transcaucasus, where appropriate publish a native-language edition of the Koran, the first in fifty years.

Balts, Ukrainians, White Russians, Cossacks, and the multicultural peoples of the Transcaucasus all possessed a history outside Russian history; they had languages, religions, or cultures (in some cases all three) that did not spring from the Grand Duchy of Moscovy. Inasmuch as they would not have been artificial creations of the German Reich, they might have survived the effort to start anew, especially if allied with a strong and supportive Germany.[2]

Better to buy or barter for the dark bread and black gold than to bomb and blast it. Each year someone would have to plant and harvest the grain anew; why not extend Bismarck's compromise of steel and rye, updated from the internal politics of the urban and rural Second Reich, to a relationship of trade in industrial goods from the Third

Reich in exchange for foodstuffs from Ukraine? But Hitler was no Bismarck. And to take the oil by force meant keeping troops, whose homeland might be 1,500 miles away in the Rhineland, in Muslim areas where the population would surely learn to hate the new enslaver as much as the former Soviet overlord.

Would any of these captive nationalities, if treated with respect, ally themselves with the German Reich? One German thought so. Field Marshal Heinz Guderian, one of the German masters of tank tactics, saw proof of this in the attitude of the civilian population. "Women came out from their village on to the very battlefield bringing wooden platters of bread and butter and eggs and, in my case, refused to let me move on before I had eaten." In his memoirs he suggests what killed this welcome. "Unfortunately this friendly attitude towards the Germans lasted only so long as the more benevolent military administration was in control." Who killed it? "The so-called 'Reich commissars' soon managed to alienate all sympathy from the Germans and thus to prepare the ground for all the horrors of partisan warfare."[3]

Did Hitler follow the reasonable, less bellicose course? No. Did he show any understanding of Clausewitz's idea of a strategic center of gravity?[4] That in the Soviet case the center of gravity consisted of the problem of the nationalities? Twice no. He grabbed for everything, and he grabbed ruthlessly. Why the museum and palace city of Peter the Great? Near enough to Leningrad, the Finns tied down whatever Soviet forces one wanted immobilized there, and the German navy ruled the Baltic Sea. Besides, many of Leningrad's factories had already traveled east toward the Ural mountains; even the masterpieces from the Hermitage had departed.

And Moscow? It had burned before, it could burn again. Unlike Paris—the center of gravity of France—the Soviet administrative capital could uproot itself. But Hitler and his henchmen, especially Herr Himmler, knew they knew best. One thing they did not know; their brutal excesses helped save a politically bankrupt and hated Stalinism.[5] And at a city bearing the tyrant's name, ordinary folk of the region soon stood, fought, and won.

Stalingrad was not a battle, it was a bludgeoning. A city mainly of wood, much of it disappeared after the Luftwaffe's Eighth Air Corps blitzed it on August 23, 1942. The city was mainly an ashheap bleached white by fire and ice; only the newer industrial facilities resisted the early flames and later freezing, their concrete cracking, but holding. At the end, the brutalization consisted of firefights around three major factories—the Tractor, the Barricades, and the Red October. Having been excoriated by Hitler as *untermenschen* (subhumans), the Russians beat him at his own slander by burrowing underground, popping up to fight and plowing down to flee—subterranean defenders at their best. In order to kill the Soviet defenders, the German attackers had to ferret them out from their dens.

Soviet soldiers slaving in this satanic ice furnace had to singe the enemy to their front. At their rear the Red Army defenders had a deep, cold river, one mile wide. With a depth of only 4,000 yards between the front and the river—Stalingrad being on the western shore of the Volga—little maneuver space remained. Soviet troops also had a commander, General Vasili I. Chuikov, through whose veins ice crystals coursed. He made famous the slogan "Fight as if there is no land across the Volga."

By January the Volga froze strong enough to offer Chuikov and ice bridge for nighttime resupply; only the seriously wounded could return with the empty supply caravans. Before the winter built Chuikov his ice bridge, he depended on civilian fishermen and rivermen of the Volga to ferry supplies and wounded.[6] Music incarnate, these boatmen of the Volga represented Tchaikovsky's soulful water music. On the river flanks of the city, the Red Navy floated a Volga River flotilla under Rear-Admiral Rogachev, with gunboats, minesweepers, and antiaircraft gunboats.

What amazed Chuikov about this battle was not the snow or the Germans. It was the Volga. Before this assignment, he had only seen Russia's northern rivers. In them, ice floes had been a harbinger of spring. Here in the south, they signaled the onset of winter: "in November appears 'sludge,' small pieces of ice, which then turn into large pieces, (float) down the river . . . communications across the Volga are halted, as shipping cannot get through it." He watched the river with amazement: "it takes weeks, months, to ice over." Even when the temperature fell to −10 degrees Centigrade, the Volga remained free of ice, steam rising from it. At −12 degrees things changed, jagged ice slabs appeared. At 15 degrees below zero, river icebergs stuck their pointed tips skyward. At that point only natives with "bold spirits and boat-hooks in their hands, jumping from floe to floe, can cross over to the opposite bank." Chuikov never forgot that river crammed with ice shards.[7]

If one selected a Soviet soldier who militarily exploited Stalingrad, one could do worse than choose Marshal Georgi Konstantinovich Zhukov. Hired, fired, and rehired by Stalin, Zhukov had testicular courage. He outlived the old Georgian-born gorgon, even though a jealous Stalin struck at him in the postwar years. Born the son of a village shoemaker in 1896, apprenticed to a furrier, drafted into the tsarist army in 1915, Zhukov ended the World War I phase as a highly decorated cavalry sergeant. He entered the Red Army in 1918, and by June 1941 Zhukov, by dint of hard work, served as chief of the General Staff.

Stalin gutted the General Staff before Germany invaded; his surrogates slaughtered mainly honest men in purges that began in 1936 and continued up to two weeks before the German invasion (the last victim, General Shmushkevich, chief of the Soviet Air Force). Stalin's state murders devastated military morale; more generals died in this butchering than perished in the war with Germany.[8] To replace some of those he ordered killed, Stalin appointed 479 new major generals in June 1941, the largest mass promotion known to military chroniclers. Too junior to count, and off with the Soviet Union's Far Eastern forces, Zhukov survived the purges and made the promotion lists.

Zhukov saw service in all three of the twentieth-century's wars. He rose high and fell low. The high point came in 1945 with the capture of Berlin, the low point in 1957 when his Kremlin bosses publicly disgraced him, charging that he questioned party leadership of the armed forces. Like General of the Army Douglas MacArthur, who also served in all three phases of a century's worth of fighting, and who also departed under a cloud of civilian–military authority juggling, in his last years Zhukov just faded away.

But during the war, Zhukov witnessed German armies fading back toward Germany after the mammoth urban battles of Leningrad, Moscow, and Stalingrad, in all three of which he held an important position.[9] The Germans clung to their forward position for as long as possible, the Soviets stubbornly defending. The middle, before Moscow, marked where the Soviet bear tried first to dislodge the German eagle's grasp.

Finally, the German talons loosened on the capital. Decades after the war, and a decade after the death of Josef Stalin, Zhukov remembered the Battle for Moscow as the high point of his career. By then he knew the brutal Stalin, but he insisted that Stalin worked hard at the war effort: "He must be given his due." Zhukov also remembered the snow: "The Soviet counteroffensive of the winter of 1941–42 was conducted under the difficult condition of a snowy, cold winter."[10]

It remained for the southern city of Stalingrad to experience the surrender of a frozen German field army. In that counterthrust, Zhukov and other senior generals had argued the cautious Stalin into using the battle as the staging point for a major offensive, Operation Uranus. In other words, it was not enough to defend cities; the Red Army must, like a flood flowing from a burst dam, inundate the grasslands of the south. Under this deluge the German war machine would sink, very much like the drowning of the Teutonic knights at the climax of Sergei Eisenstein's 1938 film, *Alexander Nevsky*.

On September 29, 1942, as plans for Operation Uranus progressed, Zhukov, now a member of the top war-fighting body, the Stavka, flew to the embattled Volga city in his *Ilyushin* (Il-2) transport. After checking the front, Zhukov hitched a ride back to Moscow in Major General Golovanov's aircraft, with the general as pilot. An early winter storm forced their aircraft to land because of heavy icing; Zhukov's own larger Il-2 came to his rescue and transported him back to the Central Airport in Moscow. Where a sandstorm in the desert had forced Rommel out of the air, likewise Zhukov experienced an aerial delay, in his case a snowstorm on the Soviet steppe. And it was on this steppe that the cream of the German army met its nemesis, the winter weather of Eurasia.

When Hitler ordered the attack on the Soviet Union, he overwhelmingly committed German power to that campaign. Of 3,800,000 men in the army at that date, Hitler sent 3,200,000 against the Red Army, assisted by 3,500 tanks and 7,184 pieces of artillery. They constituted the core of the German army in the east, the Ostheer.

The impression lingers that this force rode into battle. Not so; most had to walk. And if something had to arrive by transport, often the transporter had four legs—over 600,000 horses accompanied the invaders. Of their number, half died in the first winter. Without discrimination, the cold took soldier and steed as victim. And lack of cold-weather planning incapacitated many German infantrymen. Their regulation boots, the Kommisstiefel, had iron-nailed soles, which in winter accelerated the onset of frostbite.

At the outset of Germany's Operation Barbarossa, the troop commands went to older warlords; Field Marshal Ritter von Leeb com-

manding Army Group North, Field Marshal Fedor von Bock commanding Army Group Center, and Field Marshal Gerd von Rundstedt commanding Army Group South. Opposing them stood Marshal K.E. Voroshilov's North-Western Front, Marshal S.K. Timoshenko's Western Front, and Marshal Semyon Budenny's South-Western Front. After the failures of the first year of freezing, names and faces changed; the young lions now roared forward.

Of those lionized on the German side, Field Marshal Erick von Manstein meant most for his maneuvering of millions. Among his peers, he lived to tell his story, *Lost Victories,* and among other generals who likewise survived the war, von Manstein garnered their highest esteem as a field commander.[11] In life, most generals are realists; von Manstein was an ironist. Early in the war against the Soviet Union, two soldiers in von Manstein's corps, having been convicted of raping and killing an old woman, received the death penalty in a court martial. Von Manstein signed the death sentence without hesitating; justice done.

Before assuming command of Army Group Don (later Army Group South), von Manstein tasted Russian combat in the north, in the push against Leningrad. In that drive, in four days he raced his force to the Dvina River, some 200 miles beyond the frontier, where he had to wait while the Sixteenth German Army caught up with him.

While in the northern sector, von Manstein was near the site of the Russian naval Dunkirk, the evacuation of the Soviet Baltic fleet from its base at Tallinn to the comparatively safer base at Kronstadt. Peter the Great had built Tallinn, but that alone could not save the naval anchorage. In July 1941, refusing to admit how close danger lurked, local citizens lolled on the white sandy Baltic beaches, seemingly unconcerned that Nazi tanks fired on the few defenders only eight miles from the city center.[12]

If Stalin knew little of armies, he knew less of navies. Failing to give the command to evacuate the fleet, the warships had no recourse but to fire as long-range artillery against the encircling German guns. The flagship and pride of the Baltic fleet, the 7,000–ton *Kirov,* had only recently arrived, having miraculously escaped the German drive into Riga. Her seven-inch naval guns dueled with German army batteries.

Finally, in August, Admiral Vladimir Tributs began the long overdue evacuation, the order for the exodus having arrived from Moscow on August 26. One hundred and ninety overloaded ships tried to race the 200–mile passage to Kronstadt, perilously without air cover.

Half Loreleis, half Valkyries, Luftwaffe pilots staged a watery gotter-damerung worthy of Wagner. Of twenty-nine large transports, the Soviets lost twenty-five; in all, thirty-eight noncombatant ships went down, with a loss of life exceeding 10,000. Of warships, ten went to the bottom.

Casualties did not end on reaching Kronstadt. In Stalin's gulag-state, someone always paid for debacles. In the dash from Tallinn, Captain Viacheslav Kalitaiev commanded the transport *Kazakhstan*. An experienced Baltic skipper, he took wave after wave of Junker-88 bomber strikes. A well-placed bomb hit the bridge, blowing him into the cold water. Fires raged on the ship, which lost speed and fell out of the convoy. Surviving crew members ran the ship aground and evacuated the passengers. Seven crew went back on board; amazingly, on September 12 the ship limped into Kronstadt.

Meanwhile, the Soviet submarine, the S-322, had picked up the missing Captain Kalitaiev, wounded and unconscious. Upon his return to Kronstadt, he discovered that the secret police accused him of "leaving" the bridge of his ship during combat. For this they shot him. Heros faced fearful fates. (In 1943 Lieutenant Colonel Leonid Brezhnev tried to come ashore with elements of the Eighteenth Shock Army, which fought against the Germans holding the Black Sea port of Novorossiisk. Brezhnev was standing beside the pilot when the ship hit a mine. The explosion shot them both overboard. Luckily for the future leader, he was conscious and quickly got himself and his wet men onto a rescuing Soviet motorboat.)

As it was for Captain Kalitaiev, soon it was for senior German generals who could not snare the prizes that Hitler hunted. In the Nazi case, Hitler fired with paper, not bullets. Hence, in September 1941 von Manstein found himself traveling south to try his hand at prospecting for the black gold of the rich southern basins. (Von Manstein received the nod in much the same manner that General Montgomery inherited the command of the British Eighth Army. Montgomery took charge of Eighth Army only after the first choice, General "Strafer" Gott, died in an air encounter. Von Manstein inherited the German Eleventh Army when General von Schobert's plane blew up when it crash-landed on a Soviet minefield.)

In the south, von Manstein faced Rommel's problem. He could push further toward the Transcaucasus, but he would have a thorn in his side, an exposed right flank that presented him with a version of Tobruk. In his case the enemy stronghold in the rear rose up in the form of the Crimean naval bastion of Sevastopol. Like Rommel in North Africa, von Manstein determined to rid his flank of this ulcer, no matter the treatment.

When the German Sixth Army took Kharkov in October 1941, it secured the junction of Army Group Center and Army Group South. Despite desperate Soviet attempts to hold the Donbas, the Soviet Ruhr, attempts that included the mobilization of 100,000 miners, this important industrial basin fell to the Germans. Both von Manstein's Eleventh Army and Field Marshal Ewald von Kleist's First Panzer Army battered the remaining defenders into pockets, squeezing them down toward the sea. Once this was completed, von Manstein faced Sevastopol, a key base for the Soviet Black Sea Fleet.

To batter his way into Sevastopol's heavily fortified positions, von Manstein had huge siege guns, to include the titanic German 369–mm guns, hauled to the front. To assist the 369s, von Manstein added monstrous mortars like the Karl, which hurled a two-ton projectile. Topping the list came the three-story-tall Big Dora with a barrel ninety feet long and firing a seven-ton explosive, drawn forward by sixty rail trucks along a railway specially laid for the purpose. (Built to bombard France's Maginot line, it did destroy a Crimean ammunition dump buried ninety feet deep in the natural rock.) No wonder the defenders burrowed deep. Entire hospitals went underground.

Like Rommel in North Africa, von Manstein did not find his Tobruk an easy operation. Battling grim odds, the Soviet Black Sea fleet, commanded by Vice-Admiral F.S. Oktiabrski, brought in reinforcements.[13] The unloading of ships was done under tougher odds. Those who did that heavy work, under even heavier enemy fire, waited until dark when the ships could slip into the harbor. While waiting they drank; vodka warming them against the outside chill.[14] At the start, the Red Air Force evened the odds, for the Soviets initially had air superiority, a new experience for the Germans, who had to learn to dig in positions for everything, including the remaining horses.

Von Manstein experienced Soviet air power the hard way. To inspect the roads along the coast near Yalta, he used a small Italian E-boat. Before the crew knew it, two Soviet *Yak* fighters strafed the vessel, killing or wounding seven of the sixteen abroad and setting the ship afire. As far as it is recorded, von Manstein never went to sea again.

Then came December temperatures that shot down to −20 C. Soviet marines embarked in a Force 8 gale; they came ashore the day after Christmas in Force 5 gales with ice adrift in the Sea of Azov. Barges spilled men and material into the sea, but somehow 40,000 men, 236 guns, and 43 tanks made it onto the beaches. As John Erickson describes it, the defenders hung on, "not for days or weeks but for month after agonizing month, for 250 fire-drenched days."[15]

Red soon felt real freezing. Having grown up on land drained by North America's greatest river, Red was in for a shock. Mississippi valley weather has nothing in common with the American steppes as they work their way up toward the Rocky Mountains. These open plains offer a runway for the frigid blasts coming down across Canada from the Arctic. In November 1943 the Army sent Red to Armed Services Training at the University of Wyoming. Soon thereafter, weather reports began to arrive in California.

> November 25, 1943: Dear Folks: A big one came in. We could see it snowing up in the mountains long before it started here.
> November 29, 1943: Dear Folks: Instead of marching to chow, we slide.
> December 8, 1943: Dear Folks: This whole county has been frozen up tighter than a jug for three weeks.
> January 14, 1944: Dear Folks: Six degrees at twelve noon and eighteen below at night.

At least no one shot at Red from the snow banks of the wild West.

Did only Russians and Americans feel frosty flashes? Not according to von Manstein's memoirs. He had planned to start an offensive on November 28, 1941. What hampered him? "At this point the Russian winter overtook us, its impact being all the more devastating by reason of the two different forms it took." What forms? "In the Crimea itself the rains came, very soon rendering all the unpaved roads there quite unusable." But he feared the mainland more, for it "was already in the grip of severe frosts which promptly immobilized four of the only five railway engines then available south of the Dnieper."[16]

What were the results? Winter delayed von Manstein's offensive for three weeks, valuable time in which Stalin began to reinforce along the Kerch peninsula, making any drive on Sevastopol all the more difficult.

Why take the weather report from field marshals? They look at the weather; soldiers live in it. Siegfried Knappe lived through it; he also kept a diary. Interestingly, as a lieutenant of artillery Siegfried rode a horse into the Soviet Union. What did he record of the snow? It killed his horse. Or read the entry for December 5, 1941, outside Moscow when the temperature plummeted to 30 degrees below zero. He writes that the flesh on his face and ears froze if he left it exposed for any length of time. His fingers were worse: They froze even when he wore gloves and stuffed them into his thin overcoat pockets. Hitler's army had only summer uniforms in December. Even though freezing, Siegfried still gave off enough warmth for the body lice feeding on him; in fact, vermin constantly tormented him.[17]

Siegfried had great good luck; he was wounded. Back in the warmth of Germany, he recovered. His new commander ordered him to establish a ski school for troops going to the Soviet snow. Before he could perform this duty, his luck changed, this time for the worse. Berlin ordered him to Stalingrad. His luck changed again; he arrived too late.

Instead, he worked on the German staff in Rostov helping to organize the escape of German forces from the Caucasus. They had a bit of good luck; Russia's winter allied itself with Germany for once. It froze the Sea of Azov. All but the heaviest tanks crossed it in their headlong retreat.

Luck changed again; Siegfried had home leave, went on a ski trip to Austria with his fiancée, and received a new assignment in pastoral France. Then his combat luck changed for the last time, much for the worse. They sent him again to the Russian front, where he stayed to the last battle.

While Siegfried, like Red in America, went about soldiering, the war continued. Sevastopol, like Tobruk, finally fell, but not until July 1, 1942. In its death agony, Sevastopol's defenders had to wear gasmasks in order to fight the stench from the festering flesh of their dead comrades, long unburied in this ruinous battle that crunched the life out of youthful defenders.[18] With its capture came a fortune in equipment, stores the Soviets did not have time to evacuate or destroy.

After that, the fighting continued on the Khersones peninsula. In fact, 30,000, the last of the last, did not surrender until the fourth of July. For his victory, Hitler awarded von Manstein his field marshal's baton. His great public gain was soon surpassed by his even greater private loss. A Russian bomb killed von Manstein's only son on October 29, 1942. A youth serving on the Leningrad front, his loss for the von Mansteins only foreshadowed the draconian loss of German youth soon to follow at Stalingrad.

And what of that battle? It was terrible, yes. Stalingrad also broke the chain of German victories. While a larger battle followed at Kursk, this thrust was the killer. After Stalingrad the Germans went over to the strategic defensive, notwithstanding Hitler's ravings to hold every inch of ground. Increasing partisan activity made German movement perilous at best. In trying to visit the front, von Manstein had to travel in an armored railcar; mines twice exploded under his train.

At the peak of fighting in Stalingrad, it turned into a snowy apocalypse. The Soviets had massed 1,000,500 men, 13,541 guns, 894 tanks, and 1,115 aircraft. The night before the attack, a snowstorm roared into the region. The morning of November 19, 1942, began with a eighty-minute bombardment. The thick fog and swirling snow made artillery corrections impossible for Soviet gunners; instead, they aimed and fired their guns by quadrants. The freezing wounded howled their way to death, the outside temperature at minus 30 degrees Centigrade. By January 24 nearly 20,000 men, one-fifth of the entombed German force, lay in temporary hospitals, most of them unheated. By February 2, 1942, the shrill cries of death without mercy ceased; the Germans, those who had not surrendered to the snow, had surrendered to the Soviets.

Three years later in the snow-covered countryside of France, Red met his first Russian. The Germans had forced many Russian prisoners to work on the Atlantic Wall along the Normandy coast. When the allies landed, some Russians made their way to the allied lines. Red was obviously fascinated by his Russian.

> March 12, 1945: Hello Again: The Russian is an interesting character. He was wounded in the leg and captured by the Germans a long time ago (when the Heines first invaded Russia). He worked in labor battalions, in coal mines and stuff. They tried to get them to fight but they wouldn't. He has seen quite a bit of Germany and France. When the Yanks hit the beaches here he slipped away one night and joined forces with them. He is a brute physically or he probably never would have survived.

Earlier than Red's encounter, American civilians and service personnel began to meet their new Soviet comrades-in-arms in the cinema. When the Germans declared war on the United States, a former antagonist turned into an ally. In 1943 Warner Brothers made a motion picture, *Mission to Moscow,* from Ambassador Joseph E. Davies's book of the same name. Walter Huston starred as Davies. "Naive and controversial" sums up Bosley Crowther's review for the *New York Times.*

More cameras rolled in the same year. Walter Huston went to RKO studios for Samuel Goldwyn's production of Lillian Hellman's *The North Star.* Full of peasants suffering at the hands of Nazis, this motion picture also fell before Crowther's axe; he characterized it as a cross between a idyllic operetta and vehement reality. After the war, the House Un-American Activities Committee liked the movie even less, especially following the passage of the National Security Act of 1947, harbinger of the last phase of twentieth-century warfare, the Cold War.[19]

In 1944, MGM had also jumped onto the war-wagon. Only a few years before, Metro's screen writers had spoofed the Soviets in the delightful Greta Garbo film, *Ninotchka.* Now the front office rushed Robert Taylor (in his last pre-enlistment role) into Joseph Pasternak's *Song of Russia.* Basically ludicrous, Taylor played an American symphony conductor touring the Soviet Union prior to the Nazi attack, which sweeps him and the cast into the war. The movie engulfed the star in a postwar foray in front of the House Un-American Activities Committee, the Soviets recast by the committee as the bad guys. Taylor escaped, testifying that he hadn't wanted to do the film.[20]

And the Russian campaign gave Gregory Peck his first role in Hollywood. Ineligible for the draft because of a spinal injury, Peck came to Hollywood from Berkeley via Broadway to star in the 1944 RKO release, *Days of Glory.* Peck tried to resemble a Russian peasant leading his comrades in the resistance against the Nazi invader. Critics guffawed.

Waiting in the wings to reinforce his star status, Bogart found his Soviet motion picture at sea. This time Bogie joined the Merchant Marines and crewed Liberty ships carrying lend-lease supplies to Britain and the Soviet Union. He lost a few ships and saved a cause. The film, *Action in the North Atlantic,* released in 1943, ranks as one of the war's most popular flagwavers.

The second half of this North Atlantic movie script depicts the dangerous ocean supply of the Soviets, sneaking around Nazi occupied Norway and slipping into Soviet arctic ports, specifically Archangel and Murmansk. Here, snowstorms ranked as an ally; they blinded land-based Luftwaffe bombers and sea-based submarines from getting a fatal fix on the convoy. Fair weather favored the Nazis. Under the cover of ice and snow, Bogart's crew hoped for three Russian rewards: warm accommodations, warming vodka, and warmer women (always called "dames" and addressed by Bogart as "kid." In their postwar musical *South Pacific* Rodgers and Hammerstein have lonely sailors sing *There Is Nothing Like a Dame*).

Warner Brothers did not have to search for a script. American Liberty ships had written it as early as 1942. In *Action in the North Atlantic* Bogart and his Liberty-ship crew sink a German submarine by ramming it. Strangely, fact sometimes collides with fiction.

Launched from the Kaiser shipyards in Richmond, California, on April 14, 1942, the Liberty ship SS *Stephen Hopkins* departed San Francisco Bay with cargo and troops for Bora Bora. Off loaded, the *Hopkins* sailed to New Zealand and Australia, then across the Indian Ocean to Durban, South Africa, where she received orders to proceed to Surinam, South America, to pick up a load of badly needed bauxite for American aluminum manufacturers. Emerging from an Atlantic storm on Sunday, September 27, 1942, the *Hopkins* inadvertently interrupted a rendezvous of the German raider *Stier* and her supply ship *Tannenfels*.

Merchant vessels seldom fought, and raiders usually allowed cargo crews to abandon ship. But the German-born master of the *Hopkins,* Captain Paul Buck, with a young crew of California and Massachusetts boys, in addition to four Greek immigrants who refused to return to Nazi-occupied Greece, decided to fight the moment he saw the raider raise the Nazi swastika. Buck ran up the Stars and Stripes. Taking on the German raider, with its six 5.9–inch guns, enough armament for a destroyer, and commanded by a naval officer, Captain Horst Gerlach, who had a handpicked navy crew of 400, the *Hopkins* faced a warship disguised as a merchantman.

A four-inch cannon, vintage WW I, with worn rifling, along with several rusted shells, served as the main weapon on the *Hopkins*. Even with such poor odds, at a distance of half a mile the *Hopkins* engaged the *Stier*. Once the raider realized that the radio officer of the *Hopkins*, known as Sparks, was radioing distress signals, Captain Gerlach ordered his gunnery officer to shoot the antenna off the *Hopkins'* radio shack. He missed, striking just below the bridge. The gunnery officer tried again. On the second try, his shells collapsed the antenna. Then the *Hopkins* boatswain climbed to the roof of the shack and rerigged the antenna! Finally, the Germans blew the shack to smithereens.

All fifteen men of the *Hopkins* Navy Armed Guard died firing at the *Stier*. Edwin O'Hara, a cadet from the U.S. Merchant Marine Academy in Kings Point, New York, took over the four–inch cannon and kept firing until he too was killed. But several shells fired from the *Hopkins* hit the *Stier* below the waterline, sending it to the bottom. Unlike Bogart's escapade, the *Stier* took the *Hopkins* with it.

Only fifteen American crewman, out of a total of fifty-eight, survived the engagement. They reached the shore of Brazil after a harrowing thirty-one-day voyage in open lifeboats.[21] (Wartime lifeboat movies took form when Alfred Hitchcock, working from a story by John Steinbeck, cast fog-horn voiced Tallulah Bankhead in his 1944 *Lifeboat*. As a piece of cinema hokum, Hitchcock's lifeboat—loaded with passengers whose ship the Nazis torpedoed—became, in James Agee's appraisal, a tour de force.)

As the story of the *Hopkins* suggests, no sealane proved safe. Of the two sealanes connecting U.S. arsenals with Soviet land routes, the shortest, the northern route around Norway, posed the greatest danger. The longest, the Persian Gulf route, meant crossing the safer South Pacific and Indian Ocean. (The Germans did operate submarines and an Indian Ocean tanker from the Japanese base at Penang, on the western coast of the Malay peninsula.) Of the two routes, the Soviets favored the northern one, the easiest for them.

Easy or not, the Soviets not only had to evade the German interdiction of their sea supplies, they had also to dodge Roosevelt's energetic ambassador-admiral. A former naval officer, Ambassador William H. Standley had retired as America's senior admiral. Following retirement, the former chief of Naval Operations took up his civilian duties in Moscow in April 1942 and stayed until October 1943, through the battle of Stalingrad.

Standley spoke openly for the cause of the wartime Poles—not a way to make a friend of Stalin. Under pressure from Churchill, in December 1941 Stalin had released his 180,000 Polish prisoners and transported them via Iran to form an army under General Anders. With that force, along with Polish fighters who had made their way to French Syria, and then to British Palestine when France fell, Britain had an allied army that could fight in Egypt, even in Tobruk against Rommel. London also hosted a Polish government in exile.[22] Standley wanted more help for the Poles. Deaf ears awaited his few invitations to the Kremlin.

Standley also openly criticized the Soviet unwillingness, no matter the cost to Britain and America, to credit them for delivering lend-lease supplies.[23] In May 1942 a convoy (PQ16) lost almost a quarter of its cargo and seven out of thirty-five ships. On June 27, 1942, PQ 17 steamed from Iceland toward Murmansk: It faced constant submarine attacks, bomber strikes as soon as within range of land, and the threat of the German battleship the *Tirpitz*. Murmansk expected thirty-six merchant ships; it welcomed only eleven. Worse yet, more than four hundred tanks, two hundred aircraft, and four thousand trucks went to the bottom.[24] This was equipment that did not show for the snowy battle at Stalingrad. And for the crews of the lost ships—hypothermia, then death.

To help defend the nearly defenseless Liberty ships, the Royal and American navies tried to spare a few large warships for arctic convoy duty.[25] Sinking them proved harder, but not impossible. In early April 1942, the HMS *Edinburgh* escorted a convoy into the Kola Inlet, where the Soviets took charge. On April 30 she returned, escorting convoy QP12. In the Barents Sea, two hundred miles north of Murmansk, she took two torpedoes. With only one screw turning and making only four knots, she headed for the safety of Murmansk. Russian escort destroyers had to leave the HMS *Edinburgh* to protect other shipping. Only Russian minesweepers remained.

Awaiting their chance, three large German destroyers appeared and engaged the British warship. She took a final torpedo and sank, but not before her crew scrambled to safety on a Soviet minesweeper. Among the survivors, J.N. Thwaite, at eighteen unentitled to a tot of rum (the rum supply conveniently saved from the sinking warship) hoped for a nerve calmer. Screwing up his courage in a snow squall as his first ship sank, he went into the rum line. The master-at-arms spoke sharply, stating that all survivors deserved a tot, and a tot Thwaite took.[26] What bravery and bravado sailors and merchant mariners brought to battle and bottle, Bogart tried to recapture on celluloid.

Did any of this matter? Red and his buddies, away from home and without much money, drank their rum-and-cokes and went to the movies, both frequently. Red reviewed the latest attractions for his folks. He showed an uncanny ability for pruning the propaganda; too much of it and the film failed to win his soldierly seal of approval. The following typify his candid cinema taste:

> August 5, 1943: Dear Folks: Have you all seen "Stage Door Canteen?" I saw it for the second time last Sunday.
> August 20, 1943: Dear Folks: I saw "So Proudly We Hail." Didn't like it and don't recommend it.

Like most teenagers, Red enjoyed adventure films best. In December 1943 he sent home a rave review of *Lassie Come Home* and *My Friend Flicka*—starring a dog and a horse, respectively. In 1944 he praised *Drums Along the Mohawk*—bows and arrows. What motion pictures did Nazi and Soviet soldiers see?

In both the Nazi and Soviet cases, the state controlled the national cinemas. Of the fall of Stalingrad, German civilians saw nothing. Instead, the regime ordered that the state radio transmit Bruckner's Seventh Symphony for three days. In Moscow they held a victory celebration, parading the vanquished for the newsreel cameras to capture.

Both regimes knew how to employ cinema for propaganda; with their luck they had filmmakers of such talent that the work they created survived the regimes.[27] In Hitler's service, he had Leni Riefenstahl's masterpiece, *Triumph of the Will,* filmed before the war.

In Stalin's service, he had Sergei Eisentein's triumph, *Ivan the Terrible,* filmed during the war, Part 1 released in 1944. It boasted a score by Sergei Prokofiev; both Sergeis received Stalin Prizes for their collaborative work. The film's message clearly justified any act a tyrant took to secure the state. Fifty years after the war ended, a Manhattan retrospective of the film caused the *New York Times* to print a full page blasting "the prostitution of two great artists" to the needs of a monster like Stalin-the-Really-Terrible.[28] But the film had its impact.

With or without the cinema, battles like Stalingrad so embittered German–Soviet relations that, fifty years after the end of the war, when, in June 1989, Mikhail Gorbachev visited Chancellor Helmut Kohl in Bonn, in order to move to the future, both had to first restate the past, their experiences in World War II.[29] Stalingrad in particular, and the Great Patriotic War in general, also burnt itself into the collective memory of a Soviet generation. That generation had to hold to an official story; that story changed slowly after Stalin's death because the thaw in censorship gave the victorious marshals of the Soviet Union a chance to publish their martial memoirs.

What one misses are the memories of ordinary soldiers. Helping to fill that void, Vladimir Voinovich wrote a novel, *The Life and Extraordinary Adventures of Private Ivan Chonkin*. So unkind to the wartime regime was it that Soviet censors forbade its publication. Instead, chapters traveled underground until, in 1969, they surfaced, published in, of all places, West Germany. A monumental spoof, the secret peasant recipe for homemade vodka showed how far a Russian would go for his favorite spirits—the rum of the steppe. Vodka flows through Russian song and stories like the mighty Volga flows through Russia. In Alexander Borodin's *Prince Igor* what does Prince Galitsky offer his followers to betray Igor, who is away defending Russia from foreign invasion? Gold? Jewels? Power? No. A barrel of vodka each![30]

While vodka warmed many a Russian, many Germans found only a deep freeze. Refusing to withdraw General Friedrich von Paulus's Sixth Army from the ice-trap at Stalingrad, Hitler issued his infamous order: "We are not budging from the Volga." Resisting the advice of the General Staff, Hitler insisted that his goals of 1941—Leningrad, Moscow, and the Transcaucasus—could still be had in 1942.

In this futility, Hitler wasted vital forces in piecemeal efforts without one center of concentration. He even ordered the battle-tested Eleventh Army that von Manstein had used to take Sevastopol to move north across the entire front and throw itself into the battle for Leningrad. He insisted that the Luftwaffe could resupply the surrounded Sixth Army. Goering promised an airlift for Stalingrad, again promising what he could not deliver. By fighting everywhere, Hitler's pigheadedness lost Germany everything. He sent the Sixth Army to its martyrdom on the Volga.

Germany was lucky that it had in von Manstein a commander who could get as many units out of the way of Soviet encirclement as he did. It must be remembered that once the Red Army crossed the Volga and circled around Stalingrad, it was on the move on what had been the left flank of Field Marshal von Kleist's overextended Army Group A, whose motorized patrols had reached the shores of the Caspian Sea in the autumn of 1942. They had to retreat and retreat fast.

This von Manstein helped to accomplish, although Hitler grew to hate him for these retrograde movements, finally sacking him, the best of his field commanders. (Amazement struck Berlin insiders. Studnitz found that the military situation in south Russia kept on producing all sorts of puzzling surprises. "Manstein and Kleist were no sooner decorated with the Knight's Cross with Swords than they were both relieved of their commands!")[31]

Von Manstein observed Hitler in all his war moods; he gives him credit for having a certain eye for operational openings, an astounding retentive memory and imagination, and an amazing familiarity with the effects of the latest weapons. But in the end von Manstein suggests that what Hitler lacked in the broadest sense was "military ability based on experience—something for which his 'intuition' was no substitute." As for the Soviet invasion, von Manstein faults Hitler for underrating the resources of the Soviet Union and the fighting qualities of the Red Army.[32] Von Manstein is too generous.

Hitler's job did not entail moving field armies around the battlefield; Germany had professionals for that. The head of the German government should have seen that it would take attacks on both ends, European and Asian, to blast open the Bolshevik bastion. Other than the Germans, the only force Stalin feared, Japan, had an alliance with the European Axis. Not until he had secured a joint German–Japanese attack on the Soviet behemoth should Hitler have invaded. To obtain Japanese help, he should have promised anything; the Pacific Ocean meant little to Germany. To give Russia the German disease—war on two fronts—meant carefully orchestrating a policy with Tokyo. Missing this opportunity meant losing the war. Hitler never fully comprehended that he had stumbled into a global war, preferring instead to see the conflict in regional terms.[33]

Germany was too big for Europe but not big enough for the world. Hitler needed Japan in order to defeat the Soviet Union, and he needed to keep the United States neutral in order to limit the war to the Eurasian landmass. This he failed to understand. Hence he stunned Tokyo when he orchestrated the ghoulish Russian deal of August 22, 1939, the nonaggression pact signed by two grave diggers out to bury civilization, Foreign Ministers Molotov and Ribbentrop. Cynical thugwork.

Why Japanese consternation? Because in 1939 the Soviet Union, an old Japanese enemy with a new name, had clashed with the Imperial Japanese Kwantung Army in Outer Mongolia. At the battle of Khalkin-Gol an unknown corps commander, Zhukov, had won a battle with his tanks. But the frontier stretched for two thousand miles. How to defend it against Japanese expansion? With force, of course. Stalin stationed three-quarters of a million crack troops, supported by more than two thousand tanks and heavy air support along this Asian frontier.

Until Japan moved south, committing the bulk of its forces away from Soviet Asia, Stalin could not withdraw his strong Asian army for duty on his western front. Richard Sorge, the Soviet spy in Tokyo, alerted Stalin to Japan's decision to chose southern expansion over a Soviet campaign regardless of the pleas of Germany's ambassador, General Eugen Ott.[34] Hitler's flip-flop diplomacy toward Stalin—first peace, then war—left Tokyo out in the cold. So it warmed to a solo southern adventure, returning in kind the lack of strategic coordination with Berlin that Berlin had visited upon it.

In all this, Moscow played the better strategic game. Even after Tokyo found itself embroiled in a Pacific war it could not win, the Soviets refused to attack, regardless of American pressure to do so. Stalin did not declare war on Japan and open an eastern front until he had won his western war. No two-front conflict for that dictator.

In late 1941, did the release of the Soviet Asian armies help? Indeed it did. Advance units arrived on one side of Moscow, detrained, walked through the city, and threw themselves into the raging battle for the capital. In October and November 1941, Stalin brought ten divisions, one thousand tanks, and one thousand aircraft from his Siberian force. The result? Moscow did not fall, nor did the Red Army, the force the German generals wanted to destroy regardless of Hitler's determination to hold real estate, surrender. And without a surrender, with an expanding enemy army in the field while the German field armies had already reached their apex and begun their decline, the war turned against the unwise invader.

And it turned against Germany in the snow of Stalingrad—the turning thrust on the Russian steppe.[35] Cruel, cold death under a white blanket; folly of the highest order had taken a generation of innocents on both sides to death's deep freeze.[36] And then there was the snow, always the snow.

Notes

1. Alan Bullock, *Hitler and Stalin: Parallel Lives* (New York: Random House, 1992). Both tyrants lived in the same city, Vienna, for a few days in early 1913. Unfortunately, the Hapsburg police did not put an early end to their disastrous careers. Also see David M. Glantz, "Soviet Military Strategy During the Second Period of War: November 1942–December 1943," 115–51, and Warren F. Kimball, "Stalingrad: A Chance for Choices," 89–114, both in *The Journal of Military History* (January 1996).

2. J.F.C. Fuller, *The Conduct of War 1789–1961* (New Brunswick, NJ: Rutgers University Press, 1961), 262–66. Critics of Nazi strategy toward the peoples conquered in the East existed even within the Third Reich. These critics also suggest that the beneficial policy would have been to liberate the non-Russians and make allies of them. See Hans-Georg von Studnitz, *While Berlin Burns: The Diary of Hans-Georg von Studnitz* (London: George Widenfeld and Nicolson, 1964), 166. Others suggest that a failure of nerve on the part of the West caused the war, a failure that replaced deterrence of Hitler with appeasement. For a restatement of that view see Thomas Sowell, "An Unnecessary War," *Forbes,* August 14, 1995, 122–27.

3. Heinz Guderian, *Panzer Leader* (London: Michael Joseph, 1952), 193–94. Also see John Erickson, "Nazi Posters in Wartime Russia," *History Today* (September 1994): 14–20.

4. Carl von Clausewitz, *On War* (Princeton: Princeton University Press, 1976), 595–96. Stalin, himself a non-Russian, always played to the Russian majority, his regime suggesting that the Russian nationality won the war against Hitler. What about the other Soviet nationalities that fought? Disregarded. A case in point, Yuri Slezkine, *Artic Mirrors: Russia and the Small Peoples of the North* (Ithaca: Cornell University Press, 1994), 303–4, 309.

5. A study of Stalinism can be found in Roy A. Medvedev, *Let History Judge: The Origins and Consequences of Stalinism* (New York: Knopf, 1971). Also see Robert C. Tucker, ed., *Stalinism: Essays in Historical Interpretations* (New York: W.W. Norton, 1977). For biographical works see Isaac Deutscher, *Stalin: A Political Biography* (New York: Vintage, 1960), and Adam B. Ulam, *Stalin: The Man and His Era* (New York: Viking, 1973).

6. A prolific writers about the war, Vasili Ivanovich Chuikov wrote *The Battle of Stalingrad* (New York: Holt, Rinehart and Winston, 1964), with an introduction by Hanson W. Baldwin. Also see Chuikov, *The Beginning of the Road* (London: MacGibbon and Kee, 1963); *The End of The Third Reich* (London: MacGibbon and Kee, 1967); and *The Fall of Berlin* (New York: Holt, Rinehart and Winston, 1968).

7. Chuikov, *The Beginning of the Road,* 206–7. No one should assume that Red Army generals won the war by themselves. They had help. See Richard N. Armstrong, *Red Army Tank Commanders: The Armored Guards* (Atglen, PA: Schiffer Publishing, 1994).

8. Seweryn Bialer, ed., *Stalin and His Generals: Soviet Military Memoirs of World War II* (New York: Pegasus, 1969), 63, 318–36, 640. No better example of this state murder of former heros exists than Nikita Mikhalkov's 1994 film, the docudrama *Burnt by the Sun.*

9. Georgi K. Zhukov, *Marshal Zhukov's Greatest Battles* (New York: Harper and Row, 1969). The book is a collection of articles that Zhukov wrote. Harrison E. Salisbury edited the book and wrote its Introduction.

10. Ibid., 100–103.

11. B.H. Liddell Hart, *The German Generals Talk* (New York: William Morrow, 1948), 63.

12. Harrison E. Salisbury, *The Unknown War* (New York: Bantam Books, 1978), 44.

13. F.S. Oktyabrsky, "The Defense of Sevastopol," in *Sevastopol: November*

1941–July 1942, Eye-Witness Accounts By Soviet War-Correspondents (London: Hutchinson, 1943), 63–70.

14. Boris Voyetekhov, *The Last Days of Sevastopol* (New York: Knopf, 1943), 98.

15. John Erickson, *The Road to Stalingrad: Stalin's War With Germany* (Boulder: Westview Press, 1975), 256.

16. Erick von Manstein. *Lost Victories* (Chicago: Henry Regnery Company, 1958), 223.

17. Siegfried Knappe and Ted Brusaw, *Soldat: Reflections of a German Soldier, 1936–1949* (New York: Bantam 1992), 229–36.

18. Voyetekhov, *The Last Days of Sevastopol,* 156–57.

19. Patrick Lloyd Hatcher, *The Suicide of an Elite* (Stanford: Stanford University Press, 1990), 8–12.

20. Joe Morella et al., *The Films of World War II* (Secaucus, NJ: Citadel Press, 1975), 122–23, 153–54, 174–76.

21. J.L. Pimsleur, "S.F. Honors Liberty Ship's Heroic World War II Battle," *San Francisco Chronicle,* September 27, 1996, B1; Pat Hammond, "Claremont Man's Acts in WW II Remembered," *Union Leader* (Manchester, New Hampshire), September 25, 1995, A1; Carl Nolte, "Gallant Heroes of Liberty Ship Hopkins Are Aboard in Spirit," *San Francisco Chronicle,* April 29, 1994, A3.

22. Polish-Americans have never forgotten the Polish contribution to the victory of democracy in WW II. They have their own organization, Polonia Solidarity Association, in Reading, Pennsylvania. See Andrew Hempel, "A Nation That Never Surrenders," *Wall Street Journal,* May 20, 1995, 7.

23. George C. Herring, Jr., *Aid to Russia: 1941–1946* (New York: Columbia University Press, 1973), 80–85.

24. Erickson, *The Road to Stalingrad,* 399.

25. Dan van der Vat, *The Atlantic Campaign: WW II's Great Struggle at Sea* (New York: Harper and Row, 1988), 279–80, 355–58. When convoys to Russia were resumed in 1943, they had even larger escorts, especially escort-carriers. Critics called them "Woolworth carriers" because of their admittedly rudimentary construction.

26. A.J. Pack, *Nelson's Blood: The Story of Naval Rum* (Hampshire, UK: Kenneth Mason, 1982), 185–86.

27. Luda and Jean Schnitzer with Marcel Martin, eds., *Cinema in Revolution: The Heroic Era of the Soviet Film* (New York: Hill and Wang, 1973).

28. Richard Taruskin, "Great Artist Serving Stalin Like a Dog," *New York Times,* May 28, 1995, H22.

29. Timothy Garton Ash, *In Europe's Name: Germany and the Divided Continent* (New York: Random House, 1993), 118.

30. In tsarist days, vodka ranked high enough in value that the tsars made it a state monopoly (Richard Pipes, *Russia Under the Old Regime* [New York: Charles Scribner's Sons, 1974], 195, 208). During the Soviet period, tax on vodka accounted for up to one-third of the state's budget (Andrew Kramer, "Where Vodka Is Still King," *San Francisco Chronicle,* January 27, 1997, A8). Also see Vladimir G. Treml, *Alcohol in the U.S.S.R.: A Statistical Study* (Durham, NC: Duke University Press, 1982).

31. Studnitz, *While Berlin Burns,* 179.

32. Manstein, *Lost Victories,* 175–76, 274–75 (see chapter 11, "Hitler as Supreme Commander," 273–288). Also see William Murray et al., eds., *The Making of Strategy: Rulers, States & War* (New York: Cambridge University Press, 1994).

33. Hitler's ignorance of global strategy in regard to Japan is all the more surprising when one considers that Kaiser Wilhelm II's government was keenly aware of the role Japan could play in the Pacific, a role that would enhance Germany's security. See Ute Mehnert, "German Weltpolitik and the American Two-Front Dilemma: The 'Japanese Peril' in German-American Relations, 1904–1917," *Journal of American History* (March 1966): 1452–1477.

34. In the case of the failure of Berlin and Tokyo jointly to attack the USSR, Chalmers Johnson bluntly states: "It was this combination of German arrogance and Japanese pride that led to the eventual destruction of both states" (*An Instance of Treason: Ozaki Hotsumi and the Sorge Spy Ring* [Stanford: Stanford University Press, 1990], 148–60, quotation is from page 157). Masao Maruyama concludes that, in the case of Japan's leaders choosing an attack on the United States over an attack on the USSR, "the fateful decision was taken by men who were surprisingly ignorant of international affairs." (*Modern Japanese Politics* [New York: Oxford University Press, 1969], 84–134, quotation is from page 85).

35. The Soviet novel that tells Stalingrad's story better than any history is Vasily Grossman, *Life and Fate: A Novel* (New York: Harper and Row, 1985). I am indebted to two Russian specialists, the historian Nicholas Riasanovsky and the economist Gregory Grossman (no relation), for recommending this book. Before *Life and Fate* made its appearance outside the Soviet Union, the wartime reading public of 1945 had English translations from both London and New York publishers of Konstantine Simonov's *Days and Nights* (New York: Simon and Schuster, 1945). Simon and Schuster informed the American readers that Simonov ranked as one of Russia's outstanding war correspondents, and that his experiences at Stalingrad formed the basis for *Days and Nights.*

36. German filmmakers waited until the 1990s to tell their story in the film *Stalingrad.* Not without reason, the film stars the "paralyzing snow" (Marc Fisher, "Movie Helps Germans to Mourn War Dead," *International Herald Tribune,* April 2, 1996, 28). Earlier, the German theater had the seared memory on paper of a soldier who had served on the Russian front. See Wolfgang Borchert, *The Man Outside* (New York: New Directions, 1949).

The Sea

Sometimes pugnacious, sometimes peaceful, blue-water seafarers sailed the North Atlantic for travel and trade. This briny basin also fed them; harvested along with the land, the sea added a richness to their diets. Viking long-boats, Spanish galleons, Dutch merchantmen, British men-of-war, American clipper-ships, Swedish schooners, French luxury-liners, German U-boats, Norwegian freighters, Danish trawlers, Russian whalers, Canadian icebreakers, Portuguese fishing vessels, Greek tankers: They carried these aquatic rovers. The basin's citizens met either through the force of combat or the favor of commerce.

Naval combat had settled sea squabbles in the past: Spain and its allies at Lepanto blocked Islam's nautical ambitions in the western Mediterranean, Nelson at Trafalgar ended Napoleon's ocean-going career, and in 1916 the British Royal Navy at Jutland forced the German High Seas Fleet to retire to home waters for the remainder of phase one of North Atlantic political strife.

On three warring occasions during the twentieth century, a unique type of warship became, in zoological terms, the Alpha, or dominant, killer. For the 1914–1918 period, dreaded battleships took the place of horror; for 1939–1945, aircraft carriers supplanted big-gunned dreadnoughts; and for the last of the combat periods, the 1947–1989 frosty struggle dove underwater when the submarine gained primacy.[1] This ship triad saw duty in all three periods, and each had its impact regardless of the ascendance of any one type at any one time.

With the growth of trade during the expansive nineteenth century, the North Atlantic became the watery connection of choice. As an economic conveyer it had no rival. It witnessed a mighty exchange of goods and services, an ocean emporium. British traders in London supplanted the Dutch in Amsterdam, who had earlier supplanted the Venetians. By mid-twentieth century, New York City financiers challenged City of London bankers; in due course, the New Yorkers won.

In trade and war, if the English Channel is a barrier, the North Atlantic is a bastion. Combined with the South Atlantic, it is the second-largest ocean next to the Pacific. Excluding dependent seas, it covers 31,800,000 square miles (including dependent seas, 41,100,000 square miles). It is also the youngest, having formed late because of delayed continental drift. Each year the North Atlantic gives birth to icebergs, almost eight thousand a winter. Most come from the six-fastest moving glaciers on Earth, which release over five thousand a year into Baffin Bay.

In the North Atlantic the trade winds maintain a fairly steady current from east to west. This current swirls into the Caribbean, up into the Gulf of Mexico, and out again through the Strait of Florida. Reinforced at that point, it becomes the Gulf Stream, which heads toward Europe after following the American coast past the Grand Banks of Newfoundland.

Weather over the North Atlantic is determined largely by wind currents and air masses over the North American continent. A general forecast: several hurricanes in fall, severe storms in winter, some northeasters in spring. Summer is mildest, but still tricky.

Across this turbulence, President Roosevelt wished to build a bridge of ships. Nature helped. If one steamed north along the Arctic fringe, a string of islands hung like uncut stones across the throat of the northern reaches. Islands large like Greenland, medium like Iceland, and small like the Hebrides: All pointed downward to the pendant, the British Isles. At these islands one found safe anchorages; one could also fly from local airfields to defend approaching and departing ships.

Under this turbulence, Grand Admiral Karl Donitz wanted to sink this bridge of ships. Nature helped. Having won the Battle of France, the Third Reich scored submarine bases along the Atlantic coast, bases that placed its underwater fleet closer to this ship-bridge. If one steamed south along the Bay of Biscay, a string of ports snuggled like pearls strung across the cleavages of the French shoreline. Ports grands, moyens, and petits—Brest, Lorient (Donitz's early headquarters), Saint-Nazaire, La Pallice, and La Rochelle housed submarine pens. At these pens one found safe havens; one could also fly from nearby airfields to defend returning and departing boats.

Each side tried to cancel nature's help to its enemy. In the case of the Anglo–American rocky havens, a submarine could wait for victims in the gaps between islands, especially the Greenland Air Gap. And German submarines did not wait alone; they worked in packs, like canines of the sea. The other side could close the gaps with longer-range land-based aircraft; greater numbers of escorts for convoys, especially escort aircraft carriers; and improved sonar for hunt-and-kill sea chases.

In the case of the submarine pens along the French coast, they were in range of bomber attacks from Britain. Aware of this, German engineers had made the low-lying pens bomb-proof; twelve-foot-thick concrete roofs protected those hiding underneath. In January and February 1943, the Royal Air Force's Bomber Command dropped nine thousand tons of bombs on the pens. Headaches aplenty, but not one bomb penetrated, not one submarine sank. So durable were they that during the last phase of North Atlantic warring, the French Navy based its Cold War nuclear submarines in the largest of the old U-boat pens at Brest.[2]

Two admirals dominated Nazi naval strategy. The senior of the two, Grand Admiral Erich Raeder, protected the interests of the surface navy. The junior of them, Donitz, watched over the undersea fleet. Raeder had tried, but failed, to distract Hitler away from his Russian gambit. He had hoped to catapult the Axis into Mediterranean dominance by having Hitler coax, cajole, and, if necessary, carry Francisco Franco's fascist Spain into a war that captured Gibraltar. But Hitler, completely ignorant of naval strategy, turned against the expensive surface fleet, suggesting that its large guns could serve a better purpose by being remounted as coastal artillery to protect the continent from any Anglo–American invasion. At that juncture, Raeder retired as chief of the German Navy. In January 1943 Hitler replaced him with Donitz, awarding him the same rank that Raeder had held since 1939, grand admiral.

Donitz came out of the World War I phase of combat enamored of submarines. He initially experienced the sea with the surface navy; in 1914 he served on the light cruiser *Breslau,* whose famed dash through the Mediterranean to Istanbul, along with the battle cruiser *Goeben,* helped propel the Ottoman Empire into the war as a German ally. But two years crammed into submarines fixed his future. Despite the fact that, once given his own submarine to command in the Mediterranean, he was forced to surface and surrender his boat and crew, he remained wedded to the undersea struggle.

Unremarked at the time, the design for the submarines that Germany built originated with a former British subject, John Philip Holland, who, as an Irish nationalist and later American citizen, perfected the design in the 1870s as a weapon for the Irish Fenian Brotherhood to humiliate the British Empire. In 1914 Germany attempted the Irish task, but failed. At Berlin's surrender in 1918, Donitz had a long shore leave. But by 1935 he found himself skippering a German submarine for sea trials.

For his boats Donitz did not support single combat, in which submarines searched for one target at a time, a slow version of commerce raiding. Donitz introduced the group hunt; his tactics tied to his naval strategy of tonnage war.

In numerical terms this meant maximum enemy shipping losses per submarine per day at sea. Donitz chose the North Atlantic as the decisive waterway for ton termination. There his U-boats would rip open escorted convoys with controlled operations, massed attackers guided by radio beacons. The first submarine to site a convoy would beacon others to maneuver for the kill. After initiating the attack, each submarine hunted independently on the surface through the night, diving before dawn to position itself ahead of the convoy in order to repeat the operation the following evening.[3]

Tonnage warfare relied on statistics. In 1939, Great Britain flagged the world's largest merchant fleet; in round numbers, three thousand ocean merchantmen, for a cargo-carrying total of 17 million tons. Donitz estimated that, under wartime conditions, Britain at best could build new ships at the rate of almost 200,000 tons per month. Donitz worked on the math.

Donitz projected a force of three hundred German U-boats, which would provide him with a force of fifty on patrol at all times. As a conservative estimate, he envisaged each of the fifty boats sinking three merchant ships per month. At that rate, half of Britain's cargo fleet would go under in one year. If the German surface raiders and the Luftwaffe would pick up the slack, Germany might sink up to 750,000 tons a month, which, if maintained for a year, would force Britain out of the war. Yet it did not come to pass. Why? There are a number of reasons for the failure, three in particular.

First, Donitz did not start with 300 U-boats. By the end of 1941, he had only 236. His numbers kept increasing—331 U-Boats by July 1942—but so did enemy ships. Donitz's failed to consider the impact of American shipbuilding capacity, the capacity on hand and its ability to expand rapidly.

As for time, it never allied itself with Donitz. In a war of scarce resources, the German pecking order remained the same: the army first, the navy second, the air force third. (According to Donitz, the Navy High Command had to make strenuous endeavors to keep the Army from drafting dockyard and shipbuilding workers.)

Crippling contradictions in priorities hurt the German Navy, the Kriegsmarine. Before the war, when Raeder commanded, the priority went to the surface fleet first, underwater fleet second. Nazi admirals wanted big ships. Big they got. The *Bismarck* fulfilled their fancy for floating death machines. But the British sank it. (In on the final kill, the Polish destroyer *Piorun* proudly fired Polish shells at the German giant.)

Before its death roll into the Bay of Biscay, Hitler visited Germany's newest battleship moored at Gotenhafen, back in the Baltic away from prying British eyes. He gave onlookers the impression that he was ill at ease. Well he might have been; he consigned the *Bismarck* to its doom in 1941. Hitler didn't sink another German behemoth; he didn't have to. Surface sailors watched interservice rivalry kill their hopes for a complete blue-water navy when their best-laid keel, the *Graf Zeppelin,* Germany's first aircraft carrier, never joined the fleet. While it re-quired the U-47, with derring-do, to imperil the imperial naval base at Scapa Flow, within which it sank the British battleship, the *Royal Oak,* it took only bureaucratic pens in Berlin to zap the *Graf Zeppelin.*

Second, Britain did not live down to Donitz's projections. While he sank its surface ships, it sank his submarines. What the British called ASDIC, and the Americans called sonar, was to the battle of the sea what radar was to the battle of the sky. In other words, the enemy could find you, even in the dark depths. But what made ASDIC–sonar so good came from Hut 6 and Hut 8 at Bletchley Park and people there like Alan Turing, a math genius who deciphered codes and developed the first computer. Unapologetically homosexual, Turing found war-worried Britain willing to use his genius and then turn on him in peacetime.[4] A postwar suicide, his death indicted a constitutioanl monarchy unwilling to allow gay citizens to live in peace while allowing them to die in war. Assisting allied intelligence, the Poles first built a copy of the German Enigma machine (named after Sir Edward Elgar's "Enigma Variations"), and in 1939 they gave copies to their French and British allies. In May 1941, following an Atlantic convoy battle in which U-110 was critically damaged, a boarding party from HMS *Bulldog* captured U-110's naval Enigma coding machine and associated instructions for the following weeks.[5]

Coding coups like these made ocean defense easier. Navy escorts knew where to look; convoys knew where to avoid. And the allies kept adding warships to the convoys, especially the carrier escorts. Convoy and island-based aircraft, along with escort warships, also hunted in packs, and they got better and better at the chase. Ships and aircraft killed any way they could. A U-Boat had a menu of possible final courses: Its surface enemies might bomb, torpedo, ram, shell, mine, or depth charge it. But sink it they would.

Before Britain could bring this force to bear, Donitz almost won his war. British sea losses in 1940 and 1941 hurt. From fifty-five million tons in 1939, imports dropped to an annual rate of thirty million tons by March 1941. Cholesterol levels must have dropped as well; each British citizen received a ration of only two eggs a month (in British, one egg a fortnight). After the slaughter of the kingdom's livestock, meat made the menu for only a few meals.

Third, Britain found a shipbuilder's dream, an underemployed ally who learned new tricks quickly. Trickery here involved mass producing ships the way Henry Ford mass-produced automobiles—fast and cheap.

As old American shipyards streamlined to become tricksters, new yards raced them for first trick. The San Francisco Bay Area expanded into the largest shipbuilding center in the world. Build it and they will come, and they did.

Californians constructed instant shipyards: Henry Kaiser's vast complex in Richmond and Bechtel Company's yard in Sausalito. In the fall of 1942, Kaiser's Richmond yard set a record; it assembled a launchable Liberty ship in just four days. Exceptional? Yes. But most yards could produce a Liberty ship in twenty days.

Before the war, this was an unheard-of pace. During the war, it

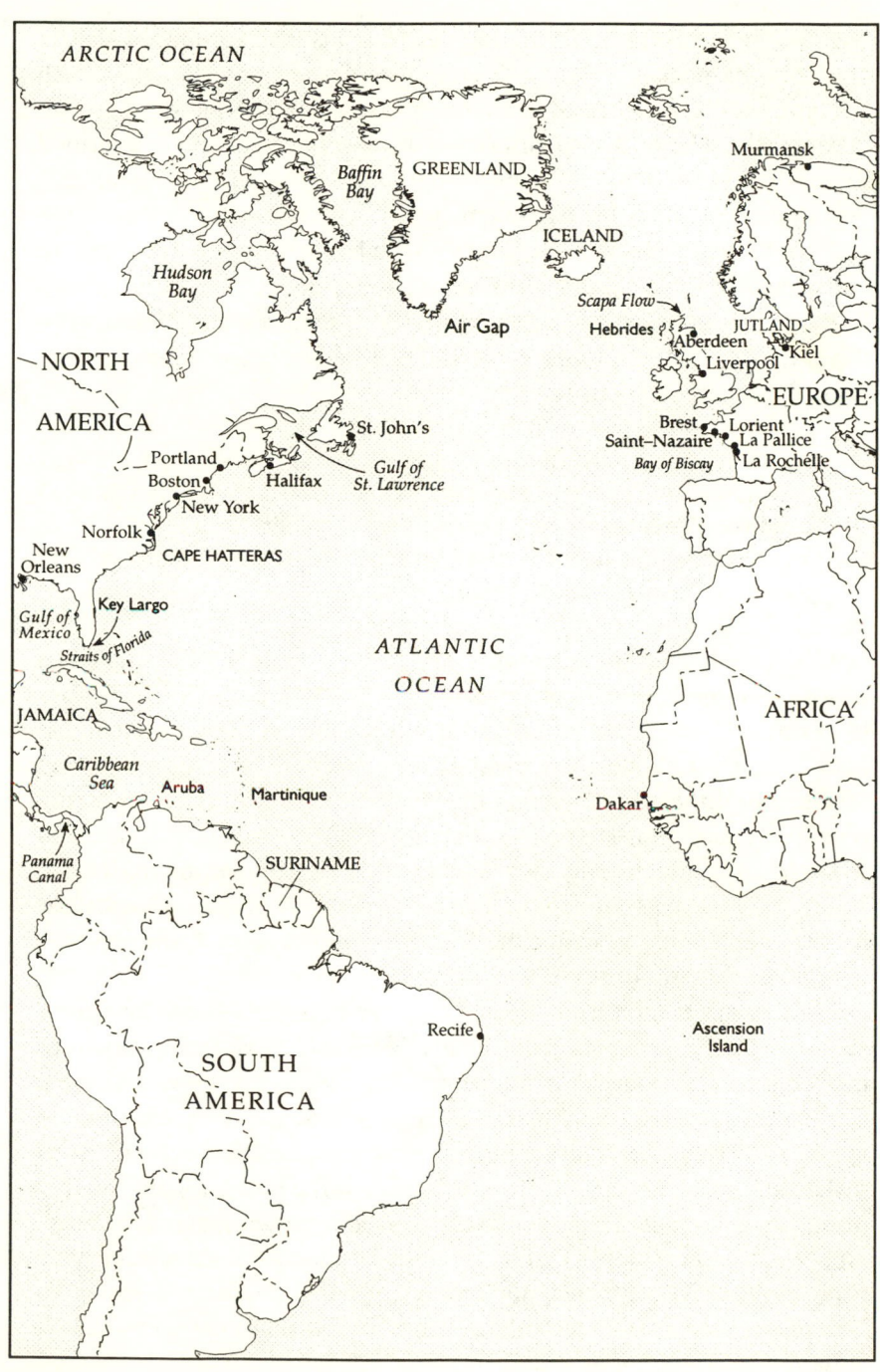

ARCTIC OCEAN

Baffin
Bay
GREENLAND

Murmansk

Hudson
Bay

ICELAND

Air Gap

Scapa Flow
Hebrides
JUTLAND
Aberdeen
Kiel
Liverpool

NORTH

EUROPE

AMERICA

St. John's

Brest
Lorient
Saint–Nazaire
La Pallice
Bay of Biscay
La Rochelle

Portland
Boston
Halifax
New York
Gulf of
St. Lawrence

Norfolk

CAPE HATTERAS

New
Orleans

Key Largo

Gulf of
Mexico

ATLANTIC

Straits of Florida

OCEAN

JAMAICA

AFRICA

Caribbean
Sea
Aruba
Martinique

Dakar

Panama
Canal

SURINAME

Recife

Ascension
Island

SOUTH
AMERICA

became the norm. The customer could have his mass-produced ship in any color he wanted, as long as it was battleship grey. For the North Atlantic people, war had industrialized into a supply contest around an ocean basin. The critical path involved transporting supplies to armed forces. The contestant who lacked that ability lost. In that sense, Liberty ships were the vehicles of victory.

Victory required Americans, many who had never seen the ocean, to come down to the coast and construct these ocean conveyers. Red's folks, newly arrived in California in 1943, represented Missouri-by-the-Bay. Replying to one of his father's letters, Red expressed his pride in his parents' contribution:

> July 2, 1943: Howdy Mister: . . . that description of the shipyards beats anything I have ever read about them. I could picture it in my mind as I read your letter. I'll bet it makes you feel just a little proud to be a part of something like that. And you can bet your boots that "the boys" will make good use of the stuff you make there.

Liberty ships tell one story-of-stuff, tankers another. With the onset of war with the United States, German U-boats raised their periscopes to peep on East Coast shipping. Donitz found America's Achilles' heel. Unknown to most citizens, tankers from the Gulf Coast carried 90 percent of the oil received in the Northeast. They formed a floating pipeline to the heartland of American industry. Insofar as the first overland pipeline, the Big Inch, was not due for completion until early 1943, America was vulnerable in its own coastal waters. Donitz had his favorite hunting grounds, the North Carolina coast: "Cape Hatteras proved particularly fruitful."[6]

For the winter months of 1942, Donitz spared six U-boats for American waters. They hunted from Sandy Hook off New Jersey, down to the Virginia Capes at the entrance of Chesapeake Bay, onward to the Carolina outer banks, southward to Georgia's Sea Islands, and around the Florida Keys. In their sinking frenzy between January and April 1942, they sent 198 ships (1,150,675 tons) to the bottom, with the loss of only one U-boat. Tanker sinkings caused a growing alarm, twenty-nine went to fire-fueled deaths in January alone. Loses would have been higher if Berlin had not ordered Donitz to divert U-boats to Norwegian waters, where Hitler, ever wrong at sea, had guessed that Britain would attempt landings.

As Navy Department staffers awoke to America's coastal danger, they learned from the British Admiralty how to drive the wolf from the door. Inasmuch as the U-boats operated in shallow coastal waters, sometimes not more than four or five fathoms, the American Coast Guard could help. With predictions of severe gasoline shortages, the Coast Guard took over private yachts, with their owners as skippers, to form the Coastal Picket Patrol, nicknamed the "Hooligan Navy." Good only for spotting U-boats, the Coast Guard armed them just in case they had extraordinary luck.[7]

Out in dry Wyoming, Red decided he might like sea life. In Cheyenne he had already helped "some sailors get a bottle" with which to celebrate. After writing his folks about that liquid adventure, he later wrote them about a possible career change.

> January 27, 1944: Dear Folks: I'm going to make application to take the Coast Guard test that is given in May.

By May, Red found himself in the infantry at Camp Robinson, Arkansas. Unfortunately for Red, the war wouldn't stand still long enough for him to hunt for submarines. But U-boats still lurked in and around American shipping; only the pack had moved.

Ever hungry, the wolves went south. Surprising the Americans, the packs now waited in the Caribbean off Aruba (oil) and Trinidad (bauxite), 4,000 miles from their pens in France. With Nazi submarines submerged in the Caribbean, it did not take Humphrey Bogart long to surface in two films about the war at the southern doorstep of the United States.

In 1942 Warner Brothers released *Across the Pacific,* which they should have titled *Saving the Panama Canal.* (The director, John Huston, received his call to active duty before he could finish this piece of film hokum.) Sailing from the East Coast to Panama, Bogart, a double agent, saved the canal and romanced the girl, Mary Astor, the woman he had sent to jail in *The Maltese Falcon.*

Not satisfied that the Caribbean was safe, Bogart convinced his next girl, Lauren Bacall, to help him save the Free French cause on the island of Martinique. Ernest Hemingway wrote the novel, William Faulkner the screenplay, and Warners released *To Have and Have Not* in 1945. In it, Bogart chartered his own small craft, big enough to shoot at Vichy gunboats, which the ever-resourceful Bogart, under questioning from Vichy officials, said looked like a patrolling German submarine to him. Bogart drank rum, and Bacall became the Caribbean version of the Rhine River's Lorelei. In Bacall's case, she lured men to their Caribbean doom with whistling lessons.

In 1945 *Life* magazine photographed Bacall vamping Vice President Harry Truman at a serviceman's party. The Missouri-trained political-pianist tried to look nonchalantly away as a leggy Bacall draped herself on the piano's top.[8] Femme fatale Bacall, a Hollywood gypsy, had a gimmick. She taught lonely men that anyone could whistle—all you had to do was put your lips together and blow. *Life* blew her photo up to man-eating proportions, her puckered lips generating enough power to jump start a quarter-ton jeep.

During the 1940s *Life* was the paramount national photo magazine, giving a snapshot-hungry America pictures of itself, its dreams, and its reality. Not only could *Time* and *Life* magazines be found in many homes, but they also circulated in many barbershops and beauty parlors where most Americans had their hair either cut, conked, or curled. And torchy pin-ups captured what fighting men hoped to find at their homecomings.

Two of the most famous shots that *Life* developed for a print-devouring America-at-war featured Rita Hayworth (dubbed the love goddess) in a negligee kneeling on a bed and the backside of Betty Grable (looking over her shoulder) in a white one-piece bathing suit. *Life* matched cheesecake photos with beefcake opposites, offering Clark Gable (grinning his Rhett Butler best) in an Army uniform and Tyrone Power, a newly minted marine. Earlier, their bear chests had meant box-office magic. Hayworth and Grable could sing and dance, Gable and Power could flex and pump, and Bacall could blow and whistle. Vertical manifestations of a horizontal desire.

Red almost made a Caribbean whistle-stop when the U.S. Army reassigned him to Camp Rucker, Alabama. He wrote his folks that he could make it to the Gulf of Mexico, only one hundred miles due south of his position. But, as always, the Army had other plans for this soldier. And Alabama turned into hostile territory once Red discovered he was too young to buy a drink there. Red groused about Alabama liquor laws in his letters home.

Finding a wartime date proved even more of a problem. When he reported in for basic training at Fort Warren, Wyoming, Red found the nearby town off-limits to soldiers. He was riled.

June 9, 1943: Dear Folks: The reason for declaring it out of bounds is that all the soldiers are getting venereal diseases from the women in town. I don't see why they don't run the women out.

At his next training location, his chance to whistle back at a local Lauren Bacall disappeared altogether.

September 15, 1943: Dear Folks: No kissing or even whistling at local gals.

Instead, the Army issued Red a pair of gym shoes.

November 8, 1943: Dear Folks: I got my gym equipment today—the shoes. They are pretty nice but I don't know how good they will wear. They are made of reclaimed rubber. (The Roosevelt Administration had rationed shoes and rubber.)

When Red arrived in Arkansas, no Scarlett O'Hara beckoned.

April 13, 1944: Dear Folks: Prostitutes in Little Rock come out to camp. Little Rock has highest VD rate in United States.

While the Army trained Red, and Bogart fought the enemy across the celluloid sea, someone had to sink submarines in the Caribbean. In this southern sea the Americans had to implement emergency measures to save vital resources.[9] As usual, Roosevelt, ever the politician, waited until after the congressional elections of November 1942 before ordering the rationing of gasoline and tires. Even with rationing, the United States needed tankers to transport the petroleum.

Replacement tankers ranked high. Unlike Liberty ships, tankers had complicated requirements, including sixteen miles of pipe whose installation required 17,000 individual welds. Bechtel's yard in Sausalito, Marinship, built T-2 tankers with 10,000–horsepower engines. With those engines, a fully loaded tanker could make sixteen knots. But it took Marinship 205 days to deliver the first T-2. Only eleven came down the shipways in 1943.

Something had to go. It went, and along came three eight-hour shifts, seven days a week. The company organized "flying squads" of specialists. No ship waited to be outfitted after launching. Marinship had eliminated any extra time or motion. In April 1945 it set a world record for tankers; Marinship delivered the *Ellwood Hills* in fifty-nine days. Two months later, it broke that record; Marinship signed over the *Huntington Hills* in thirty-three days, twenty-eight days on the shipway and five at the outfitting dock.[10]

Somehow these logistical seahorses had to survive Atlantic voyages. They had two lines of defense: they traveled in armed convoys and the U.S. Navy also armed them. (While much is made of the Anglo–American success in breaking German codes, little attention is paid to the fact that the Germans broke the allied merchant convoy code as early 1941. As if aware of this danger to themselves, in 1941 the Germans changed their submarine codes to a new system, Triton, which took the British another year to break.)

As the SS *Jeremiah O'Brien* prepared to join her first convoy, the New England Shipbuilding Corporation of Portland, Maine, installed her weapons. On June 28, 1943, while in the process of receiving her defensive armaments, the secretary of the Navy sent the master of the *O'Brien* his classified instructions on how to scuttle a merchant ship. The secretary made it very plain: "It is the policy of the United States government that no U.S. flag merchant ship be permitted to fall into the hands of the enemy."[11] Navy brass did not want this 10,000–ton cargo carrier ever to carry tons for the enemy.

On June 30, 1943, a U.S. Navy Armed Guard went on board to inspect both the three-inch and five-inch fifty-caliber double-purpose guns and the eight 20–mm antiaircraft guns.[12] They passed inspection, and the Armed Guard, under the command of Ensign Charles Lee Foote, USN, stowed their gear alongside that of the civilian crew.

The convoy sailing date set by the Boston port director called for the *O'Brien* and her crew of forty to depart Boston for the United Kingdom on July 21, 1943.[13] Before she departed for the northern route, Boston's First Naval District outfitted the crew and ship in special protective gear. The crew received winter clothing; they would have to return from the United Kingdom in the fall. The ship received splinter protection and four-inch steel around, and on top of, the bridge and the antiaircraft guns; she might have to fight.[14]

As scheduled, the *O'Brien* departed Boston harbor in a convoy of twenty-three ships and three escort vessels. The lead ships set a pace of eight knots. Commodores commanded convoys, almost always a retired naval officer who embarked on the fastest merchantman. Con-

The Liberty ship, *Jeremiah O'Brien,* **at a berth at Fort Mason, San Francisco, California** *(Photo by Gene Anderson)*

voys never steamed a straight course. Instead, they serpentined across the water, aware that deadly moccasins might strike, their fangs spewing torpedoes into thin skins. Foamy wake of death. On July 23 the *O'Brien*'s convoy reached Halifax, Nova Scotia. There they joined a convoy from New York City. On July 25 the larger convoy of seventy-three ships and ten escorts started the crossing. Almost immediately the *O'Brien* steamed into trouble.

The navy had selected the *O'Brien* to test the Mark 29 antitorpedo device. To launch and retrieve the device, the *O'Brien* had to reduce her speed to four knots. The convoy commander knew nothing about the Mark 29, and even if he had, there was no way a convoy could evade wolf packs at four knots. In fact, this convoy had increased its speed to ten knots. As a result, the *O'Brien* fell farther behind.

> Guard Report, August 10, 1943: Due to this fact we were at times several miles astern of the convoy since they apparently had no knowledge of Mark 29. On July 31 the senior Escort Commander requested, by means of blinking light, "What is Mark 29?" With the gear fully streamed the speed of the ship was decreased 1.5 knots below the speed without the gear streamed. When the convoy speed increased to 10.5 knots the Jeremiah O'Brien lagged.[15]

Danger lurked for any ship that fell behind. The *O'Brien* raced to catch the convoy, then lagged behind again as she tested the gear.

> July 25: Astern twenty hours due to Mark 29 launching.
> July 26: Dropped four miles astern
> July 27: Dropped eight miles astern while repairing Mark 29.

Then they struck. It was August 2. Daylight was fading; North Atlantic night was rising. Eight of the ten escort vessels were astern of the convoy. Ensign Foote and his team could see the white flares. The convoy dashed for safety, increasing speed to 10.5 knots. The *O'Brien,* astern of everyone, dashed also. What use was the antitorpedo test data if it was sent to the bottom by the real thing? But Neptune was with the *O'Brien;* she made Aultboa, Loch Eve, Scotland, on August 5 and hugged the British coast all the way to London, arriving there four days later.[16]

Once in the safety of the Thames estuary, the crew could relax.

Limited to a week of London pub crawling, they made the most of it. All had round-trip tickets. On August 16 a sober crew and a resupplied *O'Brien* followed a course north to Scotland. There she joined a convoy of sixty ships with five escorts. On August 17 loud explosions rocked the ship. Calm prevailed once the crew discovered that friendly minesweepers were clearing mines. As evening approached on August 19, nerves jangled again as escort ships dropped three depth charges off Aberdeen, Scotland. The convoy made a forty-five degree emergency turn, with gun crews at battle stations. The *O'Brien* returned to its base course after ten minutes. At 2050 hours that night, the escort *Commodore* ordered all ships to man guns as enemy aircraft had been spotted in the vicinity.[17]

Cursed on her maiden trip over by Mark 29 antitorpedo tests, the *O'Brien* was cursed on the trip home by leaky boilers. On August 22 her Captain reported that both boilers leaked badly. With no time to spare for breakdowns at sea, the convoy *Commodore* ordered the *O'Brien* to return immediately to The Clyde. In that Scottish haven the *O'Brien* could receive repairs. She slowed speed and came about. Worse yet, the commodore ordered the *O'Brien* to proceed back to Scotland without escort.[18] Not only an ugly duck, but almost a sitting one as well. Nevertheless, she steamed out of harm's way as quickly as her leaky boilers could take her.

Boilers repaired, the *O'Brien* joined a new convoy on August 29. By then convoys regularly crisscrossed the Atlantic like freight trains crossing the North American continent. But it wasn't Butch Cassidy and the Sundance Kid who derailed these sea locomotives. Instead, boat-mounted bandits named "Silent Otto" Kretschmer and "Snorting Bull" Gunther Prien of Scapa Flow fame racked up kills, the underwater aces of their day. Funny thing about aces, they seldom lived long enough to retire. In March 1941 Prien and boat went to the bottom, courtesy of depth charges from a convoy's escorts.

In that same month a destroyer detected Kretschmer's U-99 on its sonar. That destroyer had just rammed and sunk another ace skipper, Lieutenant Commander Joachim Schepke's U-100. When U-99 could not withstand any further depth charges, Kretschmer, having already spent all his torpedoes on a convoy, had to blow his ballast and surface. He saved his crew but scuttled his boat. As a prisoner, he faced forced retirement as Germany's greatest U-boat ace, having sunk one destroyer and forty-one merchantmen, a total of 266,629 tons.[19]

The *O'Brien* wanted no introduction to these warriors from Wotan's Valhalla. The North Atlantic proved menace enough. On the first day on its homeward passage, the sea swells made it impossible to test the Mark 29. On August 30 the sea calmed, and the crew launched the Mark 29 at 0800 hours, thereby falling astern of the convoy. Unwilling to take the risk, the crew retrieved the gear, and, at full speed, regained its position in the convoy by nightfall. The crew awoke the next morning to a rough sea.[20]

> Guard Report for August 31, 1943: Ship rolling and pitching badly. By 1900 hours it is difficult for ship to make headway. Becoming separated from main body of convoy.

Gales often separated convoys. When this happened, danger doubled. A ship's captain did everything possible to find "mother" before the wolves found him. Again, the *O'Brien* had the luck of the Irish. By 1500 hours on September 1 she regained her position in the convoy. Three days later the wolves hit. At midnight on September 4 lookouts reported two white flares. The convoy made an emergency turn. At two in the morning the *O'Brien* proceeded through a heavy oil slick. By noon nature offered a sanctuary; fog set in across the convoy's path. On September 5 the weather worsened and the *Commodore* signaled a frightening forecast—a hurricane warning. On September 6 the storm struck. The *O'Brien* rolled badly in heavy swells. Storm aside, on September 10 she made the safety of New York harbor.[21]

New York meant the Great White Way to many seamen searching for a different kind of excitement. If standing in Times Square when the government announced Victory Day, one might kiss a "Broadway Baby." At minimum, one could find rum, women, and song. For the song, America had few classical composers; instead, it had Tin Pan Alley songsmiths. Many such smiths wrote for the musical stage.[22] One, Irving Berlin, created the war's most famous musical. He did it the hard way. Awarded with frowns from the War Department, Berlin wrangled the military's grudging consent to assign him a small room in the barracks of Camp Upton. An eyewitness to mess halls, training grounds, and service clubs, he gathered material for his new show, *This Is the Army*.

Then the composer outflanked the generals. He wanted amateur soldiers for the cast. Why should the military cooperate? Because the show's profit would go to the Army Emergency Relief. An offer they could not refuse. *This Is the Army* opened on July 4, 1942, at the Broadway Theater. The *New York Times* praised it as "the best show of a generation." Hit songs included the opening chorus, *This Is the Army, Mr. Jones* and a rasping, broken-voiced Irving Berlin singing *Oh, How I Hate to Get Up in the Morning*. The Air Force had a song, *American Eagles,* as did the Navy, *How About a Cheer for the Navy.* The show even hosted an anti-Hitler dirge, *That Russian Winter.*

The demand for tickets forced the producers to extend the run from four to twelve weeks. On closing, the show toured the nation, terminating in Hollywood, where Warner Brothers filmed it. A future Cold War president, Lieutenant Ronald Reagan, starred. Only in America! Next the show went off to war—Britain, North Africa, liberated Europe. Worldwide, it grossed $10,000,000 for the Army Emergency Relief and another $350,000 for British relief agencies. And it was seen by 2,500,000 American fighting personnel. For his Herculean effort to do something the brass had not wanted, General George Marshal awarded Irving Berlin the Medal of Merit.[23]

That was the Army show. Not to be outshone, the air element wanted its own moment in the searchlight. If the playwright Moss Hart could not beat Irving Berlin at his own game, he could match him with a drama titled *Winged Victory.* This Army Air Force show had War Department big-wigs for angels, and many airmen in the cast. It went from Broadway success of 1943 to Hollywood hit of 1944, with George Cukor directing an all-star cast. The show's profits also enriched military charities. In his review for the *New York Times,* Bosley Crowther called *Winged Victory* a "stunning film version of an Air Force Show."[24]

Next came the Navy. If you were on the town in 1944, the town being New York, you could see a show by the same name. *On the Town* opened in December 1944. The plot could not have been simpler: three sailors on twenty-four hour shore leave in New York before shipping out for a combat zone. Some smart young kids put it together: Betty Comden and Adolph Green the book, Leonard Bernstein the music, Jerome Robbins the choreography, and Oliver Smith the sets. George Abbott consented to direct. What a roster! In 1960 Comden and Green, on the occasion of Bernstein's recording of the show, tried to recollect their feelings at its opening: "World War II was on, and the theme of young people caught in it, and the urgency of their desperately trying to cram a lifetime of adventure and romance into a moment, seemed to move the audience, and give the show and underlying poignancy, while never having to ask for sympathy."[25]

On the Town was a hit and later gave two young stars, Frank Sinatra and Gene Kelly, classy movie roles. In time it became a crossover classic. (In 1996 Michael Tilson Thomas resurrected the show, conducting the San Francisco Symphony in a concert version that showcased opera singers, including Frederica von Stade and Thomas Hampson, with Comden and Green narrating.)

Throughout the war years rich popular offerings were available, not to mention the political message for democracy. If you did not care for any of the above, you could sing along with Private First Class Frank Loesser of Special Services, who composed the words and music to World War II's popular anthem, "Praise the Lord and Pass the Ammunition." Recorded in 1942 by the Ink Spots, it sold over two million records and over one million copies of sheet music before a protest from the clergy set in over associating the Lord with ammunition! (The Lord took care of Loesser; after the war he created the triumph known to Broadway history as *Guys and Dolls*.) During the war, whether your taste ran to musicals, plays, films, or songs, New York and Hollywood celebrated the war experience on land, in the air, and at sea.

After two weeks of giving their regards to the music and lights of old Broadway, on September 22 the *O'Brien* and crew departed New York for Liverpool, joining sixty-six other ships and thirteen escorts. The *O'Brien* ran ahead of the convoy to stream the Mark 29 gear. Inasmuch as the convoy set a pace of ten knots, the *O'Brien* quickly fell astern. At Halifax, Canada's gateway to danger, the convoy again grew in size. Welcomed by all hands, an aircraft carrier and her escorts guarded the assembled ships. Crossing in heavy seas, the crew lashed all deck gear. The carrier kept an air umbrella up whenever possible. Within the convoy, the SS *Bartholomew Gosnold* also tested the Mark 29 gear. One day away from her destination, the *O'Brien*'s crew heard forty-three depth charges between 2100 and 2200 hours. Unscathed, on October 5 the *O'Brien* arrived safely in Liverpool.[26]

Departing Liverpool on October 18, the *O'Brien* joined a seventy-three ship convoy with twelve escorts. Their *Commodore* joyfully informed all ships' captains that they would have one aircraft carrier escorting them for the entire journey and a second carrier for the worst part of the crossing. Less joyful was the sea, never one to cooperate.

> Guard Report for October 19, 1943: Trouble. Convoy not forming into column as instructed by convoy Commodore. All vessels having difficulty maneuvering. Two ships colliding, one of which caught fire.[27]

By the next day the ships rolled badly and the storm scattered the convoy—not an auspicious beginning. On October 21 danger loomed. The convoy made three twenty degree turns to starboard in quick succession. On October 24 the *Commodore* ordered three more changes of course. Somewhere the sea-wolves waited. Again they struck:

> Guard Report for October 26, 1943: Two white flares reported. These were followed in quick succession by six more white flares and a Roman candle. These were apparently sent up by ships on port wing of convoy, forward. No details could be determined. General alarm was sounded.[28]

At first light on October 27 a four-engine bomber circled the convoy along with aircraft dispatched by the carrier. Without further incident, on November 3 the convoy reached New York.[29]

During 1943 the Royal Navy began to increase its kills of German U-boats. On a few occasions a dying U-boat took a warship with it. On March 10, 1943, the HMS *Harvester* rammed the U-444. For ten minutes the U-boat remained wedged under the stern of the *Harvester.* When it broke free and sank, an explosion crippled one of the *Harvester*'s engines. Able to make only ten knots, she presented an easy target for the enemy; U-432 found her the next morning. One torpedo did it. (The Free French corvette the *Aconit* then found U-432 and sank it.)

As the *Harvester* began to sink, a crew member, Harry Newson, made his move. The pusser's tot (pusser is British naval talk for purser; sailors are "jack tars") had just started its morning round when "Jerry" struck. As the crew dashed for safety, Newson dashed for the rum. Gulping it down, he hit the icy water, his internal warmth supplemented.[30] And he lived to tell the tale. Saving a ship's liquor must have entered the Anglo-Saxon gene pool as early as Tudor days. In Shakespeare's sea-drenched *Tempest,* lowly sailors raced for the flagon as their ship went on the reef. The Bard has Stephano rescue his ship's bottle, then use it to lure the creature Caliban to work for him and his mate Trinculo.

The *O'Brien*'s crew had to buy their rum ashore; no Caliban to fetch for them. They would have had something to celebrate if they had known that Donitz had lost the Battle of the Sea. During "Black May" 1943 forty-one U-boats did not return. This marked a rapid reversal from March 1943, when his boats had sunk 590,000 tons of allied shipping; in one March convoy battle, his aces sank 141,000 tons in six days.[31] Now his monthly tonnage loss spelled disaster. Donitz repositioned his remaining assets to try and hold allied gains to a minimum.

In the *O'Brien*'s case, the crew could still die as easily in a submarine defensive as in an offensive. They learned this on their next voyage from New York to Immingham Dock in Britain. Departing New York on November 26, the *O'Brien* took up position #91 in the convoy. Later that night (2330 hours) the ship holding position #81 had steering troubles. It swerved, nearly colliding with the *O'Brien*. Then the sea erupted, making it impossible to man the forward gun while huge waves broke over the bow.

The heavy weather increased until, on December 1, the *O'Brien*'s captain had to admit that he was separated from the main body. With visibility poor, the *O'Brien*'s watch identified five other lost ships in the vicinity, all looking like set designs for Richard Wagner's opera, *The Flying Dutchman*. By December 2 no other ships could be seen, which meant that the *O'Brien* had to take what the Admiralty called the straggler's route, a lone sea-sheep prey to any ocean-wolf. As dawn broke on December 3, the loner sighted two ships and one escort, only to discover that the convoy lay astern of the *O'Brien,* a first in her log. By noon the *O'Brien* had retaken her convoy position.

As if that had not been enough for one leg of the journey, in the early evening of December 6, the *Commodore*'s flagship hoisted a flag warning of enemy submarines in the vicinity. The next morning the *Commodore* warned all ships, via flag hoist, that an enemy submarine was shadowing the convoy. As the ships arrived off northern Scotland on December 11 (0630 hours), the *O'Brien*'s crew heard loud explosions astern of their position in the convoy. The watch identified eleven white flares as a nearby cruiser began firing its guns. More white flares appeared. Meanwhile, the convoy dashed for safety, and on December 13 the *O'Brien* docked at Immingham Dock in the River Humber.[32]

The Battle of the North Atlantic peaked in 1943. From September 1939 to May 1943 the current ran in favor of the Nazis; from June

1943 to May 1945 it ran in favor of the allies. During 1943, the *O'Brien*'s crew focused their attention on surviving their first year of service.

Meanwhile, Warner Brothers focused their cameras on the ever-ready Humphrey Bogart. He gave the U.S. Navy its war-at-sea film, but instead of a glamour ship like the USS *Missouri,* named for Red's home state, Bogart served on an ugly duckling, a Liberty ship.

In the 1943 release, *Action in the North Atlantic,* Bogart experiences his ship being torpedoed out from under him and his mates. But Bogart bounced back, bashing Nazis back and forth across the Atlantic. Like a sea-going Scarlet Pimpernel, you saw him here, you saw him there, you saw him everywhere. Surviving the sinking, he is assigned to a new Liberty ship, much like the SS *Jeremiah O'Brien.* Once the captain "takes a round" from enemy aircraft, Bogart takes the ship in, fighting all the way. His was probably the only Liberty ship to sink a submarine, in his case ramming it. Of greater importance, on screen he delivered the supplies, and in theaters he delivered the thrills.

With Bogart on their side, the crew of the *O'Brien* still had two years of danger ahead. They discovered this on Christmas Day 1943 when they were ordered to depart Britain. Fifty ships with seven escorts and one aircraft carrier formed a convoy off of Oversay Island Light, Scotland on New Year's Day 1944. With heavy weather and the ship rolling badly, the *O'Brien*'s captain found he had insufficient ballast to cross the North Atlantic in winter gales. This necessitated filling the number three deep tank in order for the ship to make head way in rough seas. As usual in winter, things got worse.

Guard entries telegraph the ordeal:

January 3: Frequent changes of course.

January 5: Flag hoist—enemy submarine in vicinity.

January 8: Heavy seas. Convoy speed very much reduced.

January 9: Ship pounding heavily. Wheel did not respond. Necessary to heave to for one hour of repairs.

January 10: (0630 hours) Unable to sight convoy. Visibility very low. At 0815 hours contacted ship #122 by blinker. She stated convoy was to her port side.

January 11: Very heavy seas during the night. Three ships showing breakdown lights and dropping our of convoy. Difficult to maintain steering. Convoy badly dispersed.

January 12: Running alone during night. (1700 hours) Regain convoy.[33]

That should have sufficed for one hellish crossing, but more lay in store. Sometimes dispersed ships found each other at the last minute. Discovery, at any speed, was unsafe. Nighttime discovery in storms almost always meant a collision. The Armed Guard Report for this crossing records the following:

> Armed Guard Report, January 16: SOS signal (0158 hours) from ship; sinking condition as a result of collision. Her position near ours. Receiving (0200–0900 hours) radio signals from distressed ship, and sending radio message in order that she might take a bearing on us. (So might a submarine.) Sighting (0900) two ships and one patrol boat. Both ships damaged as a result of collision; one British vessel and one U.S. Liberty Ship, the SS George Washington. The George Washington had been sending the distress messages. Her Captain stated that the number one hold was filled with water to the water line and asked us to stand by. Escort vessel took her under tow and released us to proceed to our destination. On January 17, 1944, the O'Brien arrived in St John, New Brunswick.[34]

In Canadian waters for a respite, the O'Brien had a change of command. Ensign Charles Lee Foote turned over his Naval Armed Guard unit to Lieutenant A.R. Memhard, Jr. With that the ship joined sixty-five others, escorted by six corvettes, twelve destroyers, and three aircraft carriers. Canadian warships were few but feisty, especially the fleet of small, lightly armored corvettes.[35]

From St. John, New Brunswick, to Leith, Scotland, the convoy made an average speed of ten knots in exceptionally good weather. On February 15 the flag hoist indicated enemy submarines in the vicinity, but the escort pack kept them at bay. On the morning of February 19 loud explosions were heard abroad the O'Brien, shaking the ship noticeably. They seemed to come from the center of the convoy. That afternoon, trouble found the O'Brien in the form of two floating mines spotted fifteen hundred yards off the port side. Again, the O'Brien's luck held. She arrived in Scotland unscathed.[36]

For the remainder of the spring the O'Brien plowed the sealanes, hoisting supplies across the Atlantic bastion. Then in June 1944 she had a new mission, ferrying supplies from British to Norman shores. But that is another chapter, the Battle of the Shore.

Cumulatively, a deficit in technology and time defeated Donitz. Just as Germany developed jet aircraft too late to win the battle of the air, just as it developed the *Tiger* tank too late to win the battles of the sand and the snow, so it developed the "Walter" boat too late to win the battle of the sea. The latter, named for its inventor, Professor Helmuth Walter, used a closed hydrogen-peroxide fuel system and ventilated through a snorkel breathing tube.

Kaptein-luitenant J.J. Wichers of the Royal Netherlands Navy invented the snorkel in 1927, but neither side took advantage of his work until late in the war, even though, in 1940, four Dutch snorkel-equipped boats escaped from their base at Den Helder as the Germans occupied their country. The four escapees then fought alongside the allies. Germany trial-tested four "Walter" boats in the last year of the war. Submerged, they had a top speed of 24 knots, with no need to surface to recharge batteries.[37]

In contrast, the diesel-driven U-boats of the Battle of the Atlantic, the Type VII and Type IX boats, had a surface speed of 17 knots, but a submerged speed of only 7 knots. And they could submerge for only twelve hours at best. With convoys running at ten knots, and with large numbers of sea and air escorts, U-boats had to stay under or stay away.

Named as Hitler's successor, Grand Admiral Donitz paid a high price for defeat. He lived, but his two sons did not. Like Field Marshal von Manstein, who lost his only son in the battle of the snow, Donitz lost both his sons in the battle of the sea. High rank, but empty heart; a burnt-out space where a soul should rest. When arrested by the Allied Control Commission, the second and last führer said: "Words at this moment will be superfluous."

Were the submariners' souls who served Germany also superfluous? They totaled 40,900, of whom 25,870 died while more than 5,000 were captured. The Third Reich placed 830 U-boats in combat and lost 784 of that total. The allies lost 2,452 merchant ships (12.8 million tons) and 175 warships in the Atlantic. The majority of deaths in the British Merchant Navy (30,248) and the Royal Navy (73,642) occurred in the Atlantic. Even the Canadian Navy lost more men (1,965) in the Atlantic than did the U.S. Navy.[38]

As sea battles went, the North Atlantic has no rival in the march toward allied victory. Win there, the supplies and soldiers flowed. Lose there, lose everywhere. Britain and America won the battle of the sea, the arsenal's flow became a flood, and the allied side triumphed.

Notes

1. John Keegan, *The Price of Admiralty: The Evolution of Naval Warfare* (New York: Viking Penguin, 1989), 317–19.

2. Dan van der Vat, *The Atlantic Campaign: WW II's Great Struggle at Sea* (New York: Harper and Row, 1988), 377. In May 1981 the author escorted university students to the pens at La Rochelle: good as new.

3. Edward P. Von der Porten, *The German Navy in World War II* (New York: Thomas Crowell, 1969), 174–75.

4. Andrew Hodges, *Alan Turing: The Enigma* (New York: Simon & Schuster, 1983).

5. Vat, *The Atlantic Campaign,* 109–15, 184–85, 198–200.

6. Karl Donitz, *Memoirs: Ten Years and Twenty Days* (Cleveland: World, 1959), 215.

7. Samuel Eliot Morison, *The Two-Ocean War: A Short History of the U.S. Navy in the Second World War* (Boston: Little, Brown, 1963), 130–31.

8. Margaret S. Truman, *Harry S. Truman* (New York: William Morrow, 1972), 199–200.

9. Donitz, *Memoirs,* 202–12, 219–21.

10. Charles Wollenberg, *Marinship at War: Shipbuilding and Social Change in Wartime Sausalito* (Berkeley, CA: Western Heritage Press, 1990), 35–39. Also see Walter W. Jaffee, *The Last Mission Tanker* (Sausalito: Scope, 1990), 12. After the war the U.S. Army Corp of Engineers built a hydraulic model of San Francisco Bay and the Delta, in Sausalito. The U.S. Park Service gives tours. Within the complex is a small museum dedicated to the shipbuilding years of WW II.

11. Letter, Department of the Navy, June 28, 1943, From Secretary of the Navy, To Master, Jeremiah O'Brien, Subject: Instructions for Scuttling Merchant Ships, National Archives, Washington, DC Copy also in files of *Jeremiah O'Brien* Office, Fort Mason, San Francisco, California.

12. Restricted Cable, July 24, 1943, From Commandant 1st Naval District, To Vice Chief of Naval Operations, Subject: Report on Arming the Jeremiah O'Brien; National Archives.

13. Port Director's Report, July 21, 1943, Subject: Jeremiah O'Brien's Sailing Date; National Archives.

14. Cable, July 26, 1943, From Commandant First Naval District, Boston, To Chief of Naval Operations, Washington, Subject: Armaments and Supplies Issued to the O'Brien; National Archives.

15. Armed Guard Report, August 10, 1943, From Ensign Charles Lee Foote, USN, Commanding Officer Naval Armed Guard of SS Jeremiah O'Brien, To Vice Chief of Naval Operations, Washington, Subject: Report of Voyage from Boston to London.

16. Ibid.

17. Armed Guard Report, September 11, 1943, From Ensign Charles Lee Foote, USN, Commanding Officer Naval Armed Guard of SS Jeremiah O'Brien, To Vice Chief of Naval Operations, Subject: Report of Voyage from London to New York.

18. Ibid.

19. Von der Porten, *The German Navy in WW II,* 176–78.

20. Armed Guard Report, September 11, 1943.

21. Ibid.

22. Laurie Winer, "Theatre: A Devilishly Tough Thing to Do," *Los Angeles Times,* October 15, 1995, 48; George W. Hunt, "Of Many Things: The Power of Popular Music During WW II," *America,* August 12, 1995, 2.

23. David Ewen, *Complete Book of the American Musical Theater* (New York: Henry Holt and Company, 1959), 54–55.

24. George Amberg, *The New York Times Film Reviews, 1913–1970* (New York: Quadrangle, 1970), 215–16.

25. Betty Comden and Adolph Green, "Reminiscences," reprinted in *Stagebill* (March 1996): 10, 50–52.

26. Armed Guard Report, October 6, 1943, From Ensign Charles Lee Foote, USN, Commanding Officer Naval Armed Guard of SS Jeremiah O'Brien, To Vice Chief of Naval Operations, Subject: Report of Voyage from New York to Liverpool.

27. Armed Guard Report, November 3, 1943, From Ensign Charles Lee Foote, USN, Commanding Officer Naval Armed Guard of SS Jeremiah O'Brien, To Vice Chief of Naval Operations, Subject: Report of Voyage from Liverpool to New York.

28. Ibid.

29. Ibid.

30. A.J. Pack, *Nelson's Blood: The Story of Naval Rum* (Hampshire, U.K.: Kenneth Mason, 1982), 187.

31. Von der Porten, *The German Navy in WW II,* 193–94.

32. Armed Guard Report, December 13, 1943, From Ensign Charles Lee Foote, USN, Commanding Officer Naval Armed Guard of SS Jeremiah O'Brien, To Vice Chief of Naval Operations, Subject: Report of Voyage from New York to Immingham Dock, England.

33. Armed Guard Report, January 17, 1944, From Ensign Charles Lee Foote, USN, Commanding Officer Naval Armed Guard of SS Jeremiah O'Brien, To Vice Chief of Naval Operations, Subject: Report of the Voyage from Immingham Dock to St. John, Canada.

34. Ibid.

35. Michael Clugston, "Cheap, Nasty Navy: Canada's Wartime Fleet of Corvettes Battled U-Boats and the Pounding North Atlantic," *Canadian Geographic* (May–June 1995): 66–73; Desmond Morton and J.L. Granatstein, "Canada Comes of Age," *Maclean's,* May 1, 1995, 64–68.

36. Armed Guard Report, February 23, 1944, From Lt. A.R. Memhard, Jr., USNR, Commanding Officer Naval Armed Guard of SS Jeremiah O'Brien, To Vice Chief of Naval Operations, Subject: Report of Voyage from St. John, Canada to Leith, Scotland.

37. Keegan, *The Price of Admiralty,* 314. Also see Vat, *The Atlantic Campaign,* 345–349.

38. Vat, *The Atlantic Campaign,* 382.

The Shore

Europe is a peninsular continent. In size, only Australia is smaller. Yet it concentrates infinite riches in a small space. Attached to Asia, it is part of the gigantic Eurasian land mass. Continental Europe, like Caesar's Gaul, *est omnis divisa in partes tres.* At its eastern terminus lies European Russia; in the center, Mittel Europa; and at its western terminus lies the peninsula's ocean-washed tip.

By 1941 the Third Reich had ejected democracy from this western extremity, Europe's center had fallen to German domination, and huge chunks of Russland lay beneath the German boot. The Wehrmacht had exploited a geographic feature; the North European plain, stretching from northern France across Germany and Poland into the Soviet Union, offered tank commanders the high-speed avenue of approach favored by armored units.

Following their Dunkirk-like decampments, democratic orphans pined for their return home. Beached in Britain—democracy's off-shore platform—they dripped foglike despair. Of their homelands the Nazis had welded together a fortress with no easy access. Stranded, governments-in-exile wondered if they would ever recross the Channel. Once the Nazis fortified the ports, they effectively locked all peninsular doors. Only a few windows—stretches of shoreline—offered a chance to pry open the Nazi *festung.*

A forced entry into the House of Europe meant much luggage and many passengers—the tools to break in, the troops to wield them. Recapturing a port meant less luggage, more casualties, and a good possibility of defeat. Recapturing a shoreline meant more luggage, fewer casualties, and a good possibility of victory. Hence the scales favored the shore.

For a shore landing, the attacking force would have to bring its own harbor, an artificial floating port facility. (The allies tried for two, a "Mulberry" at Arromanches, a smaller "Gooseberry" off Omaha Beach; they lost the latter in the storm of June 19, which raced in faster, and did more damage, than Field Marshal Rommel's tanks. Like the storm of 1588, it was an armada smasher.)[1] Of even greater difficulty, until they anchored the artificial harbors, liberators would need special ships that ferried tanks, artillery, trucks—the heavy equipment of modern warfare—up onto the beaches.

Since these specialty ships would convey armored units into shallow waters, they required flat bottoms, thus poor deep-water travelers. And they would move with all deliberate slowness, thus make great targets. The British, who designed the largest of these sea-swimming, shore-climbing conveyer-belts-of-war, called it the Landing Ship, Tank (LST). Its passengers renamed it the Long Slow Target!

Success or failure of an amphibious assault depended on the ability of the Norman shore to support heavy traffic. Much was known, some of it frightening. In antiquity, the Romans had surveyed the wind-whipped coast of Normandy; their old port at Calvados lay two kilometers out to sea from the 1944 coastline, erosion having reshaped things over two millennia. The allies consulted a Roman map (smuggled out of Paris) and a copy of the Roman survey of that part of their empire. Roman Gaul did not fear a cross-Channel invasion from Britain; Rome had pacified that island, minus the northern highlands of the Scots, since the time of the Emperor Hadrian.

Inasmuch as the Romans contrasted the cold Norman north to their milder Mediterranean base, they wanted information about fuel supplies. Consequently, they gathered peat from extensive areas along the Norman coast. Boggy peat fields under a layer of sand spelled disaster for heavy vehicles. What the allies needed was a current sample. On New Year's night 1943, the British sent a two-man party ashore from a midget submarine. They came, gathered, and went (with samples). The shore would hold up.[2]

The shorescape's distinguishing landmark towered in the form of chalky cliffs. Dover's white bluffs had twins across the channel. And just as Dover had its defenses, so had its Norman cousin. From Channel level the bold Dover and Norman outcroppings looked as if they had been blasted up from the earth's core a long antiquity ago.

The elder statesmen who sent their young against these shore buttresses had qualities that a rocky New Englander discerned in earlier leaders: "long-tried integrity, solid wisdom and sad-colored experience . . . fortitude and self-reliance, and, in time of difficulty and peril, (they) stood up for the welfare of the state like a line of cliffs against a tempestuous tide."[3] Norman tempests pounded in and out, hard to predict at any time, any season. As often as not, the Gulf Stream collided with Europe in a series of showers that kept Normandy's grass green and cows fed; voilà, the cheese capital of the North Atlantic world. But, on occasion, the collision produced a Channel storm that both dairymen and mariners feared. Woe to the cow or sailor caught by such a sea devil.[4]

Once Dwight David Eisenhower received the command that some had thought would go to his boss, George Catlett Marshall, the two American generals worked at making a cross-Channel liberation succeed. In the process, Marshall had to pacify commanders in the Pacific theater, star-studded temperaments such as Douglas MacArthur. He also had to pacify Eisenhower, himself busy pacifying tart-tongued, temperamental star-holders such as Bernard Montgomery and George Patton. Churchill called Marshall the great organizer; perhaps great pacifier would better describe him.[5] He resembled an impresario of a touring Italian opera company with too many tenors, each wanting to sing the lead. In Marshall's case, his warring tenors all demanded more landing craft.

Even Eisenhower staged a Rossini-like scene upon his arrival in Italy, where he landed after the battle of the sand and the conquest of Sicily. He ordered his forward headquarters out of Algiers before his staff could become hidebound. A comfortable Naples villa served Ike. While moving in, a member of his party discovered a rat in the upstairs bathroom. Ike, always at the ready with his pistol, rushed upstairs to finish off the rodent. The general fired four shots at the frightened intruder, who, agile at dodging bullets, outmaneuvered the general. Another officer joined the chase, finally eliminating the enemy with a stick.[6] The scene cried out for the Neapolitan laughter of Rossini's genius.

If Ike in Naples calls to mind the comedic Rossini, the Italian campaign had the despairing quality of a Verdi score. Marshall rebuked Ike's generalship; Ike steamed. Marshall suggested a dash to Rome, perhaps by amphibious means. To fight one's way up the Italian boot meant mountain combat, many casualties. Avoiding casualties always dominated American strategy; it dominated even more as Roosevelt prepared for another election campaign.

To stage an amphibious assault on the Italian coast meant obtaining more landing craft, an item in short supply. To avoid delay and casualties, Ike received additional sealift capacity. With that he set in motion the plans for the Anzio landings, landings that included the small port of Nettuno within the Anzio beachhead.[7]

Each campaign has its own lore, the Anzio beachhead no exception. Recounted numerous times at postwar veteran reunions is the story of a kid infantryman, not twenty minutes on the beach, crawling speedily back to an aid station and requesting a prophylactic (World War II code for condom) from the onshore medics. Lucky he had made the quick acquaintance of a willing lady who wanted to give her very best to a liberator. While the war waited, the GI reestablished friendly relations with the former enemy.[8] Even in the midst of war, British imperial forces broke for teatime and Free French forces for a long lunch, so American lotharios broke for a little love. Groundlaying for peace. And they had not even found the rum yet. When love was scarce, they played baseball in the beachhead. Crazy Americans.

They had to be crazed—it made it easier to die in that killing zone called Anzio. Surrounded on three sides by battle-wise Germans determined to blow them back into the sea, they faced a 3,000–foot defensive line consisting of extensive minefields (protected by barbed wire) in front of deep antitank ditches. Hundreds of machine guns fired from zig-zag trenches, fortified houses, and deeply dug bunkers. Behind these defenses, German artillery and mortars had zeroed in on what remained of a flat and featureless beachhead.

The day of the Anzio breakout, May 13, 1945, the U.S. Third Infantry Division suffered 995 men killed and wounded, the most casualties for a U.S. division in World War II in one day's worth of fighting. Some troops, trying to present the lowest target possible, lay on sleds pulled forward by tanks. One tank deposited nineteen-year-old John Shirley, sled and all, in a German minefield. Luckily it had rained, thereby exposing the mines. He crawled out unscratched, hugging the ground as he went. He and the remnants of the beachhead force fought their way onto the road leading toward Rome. On June 4, 1945, Sargeant Shirley, a carpenter's son from orange-growing Costa Mesa, California, marched with his men into the city of Saint Peter and the early martyrs who had died believing in another carpenter's son.[9]

Unbeknownst to Ike and his staff, in Nettuno rested a refugee hoard of liquor that had escaped recapture in the Libyan sand but awaited an allied race to Rome. Among the thousands of gallons lay Red's rum. Before Ike could taste any recaptured liquor, the president reassigned him.

On December 7, 1943, an unsuspecting Ike had flown back to the sands of Tunisia in order to brief Roosevelt on his return from a late November conference with Churchill and Stalin in the Iranian high-desert city of Tehran. FDR surprised Ike with a verbal shot across his brow: "Well, Ike, you are going to command Overlord."[10]

Stalin had demanded a commander's name as proof that the allies were serious this time; others had demanded that Roosevelt give up his dream of giving the Overlord command to Marshall. Recognizing Marshall's indispensability to the Washington war effort, Roosevelt had at last surrendered. On Christmas Eve, 1944, back in the warmth of the White House, FDR announced to the nation that he had appointed Ike as the Supreme Commander, Allied Expeditionary Forces. Democracy's army would return to the continent.

And a man from the demos would lead them. Good choice, as it turned out. Ike had qualities that others did not. The lofty MacArthur, the aloof Marshall, neither could compete with Ike, the press favorite, in a popularity contest. As for British competitors, General Sir Alan Brooke, to whom Churchill had promised the command, knew that in the end it would go to an American, as did General Montgomery, who accepted the second-tier assignment of ground commander of D-Day.

One of Ike's key strengths lay in his appreciation for the power of the camera. A Bogart type in general's attire, his earthiness won plugs; he spoke the language of the GI. His grin wowed them. He willingly appeared in newsreels that played the local cinemas. Soldiers would follow this guy anywhere.[11] But how would they get off the island depot called Britain? Ocean-going ships like the *Jeremiah O'Brien* had braved the battle of the sea and brought the soldiers and their supplies to British ports, but they could not take the liberators up onto the Norman shore. Landing craft could.

Irate staffers in London felt betrayed over the landing craft issue.

They knew that some landing craft remained committed to the resupply of Anzio, some for Operation Anvil, the landings in the south of France. What goaded them was their belief that Washington, especially the Anglophobe chief of naval operations, Admiral Ernest King, diverted craft to the Pacific.

Ike put his considerable weight behind his staff. Writing an "Eyes Only General Marshall" letter in February 1944, Ike made clear his concern over adequate landing craft. A diary entry for March indicates that the concern continued.[12] Even Churchill entered the fray, disgusted that "the destinies of two great empires . . . seem to be tied up in some Goddamned things called LSTs."[13] Later research indicates that the shortages came more from misallocation within Europe, but Ike's staff believed otherwise, and they acted on their belief.

The Americans held the key; they had gained power in the Anglo–American alliance once the numbers they committed surpassed those of the British. Knowing this, Ike tried not to offend their sensibilities. Nevertheless, Mayfair wags, counting the ever-increasing number of Americans at Ike's London headquarters on Grosvenor Square, renamed it Eisenhowerplatz. Fittingly, his London statue stands today near where he worked when in town. Outside London, he favored his country residence near Bushy Park. Here Churchill and other VIPs could not drop in so easily. While diplomatic with London, Ike was blunt with Washington. He saw Marshall as the conduit to more landing craft; his correspondence with his military boss was both detailed and constant. Marshall juggled; Ike received.

While Ike lobbied in London, Red languished in Alabama, half afraid, and half glad, that he would miss his war.

> May 19, 1944: Dear Folks: By the way—you know this invasion is going to come off pretty soon and the worst part of the whole bloody mess should be over before I leave Alabama.

Nine days later:

> May 28, 1944: Dear Folks: Mama, if you ever feel sorry for anyone or if you ever pray for anyone, why, do it for those boys who are in England who are waiting for this invasion. They need it.

They knew, they waited, they prayed. As all the world knows, on June 6, 1944, the allies came, saw, and conquered.[14] That day's story has been told often and well, and was caught on film by Hollywood

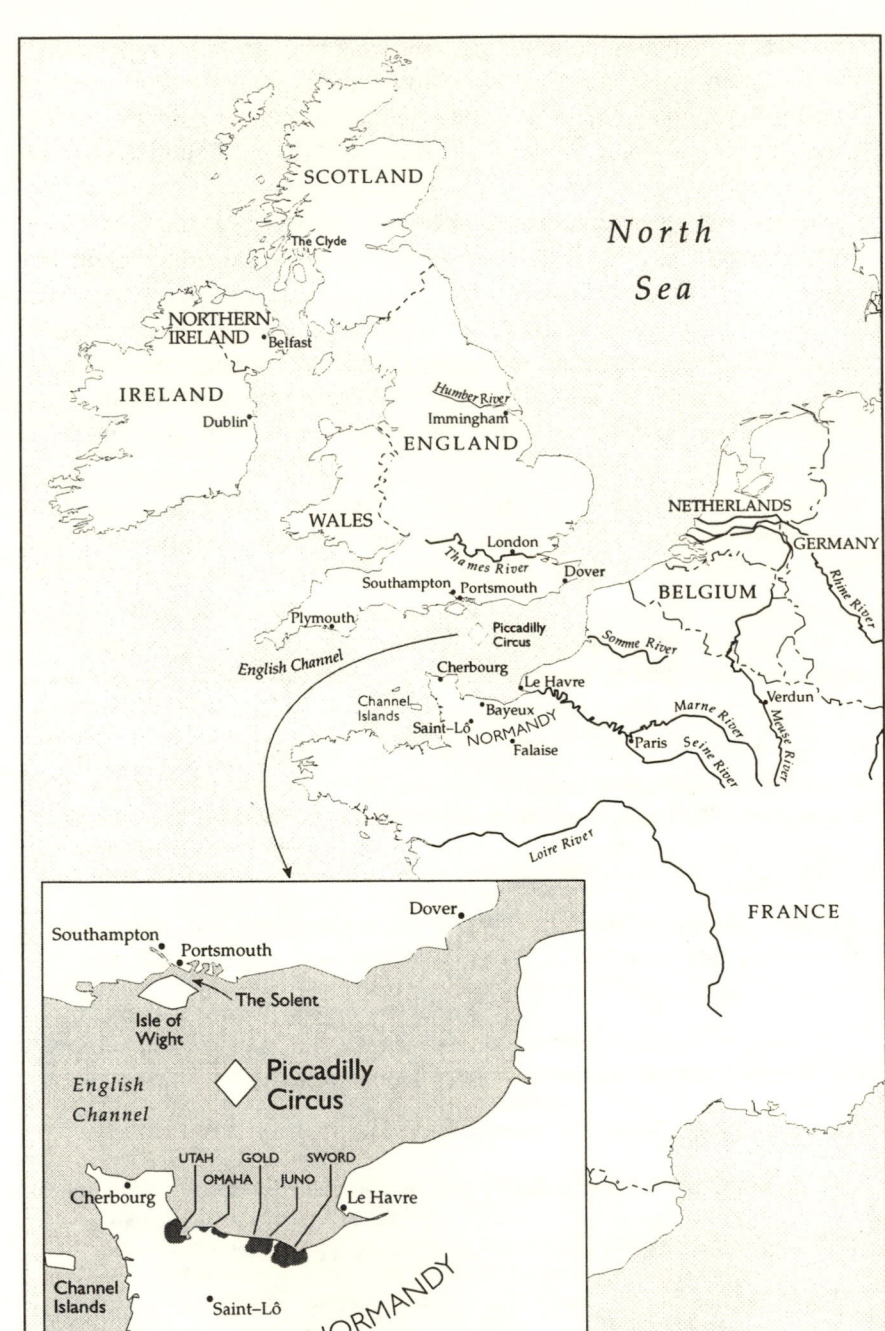

director George Stevens, whose job while in uniform was to shoot film with Army camera crews.

Ike, not unaware of the power of filmed history, had expressed his unhappiness with the North African coverage and asked for a topnotch cameraman. He got Stevens. In Italy the Army asked him to film a documentary. Local Army types, unhappy with Major George Stevens, replaced him with Captain John Huston. Huston, unhappy with the Army script, shot his own, in the process making himself unbearable but also making perhaps the war's best documentary, *San Pietro*. Huston, Bogart's best director, might have shot the best film, but Stevens, Hollywood's favorite director, shot the best color photography, including of Normandy.[15]

Normandy made Ike. He found himself fawned over by a bevy of new "friends," adored by strangers. But no person singlehandelly won the shore. Foes fought front to front, foxhole to foxhole, face to face. Democracy's doughboys did the dirty work and won. Their reward— Normandy.

It is sometimes forgotten that the battle for Normandy was not over in a day, a week, or a month. Troop units landing there suffered fatalities as late as Christmas Eve 1944. That is when Red's unit finally crossed to Normandy. And during the summer and fall before Red arrived, the *Jeremiah O'Brien* made eleven dangerous round-trip shuttles.

On June 9, 1944, the *O'Brien* received orders to proceed from Southhampton to a beachhead in an assault area off Percée Point, Normandy. The Guard Report for the night of June 9–10 records sightings of numerous flares, as well as tracer fire. Navigating with caution, the *O'Brien* narrowly avoided several mines. At 0230 hours a ship two miles on the port beam was seen to explode and burn brilliantly for hours. By 0330 the tracer fire came within two miles; the captain called an alert.

The following night more bad news arrived: Headquarters expected German air attacks on beachhead shipping—as soon as the weather cleared. It cleared. At 0345 in the morning enemy planes circled at 10,000 feet. To no avail, some ships opened fire. At 0400 three enemy aircraft came down low, and one, a *Junker* 88, dove in the direction of the *Jeremiah O'Brien*. The *Junker* dropped four five-hundred pound bombs, one splashing about two hundred yards from the *O'Brien*'s port bow and the other three falling just on the other side of another Liberty ship.

At 0425 hours a *Focke-Wulf* 190 fighter attacked the *O'Brien,* which engaged it with all guns. At 0500 three groups of FW 190s, three aircraft to a group, headed for the *O'Brien*'s area. Again all guns opened fire. Lieutenant Memhard, still commanding the Armed Guard, could not confirm any hits, but several gunners insisted that they saw an enemy aircraft "go down in smoke."

On June 12 things went from bad to worse. U-boats joined the attack, trying to penetrate the destroyer ring with a strike from below at ships in the anchorage, while aircraft attacked from above.[16]

The *O'Brien* quickly unloaded and steamed back to Southhampton for a new cargo of military personnel and their equipment. She departed on June 17, headed again for the Percée Point anchorage off the Normandy coast. The *O'Brien* had hardly reached mid-Channel when the captain sounded a general alarm; escorts had started dropping depth charges 2400 yards off the *O'Brien*'s starboard beam. It was mid-afternoon. Four other escorts arrived, all flying contact pennants. Enemy aircraft again appeared, this time at a distance from the *O'Brien.* The *O'Brien* departed the anchorage on June 20 heading for Ireland.[17]

On July 6 a fully loaded *O'Brien* departed Belfast for Utah Beach, her cargo again personnel and equipment. On July 8 an escort four thousand yards off the starboard beam hoisted the contact pennant, which it flew for an hour. No depth charges were dropped. At 2230 hours that night the escort commander signaled by hoist that the convoy could expect enemy air attacks by dawn. None materialized. On July 9 at 0330 a close-by escort dropped depth charges; a general alarm was sounded. The next day the *O'Brien* unloaded her cargo and returned to the Solent anchorage off Southhampton.[18]

To and fro the *O'Brien* hauled; fully loaded going over, almost empty coming back. On the fifth voyage (July 21 to July 26) the *O'Brien* went to the other American beachhead area, Omaha Beach. Here the action came in air attacks with shore batteries firing their antiaircraft guns in response. The ships rode dark at anchor, not firing their guns. Nevertheless, shrapnel from the shore batteries fell on their decks.[19]

On the eighth voyage over (August 23 to August 26) the ship directly astern of the *O'Brien,* the SS *Louis Kossuth,* was damaged by an acoustic mine. The damaged vessel continued on the resupply mission to the Utah beachhead area.[20] On the next crossing (August 31 to September 2) a crisis arose when the captain rang a general alarm based on a report of an on-board fire in the number four hold. No fire actually started, but sparks flew, coming from trucks banging together due to the rough sea. The *O'Brien* hove to while the crew secured the cargo.[21]

On September 24 the *O'Brien* made her last Channel crossing, dropping anchor in the reopened port of Cherbourg. Ashore, the crew tasted a powerful local brew, the fiery apple-based Calvados. (Calvados is to the apple what cognac is to the grape.) A happy ship's crew departed the Norman port for New York on October 12, 1944. Red arrived there the same month, on his way to Cherbourg. Many paths crossed in New York City, the great North Atlantic entrepôt that teamed with shipping. The war had increased this sea traffic.

To celebrate New York City's war role, Warner Brothers chose its harbor for the site of Humphrey Bogart's 1942 film, *All Through the Night.* In that one Bogart saved the U.S. Navy's latest battleship, which steamed out of the Brooklyn Navy Yard just as Nazi spies planned to sabotage it. In a small speedboat, Bogart diverted the saboteurs so that the giant warship could survive to fight the Battle of the Sea and the Battle of the Shore. (With those two battles won, Bogart went to Paramount Pictures to make the 1945 film, *Hollywood Victory Caravan.*)

Battleships mattered at Normandy. Admiral Sir Bertram Ramsay, who had commanded the vessels that had evacuated democracy's armies from Dunkirk in Operation Dynamo, now protected those same armies as they went back. One of his headquarters was located in tunnels at Hellfire Corner, a place in the Dover cliffs where the British had started tunneling in the time of Napoleon. With 7,000 ships (over 1,200 warships, more than 4,100 landing craft, and almost 850 supply ships), Ramsay had to make the passage safe. He had waited four years for Operation Neptune, the naval side of Overlord.

The minesweeper fleet, 255 ships in all, went first. From the British side it cleared a wide channel to a marshalling-point, christened "Picadilly Circus," which had a radius of five miles. From "Picadilly Circus" the minesweepers swept ten lanes toward the Norman shore. For protection, a destroyer fleet covered the minesweeping operation. In the lead, the Polish destroyer *Slazak,* commanded by Captain Romuald Nalecz-Tyminski, followed by the Norwegian destroyer *Svenner.* Naval elements from many Atlantic allies now returned to Europe's coastal waters.

A Royal Navy traditionalist, Ramsay ordered a tot of rum for every man going ashore in Normandy. Many an American, ferried ashore by a British crew, had a potent taste of amber fire before he faced German guns.[22] Ramsay's staff also had a private laugh on "Jerry"; their headquarters high inside Hellfire Corner had a loo-with-a-view. While relieving oneself, one could also moon (to display one's buttocks) the Nazis across the Channel. Small enjoyment, but one that appealed to the British sense of water-closet humor.

To enjoy his last leave stateside, in early November Red went sightseeing in Manhattan. Basically a country boy, Bogart's big city did not impress him. But Roosevelt's reelection for a fourth term did.

> November 11, 1944: Dear Folks: What did you think of the election? Roosevelt seems to be pretty durable doesn't he?

Typical of franchise democracy, elections rated serious attention, even from a kid in the midst of total war.

If nothing else, in war soldiers can count on confusion. By December 23, 1944, two troop transports waited at Southhampton for their passengers. Two thousand paratroopers boarded one of the ships, the SS *Léopoldville,* only to discover themselves on the wrong ship. They disembarked in time for the designated passengers to board. The SS *Léopoldville* and the SS *Cheshire* had orders to carry the three regiments of the Sixty-sixth Infantry Division on a nine-hour crossing to the tip of the Norman peninsula, the port of Cherbourg. At that late date the allies still crossed in convoy, in this case guarded by three British destroyers and a Free French frigate, the *Croix de Lorraine.*[23]

Waiting on Pier 38 to board, soldiers complained that the Army had ruined another holiday, this time Christmas. Others started caroling; after all, it was almost Christmas Eve, even on a British pier. They spotted the Red Cross stand; while it offered doughnuts and coffee, what it really offered was a last chance to talk with genuine American girls who worked into the frosty night.

Most of the GIs present had filled out the division's ranks only recently. On their North Atlantic crossing they had celebrated Thanksgiving Day on the converted passenger liner the *George Washington.* It was rough Thursday at sea; many of the turkey dinners were heaved overboard almost as soon as ingested. Red joined the Sixty-sixth division on April 3, 1944, at Camp Robinson, Arkansas; he crossed the North Atlantic in mid November on the troop ship the *General George O. Squire.* One letter arrived, marked sea mail:

> November 1944: Dear Folks: (Somewhere at Sea) I have gotten so I can talk pretty salty by now. . . . These boats aren't exactly luxury liners.

In fact, the allies converted their luxury liners to troop ships, space taking precedence over luxury. The Grand Tour had vanished, replaced by a combat tour. Already commissioned, the liners had a great advantage in their speed. As the fastest, the 81,235–ton *Queen Mary* could maintain a steady 28.5 knots, so fast that U-boats could not keep up with her or keep her in their sights. Placed into service in August 1942, this Blue Ribbon–winner sped across the Atlantic without escort, in one crossing carrying as many as 15,000 troops.

After landing in Britain, Red and his new mates got to know Camp Piddlehinton, Dorchester. Pubs welcomed them; inside they could enjoy the British nightingale, Vera Lynn, as they listened to a BBC broadcast of her songs of longing: "Yours," "I'll Be Seeing You," "As Time Goes By." Popular culture and its music had a universal appeal during the war; people of all ages listened to the same hit songs on radios and jukeboxes.[24] Transatlantic music included Bing Crosby and the Andrew Sisters singing "Comin' In on a Wing and a Prayer," Kay Kyser and his orchestra with "The White Cliffs of Dover," Bing Crosby with "Boogie Woogie Bugle Boy," and Vaughn Monroe with "Der Führer's Face."

Red got to know this scene all too well. In a letter of December 1, 1944, he gave his folks the bad news: Red was "busted back to Private." Never one to lose hope, he ended the letter on a cheery note: "the countryside here is beautiful." It seems that Red had gone into town without a pass, a chance many others in his unit also took. He just happened to be one of the unfortunates who bumped into the military police.

Red was not long for the beauties of southern England. On December 16 Hitler launched his Ardennes offensive, Autumn Mist, known to the Americans as the Battle of the Bulge. Within hours the brass decided that they needed more troop units to plug the gaps behind those engaged in the fighting. Down to the ships Red's regiment raced.

A dog-eared hulk, the *Léopoldville* looked as old as a ship could look and still make headway. Built in 1929 in Hoboken, New Jersey, and long overworked on the Antwerp-to-Congo route by the prewar Belgian owners, the ship's conversion to a troop ship by the British had brought a record of sorts. The *Léopoldville* had carried 120,000 men over 220,000 miles. A small contingent of British personnel stayed on board as the ship was under the protection of the Royal Navy. The captain for this voyage, Charles Limbor, was a Belgian; his crew was Belgian and Congolese, a group more suited for the novels of Joseph Conrad than the sea-yarns of C.S. Forester. During the crossing, Limbor spoke hardly a word; his wife and son remained trapped in occupied Belgium, his loneliness apparently alleviated in part by his recordings of classical music.

Both ships took on an excess number of passengers; the excuse being that the crossing would take only nine hours. The GIs found space to sleep, and sleep they did, in hammocks, under benches, on tables, or wherever space afforded a prone position. The decks were too cold, the toilets too disgusting, but somewhere; an American GI can sleep anywhere. In the second letter Red wrote after his induction into the Army, he complained about the lack of sleep.

> May 27, 1943: Dear Folks: The minute we get to sit down or lie down we fall asleep.

Loaded, the two ships departed Southhampton on Christmas Eve. Both troop ships dropped their pilots when they reached the antisubmarine nets. At that point their four escorts joined them and set a speed of thirteen knots. As they reached Buoy A-3, zigzagging commenced; the Admiralty had reported increased Channel activity by German U-boats. The *Léopoldville*'s captain ordered a boat drill. Some soldiers hunkered down, feigning deep sleep. Others went; to their surprise, there was a shortage of life preservers. Worse, the *Léopoldville* carried only fourteen lifeboats with a capacity for 797, but she carried 2,400 passengers. The crew reserved 230 spaces in the lifeboats for themselves; this left fewer than 600 places for more than 2,000 soldiers.

Across the Channel waited a lone wolf. Almost new, U-486, with a crew of forty-eight, had joined the German fleet nine months prior to its arrival in Norman waters. Commissioned at the Kiel Shipyard, the Germans had equipped this Type VII C submarine with the latest snorkel device. Commanded by Oberleutnant Gerhard Meyer, first it practiced off the German Baltic coast, then off Norway, and finally off Normandy. On December 23 Meyer received orders to take up position five miles away from the breakwater at Cherbourg. By December 24 his boat settled on the bottom, waiting.

Rough sea had brought on nausea among the soldiers jammed below deck. Tension increased when the senior escort destroyer, the HMS *Brilliant,* raised a black flag—a submarine alert. The four escorts went into hunting patterns, dropping depth charges. After fifteen minutes without results, the *Brilliant* lowered her black flag. Fifteen minutes later came another alert. Again, no results. The convoy, under blackout conditions, ran a diamond formation.

All seemed well. Cherbourg harbor lay only five and a half miles away. Slowly, U-486 rose from the bottom to feed. Her target: the overloaded *Léopoldville.* She fired; a torpedo blasted through the hull on the starboard side aft and exploded in Number Four Hold, thus opening the ship to the sea and killing 350 men outright. The U-486 raced back to the bottom. The *Léopoldville* began to list to port by some eight degrees. The engine room began to flood. Worse yet, two of the too-few lifeboats had been destroyed by the explosion.

Lookouts on the HMS *Anthony* had seen the torpedo; their sonar operator had heard it. The escorts turned against the enemy; the *Anthony* headed over the estimated course of the torpedo, depth charging all the way. Confusion reigned. Communications links went back to Britain, not forward to Normandy. More than a hundred possible rescue boats remained in Cherbourg harbor; no one ordered them to sea. On shore the crowd celebrated Christmas Eve. Offshore the dying began.

Another five hundred GIs died, "after they had stood, many of them for two and a half hours, unhurt and unafraid, on the decks of a ship that was only one hour from port."[25] When the *Léopoldville* went down, it dragged some to their death; the icy water killed others who made it overboard. No swimmer is known to have reached the shore; all those who survived were picked up by rescue ships, which had finally arrived at the disaster site. These ships had no room for the dead; they picked up only the living. Crews pulled bodies from the sea up to the railings. "If their eyeballs moved they were living, if not we dropped them back into the water."[26]

The living were freezing; "screams of men in the water were coming from all directions." In many cases the Army-issue wool overcoats proved to be shrouds. Quickly water-logged, they pulled their struggling owners down into watery crypts. Hundreds of teenage boys drowning, begging for life, wails for their mothers the last words before water filled their unwilling lungs. Bodies never found, bereavement never completed.[27]

Crews did everything possible to keep the rescued warm. One ship carried three gallons of homemade gin; it was gulped down. Liquor materialized like gifts from Saint Nicholas. One PT boat carried a carton of two-ounce bottles of brandy. A British sailor from the *Léopoldville* awed the crew by drinking eight of these bottles in quick succession.[28]

According to the historian of this tragedy, Jacquin Sanders, himself a soldier on board the *Cheshire,* he and others had heard and "softly felt an explosion, and they could see that the other vessel had developed a list."[29] Almost all of the *Cheshire*'s passengers had come on deck and were less than a one hundred yards away. Red was on the *Cheshire;* he lost one of his best buddies, Richard R. Cuskelly, who was on the *Léopoldville.* Barely twenty years old when he witnessed this night of drowning, Red never wrote about it. Some things a letter cannot convey. A night of waste, weeping, winter, wolves, and wumps (caused by the collapsing internal decks and gangways).

The U-486 continued to hunt in the same waters. On December 26 two British corvettes took torpedoes in the same general area where the *Léopoldville* went down. The U-486 stayed for nine days; in mid-January the German Navy ordered her captain to take up position off Bergen, Norway. On April 4, 1945, the U-486 developed snorkel problems while in Norwegian waters. It surfaced, was sighted, and was sunk. The British submarine *Tapir* had torpedoed the U-486, which went to the bottom with all hands.

Once the horror ended, *Léopoldville* stories circulated. The Germans announced the sinking first. The U-486 had not claimed it as a kill because her captain saw nothing while he busied himself avoiding the four escorts. But empty *Léopoldville* lifeboats and equipment displaying the division's markings had drifted into the German-held ports on the Channel Islands.

The Allied High Command remained mute. News from the Battle of the Bulge had rocked confidence; the American government had only just recently lifted some rationing on the home front. Now it felt forced to reimpose it. And no one wanted to raise German naval morale. Both the British Admiralty and the U.S. Navy ordered inquiries, neither of which came into the hands of the wartime press.[30] Ten of the Belgian crew survived. They returned to Britain on the *Cheshire,* received new assignments on the Belgian-owned *Persier,* which the Germans torpedoed in the Channel on February 11, 1945. No luck there.

The allies had captured Cherbourg on June 26, 1944, by coming in the back door. Immediately they sat about opening the damaged port. Within the town the population looked and sounded like the United Nations. Many Eastern and Central Europeans mingled with many Western Europeans, the multitude that Germany had forced to build the West Wall in Normandy. And German prisoners abounded, POWs from the vaunted Wehrmacht that, through four years of venal occupation duty, had lost much of its luster.[31] Even their commander, Field Marshal Rundstedt, never a firebrand, spent much of his working hours at his headquarters in Saint-Germain, outside Paris, reading detective stories, a genre Bogart made famous in prewar films.

Two illustrious Wehrmacht names, Rundstedt and Rommel strove to secure the Atlantic Wall, but neither field marshal could stem the allied surge, and like a Dutch dike under pressure, the wall cracked and the flood commenced. Rundstedt held the senior command, Oberbefehlshaber West (OB West) while Rommel commanded Army Group B, stationed north of the Loire River including Normandy, northern France, and Belgium. Here the Westhere (western army) concentrated its panzer strength.

Rommel, before 1944 one of the few German marshals to have fought the Anglo–Americans, feared their airpower; therefore he favored defeating the allies at the shore, a static defense. Rundstedt, the senior of the two, feared their seapower; therefore he favored defeating the allies away from the shore, a mobile defense.[32] And Hitler, always convinced he knew best, favored running the defense from Berlin. Not an effective command arrangement.

An austere Prussian, Karl Rudolf Gerd von Rundstedt, chose the joie de vivre of Paris's Hôtel Georges V for his residence, while the more jovial Wurtenberger, Erwin Rommel, chose the austere Norman Château La Roche-Guyon for his. Previously, the hotel had hosted many rich Americans, while the château had hosted some rebel ones, including Thomas Jefferson. Red saw neither piece of real estate. He landed too late for the August 24 liberation of Paris by Free French forces under General Philippe Leclerc.

Nor did Red have an introduction to the rag-tag group of Americans, among whom were Ernest Hemingway and David Bruce, who liberated the bar at the Hotel Ritz. Libation liberators! Back in harness as a journalist, "Papa" Hemingway, America's premier war novelist, had ridden to the Norman shore in a LST on June 6. He rode back out the same day; no journalists on the beach that day. Undaunted, he moved his movable feast back to Paris as soon as he could. Machismo haunted, Hemingway's off-screen bravado often matched Bogart's on-screen performances. Bruce, a courtly Virginian, added cachet; he headed the Office of Strategic Services for France.[33]

Red saw another side of France, the muddy side. Hemingway could have his bar; Red wanted a bath.

> January 24, 1945: Dear Folks: I'd give a million bucks for a bath."

(In the same letter he announced that he had been promoted back to Private First Class.)

Red discovered the Black Market.

> February 2, 1945: Dear Folks: Any French kid will give you a hundred francs for a pack of cigarettes.

With constant falling rain, Red could not avoid war's muck.

> February 6, 1945: Dear Folks: Mud, mud, mud; we're getting a taste of what we've heard about from the boys of the last war."

(In this letter he allowed how, since his folks were now Californians, he would become one after the war. Perhaps it was the lure of sunshine.)

By March Red had a bath and saw a motion picture!

> March 19, 1945: Dear Folks: Saw "A Tree Grows in Brooklyn."

In April he heard he had lost his commander-in-chief:

> April 15, 1945: Dear Folks: Was shocked to hear about Roosevelt; the world has had a great loss there. He will go down in history as one of the greatest men of all time—and he was.

(Red, like most in the Armed Forces, had known no other president but Roosevelt.)

And then there was the war: nasty, dirty, ugly. Red wrote little about his experiences under fire; only once did he allow the combat to peak through.

> May 4, 1945: Dear Folks: I got scared up there (the front) when we were on the line the last time. I was running across an open place when

two rounds of time fire went off right over my head. Time fire is when the shell is fuzed [sic] so that it bursts in the air, scatters shrapnel over a great area that way. Anyway the darn shrapnel kicked up the dust all around me, right behind and in front of me. Someone must have been praying for me.

Before Red received his initiation into combat, Jerzy Solak had flown a P-41 into Norman combat with his American comrades from the Ninth Air Force. He was still their Polish liaison officer, but now the Americans were not so green. Hunting tanks at tree-top level, Solak was shot down, captured by the Germans, sent to a POW wing of a Paris hospital, escaped with the help of the French resistance, witnessed the liberation of Paris, and made his way back to his unit. He, like Red, wanted only one thing: a bath. Solak liked flying with the Americans; they never failed to amaze him from the time in 1942 when he first saw them near Naples. They were the rich fighters. In what way rich? They had baths and movies behind the front lines.[34]

Over Red's head flew another pilot, another boy from Missouri who at age fourteen had hitchhiked to Los Angeles searching for a good diving coach. From Hollywood High to the University of Southern California to the 1932 Los Angeles Olympics, where he won a bronze medal, he dove. Then he flew. Colonel Frank Kurtz, the most decorated Army Air corps pilot of World War II, flew more than sixty missions over Italy and Germany. It did not pay to mess with men from Missouri.[35]

As the war gave off its death rattle in May 1945, the boy who had been swept into it back in Missouri was now a man headed for occupation duty in Austria. Red had changed. Some changes he noted himself. In a light-hearted manner, he listed his Army achievements: He had learned to cuss and to drink. Both came easily. An acting platoon sergeant, Red informed his parents that "I would also cuss in a military manner." He suggested that "to be a sergeant or something, you have to learn to cuss beautifully and scientifically."[36]

With alcohol Red experimented. First he started with a gin concoction, a Tom Collins. But he settled for an even sweeter drink of rum and Coke with a slice of lime, known as a "Cuba Libre." A hit song came with his favorite drink; the crooner Dick Haymes popularized "Rum and Coke" for jukebox teenagers. On Red's transfer north, he was delighted to write his folks that "Cheyenne has rum." While there, he helped organize a baby shower in the barracks. The soldier-father, minus his wife, took the honors. "We sent a telegram (to Mom and Baby in Chicago) and bought a half gallon of rum . . . which didn't go very far between twenty-five guys."[37]

Excuses for parties continued until housekeeping became a problem. A month after the baby shower, Red wrote that the "floors and walls (were) all covered with Coca-Cola and rum and mud." Five days later, after a GI clean-up party, Red wrote that he was "limiting his drinking for now to two beers max!"[38]

Little did Red know that a well-traveled bottle of rum would come into his possession in Austria, where he would also encounter the Red Army. That army had fought its way up the Danube and stayed for joint occupation duty. Both Soviet and American soldiers fell heir to select bottles of rum that the Americans started moving from Italy into Austria in late 1945. And Red learned from Red Army soldiers how to trade things, legal and not so legal. He wrote from Bischofshofen, Austria:

> October 24, 1945: Dear Folks: I could sell my watch for five hundred dollars in Salzburg (to the Russians).

The Soviet ally had burst into the Third Reich from the east, with massive Soviet army groups flooding the North European plain. The Third White Russian Front had actually entered East Prussia as early as August 17, 1944. A bloodbath began. Even as the winter snow arrived, frigid fornication continued. Women were raped with atavistic vengeance, then nailed by their hands to the farmcarts carrying their families. Fathers huddled in ditches, determined to shoot their own children rather than give them up to the Cossack horde. No angel of the Lord appeared to save these latter-day Isaacs. Savage payback for the German ravaging of Mother Russia. In this way, both Nazi and Communist fanatics brought North Atlantic civilization to its near nadir. They proved Thomas Hobbes correct—life could be nasty, brutish, and short. Only nature's barriers slowed the frenzied penetration by the Red Leviathan.

Like the Anglo–American force from the west, forward movement temporarily stopped at the large geographic drainage systems, the north–south rivers. From one bank to the other, each of the advancing armies had to leap the water barrier. For the Anglo–Americans, the

Ruel ("Red") Crocker and his bottle of rum *(Photo courtesy of Red's grandchildren, Timothy Crocker O'Neill, Brett Ruel Cutler, and Victoria Elizabeth Cutler.)*

Rhine; for the Soviets, the Oder-Neiser. In order not to collide, they reached an agreement to halt on opposite banks of the Elbe.

The Second and Third Ukrainian Fronts had taken the southern route, the Danube River Valley, into the Reich. In early May elements of the Third Ukrainian Front "gained Linz and Klagenfurt, where they made contact with Allied troops."[39] This was the force that Red later encountered in the Austrian snow, especially after November, when he settled into occupation duty in Hofgastein.

For both victor and vanquished, the war was their generation's most momentous event. For the western soldiers, they would not have been there if they had not succeeded in the battle of the shore. With victory there, the rest was history. Fascist Germany could conquer, but it could not endure. By 1944 the German nightmare, war on two fronts, was the reality. Of many things that foretold defeat, German geography rates a place near the top.

When one examines the capabilities of both sides, it is easy to see why Rommel was correct. Either you defeat the Americans at the shore or all is lost. Why? Because the United States was a giant Gulliver traveling to a strange land. To defeat this giant, the Germans needed to be as crafty as Lilliputians; they had to catch him at a moment of delicate balance. Living on one side of a great lake, the giant had one foot resting on his home shore, the other foot on an island—a good stretch even for a giant. The giant wanted to bring both feet to rest in the British Isles, which he did by winning the battle of the sea, and then to place one foot at a time on the shore at Normandy.

The moment the first foot touched the continent was the critical time to strike at it, throwing the giant off balance. This could be done by giving the giant what Americans call a hot-foot (fire on the underside of a boot or shoe), or in military terms, a powerful armored counterattack. This hot-foot should cause him to withdraw and ponder the cost of trying again. Even better, if the Germans could cut the giant's Achilles' tendon, then they would hobble him for years. If, instead, he were to succeed in getting both feet onto the shore, his strength would overcome any adversary.

Not that the giant had better weapons, nor was he better at soldiering. He simply had a lot of the stuff-of-war, what appeared to Rommel to be endless, an inexhaustible warehouse. The giant had another battle raging across another lake, yet could concentrate enormous force around the Atlantic lake. With a secured homeland, a well-fed civilian population, a productive industrial base, he had come late to the war and hoped to win it with minuscule casualties.[40]

For example, to make sure that medical facilities hit the Normandy beaches on June 6, 1944, the Third Auxiliary Surgical Group landed with the troops rather than waiting back in England for casualties to be evacuated to them. Surgeons established medical centers in abandoned German bunkers. Thanks to a crash program, they had blood available for immediate transfusions.[41]

The giant had also harnessed science to do his fierce warrior bidding, but he had a soft spot for his armed forces. Another example suffices. Having taken only the most fit to serve, the giant determined not to lose a single one to disease. And he almost succeeded. His heavy investment in wartime medicine brought him such miracles as mass-produced penicillin. As radar was to the battle of the sky, sonar to the battle of the sea, penicillin was to the battle of the sick. Compared to the 1914 phase of warfare, during the American involvement in the second phase (1941–1945) the death rate from disease in the Army fell from 14.1 to 0.6 per thousand soldiers.[42] Such miracles the Germans could not match.

Science mattered in all phases of the twentieth century's trio of wars. In the 1939–1945 phase it came into its own as Big Science, which later gave birth in the United States and the Soviet Union to the military–industrial–education nexus.[43] Into that nexus flowed a Cold War fortune: Big Science costs. As a pitched battle, the Norman shore had also cost precious pennies.

Why choose the battle of the shore? Without an Anglo–American landing somewhere on the continent's Atlantic beaches, the war would have had a different character. Free of a two-front war, Nazi Germany would have had more resources to throw at the Red Army's advance in the East. This would have led to either a longer war ending in Soviet victory or a truce in which some remnant of Nazi Germany survived. Neither scenario bode well for the survival of franchise democracy. One should not dismiss the notion that, minus an Anglo–American attack in the West, Germany could defend against the Red Army. That army suffered 304,887 killed, wounded, and missing in the siege of Berlin alone. Breslau held out longer, costing the Red Army 60,000 dead and wounded. Victory in Germany did not come cheap.

To have American participation in the battle of the shore, Britain had to give way to American thinking. (With Americans on the continent, the Soviets also had to accommodate these strange political participants from the other side of the Atlantic.) Depleted after the battles of the sky, sand, and sea, no earthly power outside the United States could assist Britain in gaining the shore. (Denuded of many resources after the battles of the snow, no other power but the United States could furnish lend-lease material to the Soviets.) Whether American policy toward its allies was cooperative or not, for as long as the war lasted, both the United Kingdom and the USSR had to cooperate.

Among American strategists—few as always—Marshall mattered most. He seriously doubted that the American people had the patience for a long war, warning the British that no American government could fight a Seven Years' War.[44] London leaders understood his point. Translation: The Americans wanted this annoying war ended as quickly as possible. To the Yanks, Normandy was situated along the closest direct approach to Berlin. Therefore, Normandy it was. There were to be no political sideshows along the way, no race to liberate Prague before the Soviets did. Even Paris was left to the Free French. Not a single American's life was to be traded for internal European politics. Such is the strategic price of democracy in extremis.

But the shore was gained, the war was won.

Notes

1. Alan Harris, "Gathering Mulberries: The Mulberry Harbors of WW II," *History Today* (May 1994): 15–18.

2. Stephen E. Ambrose, *D-Day: June 6, 1944—The Climatic Battle of WW II* (New York: Simon & Schuster, 1994), 74–75.

3. Nathaniel Hawthorne, *The Scarlett Letter* (Franklin Center, PA: Franklin Library, 1979), 263.

4. Mildred Berman, "D-Day and Geography," *Geographical Review* (October 1994): 469–75; and Ron Cowen, "The Tides of War: D-Day's Lunar Connection," *Science News*, June 4, 1994, 360–62.

5. Forest C. Pogue, *George C. Marshall: Organizer of Victory, 1943–1945* (New York: Viking Press, 1973), 585.

6. Stephen E. Ambrose, *Eisenhower: Soldier, General of the Army, President-Elect, 1890–1952* (New York: Simon & Schuster, 1983), 266. Naples is not one of Italy's big three—Venice, Florence, Rome—but it holds a historical pedigree as old as classical Rome's. The emperors kept a fleet near there, as did the Americans during the Cold War. Both are located north of Naples: Rome controlled its fleet from Miseno, America from Gaeta. (Misenus, companion of Aeneas, is buried on Monte Miseno; the Emperor Tiberius, dining in his villa there, choked to death in A.D. 37. Munatius Plancus, friend of Caesar's, is buried

on Monte Orlando in Gaeta; in nearby caves Tiberius narrowly escaped death when part of the roof collapsed.) The author started visiting naval Naples in 1966, expanding on that visit each time he returns to Itlay.

7. Fifty years after the bombardment, little evidence of a major battle remains in the Anzio area. Unlike the lonely Norman beaches, this coast had always been an inhabited resort. The Romans called the town Antium; Coriolanus took refuge here, it was also Nero's birthplace. Two large cemeteries, the British at Anzio, the American at Nuttuno, along with the small Museum of the Allied Landings, remain to remind the visitors of January 22, 1944.

8. Colonel Barney D. White told the author this bit of Anzio beachhead lore. He was there as Operations Officer (S3) to the Thirty-ninth Field Artillery Battalion and later commanded the Forty-first Field Artillery Battalion.

9. John Shirley, *I Remember: Stories of an Combat Infantryman in WW II* (Livermore, CA: Camino Press, 1993).

10. Dwight Eisenhower, *Crusade in Europe* (New York: Doubleday, 1948), 206–7. Leaders of the three allied nations attended three war conferences: Tehran, Yalta, and Potsdam. Afterward, Cold War historians tugged left and right to explain the consequences of these meetings. With the end of the cold, third phase of North Atlantic warfare, it seems that one of the first books, somewhat a court history, reported rather accurately. See Herbert Feis, *Churchill, Roosevelt, Stalin: The War They Waged and the Peace They Sought, a Diplomatic History of WW II* (Princeton: Princeton University Press, 1957).

11. On the fiftieth anniversary of D-Day, the editors of *Time* magazine published a WW II photograph of Ike on its cover. In addition, below the photograph they printed: "The Man Who Beat Hitler." After fifty years, Ike remained *Time*'s and the people's hero. Bruce W. Nelan, "Ike's Invasion," *Time,* June 6, 1994, 36–49.

12. Alfred D. Chandler, Jr., ed., *The Papers of Dwight David Eisenhower, The War Years: III* (Baltimore: Johns Hopkins University Press, 1970), 1724–1725; Robert H. Ferrell, *The Eisenhower Diaries* (New York: W.W. Norton, 1981), 113.

13. Gordon A. Harrison, *Cross-Channel Attack* (Washington, DC: Department of the Army, 1951), 68. On misallocation of landing craft within Europe, see John Keegan, *The Second World War* (New York: Penguin, 1989), 377. While the British built many landing craft, once the Americans entered the war, they outstripped British efforts. A total of 82,000 were built in the United States. Also see Winston S. Churchill, *Closing the Ring* (Boston: Houghton Mifflin, 1951), 27–28, 253–54, 364–65, 446–48, 513–14.

14. My favorite retelling of the historic day is Ambrose, *D-Day: June 6, 1944.*

15. George Stevens, Jr., "Shooting D-Day," *New York Times Magazine,* June 5, 1994, 30; Peter Maslowski, *Armed with Cameras: The American Military Photographers of WW II* (New York: Free Press, 1993), 61, 84. Some of Stevens's war photography can be seen in Max Hastings, *Victory Over Europe: D-Day to VE Day* (Boston: Little, Brown, 1985).

16. Armed Guard Report, June 14, 1944, From Lt. A.R. Memhard, Jr., USNR, To Chief of Naval Operations, Subject: Report of the Voyage of the Jeremiah O'Brien from Southhampton, England, to beachhead off Percée Point, Normandy, and return to Southhampton.

17. Armed Guard Report, June 20, 1944, From Lt. A.R. Memhard Jr., USNR,

To Chief of Naval Operations, Subject: Report of the Voyage of the Jeremiah O'Brien from Southhampton, England, to beachhead off Percée Point, Normandy, and return to Ireland.

18. Armed Guard Report, July 12, 1944, From Lt. A.R. Memhard Jr., USNR, To Chief of Naval Operations, Subject: Report of the Voyage of the Jeremiah O'Brien from Belfast, Ireland, to Utah beachhead area in Normandy.

19. Armed Guard Report, July 26, 1944, From Lt. A.R. Memhard Jr., USNR, To Chief of Naval Operations, Subject: Report of the Voyage of the Jeremiah O'Brien from Southhampton, England, to Omaha beachhead area in Normandy.

20. Armed Guard Report, August 27, 1944, From Lt. A.R. Memhard Jr., USNR, To Chief of Naval Operations, Subject: Report of the Voyage of the Jeremiah O'Brien from Southhampton, England, to the Utah beachhead area in Normandy.

21. Armed Guard Report, September 3, 1944, From Lt. A.R. Memhard Jr., USNR, To Chief of Naval Operations, Subject: Report of the Voyage of the Jeremiah O'Brien from Southhampton, England, to the Utah beachhead area in Normandy.

22. A.J. Pack, *Nelson's Blood: The Story of Naval Rum* (Hampshire, UK: Kenneth Mason, 1982), 140.

23. Ever watchful over his nation's glory, Charles de Gaulle nevertheless paid tribute to the Royal Navy and the support it gave the Free French Navy during the war. See his *War Memoirs: The Call to Honor* (London: Collins, 1955), 283–84.

24. George Hunt, "Of Many Things: The Power of Popular Music During WW II," *America,* August 12, 1995, 2–3; and Leon Botstein, "After Fifty Years: Thoughts on Music and the End of WW II," *Musical Quarterly* (Summer 1995): 225–31.

25. Jacquin Sanders, *The Night Before Christmas* (New York: G.P. Putnam Son's, 1963), 314. Sanders watched this tragedy from the deck of the SS *Cheshire.* I am in debt to him for the story as told here.

26. Ibid., 286. Also see Dennis Hevesi, "A Fight to Honor Forgotten Men of the Leopoldville," *New York Times,* May 8, 1955, B3.

27. To bring closure to the tragedy, on September 29, 1989, veterans of the Sixty-sixth Division, escorted by a French admiral, boarded a French mine-sweeper in Cherbourg harbor. They preceded to the spot where the *Léopoldville* sank and held a memorial service, followed by a French sailor blowing taps. See Carol Coffee, *From Tragedy to Triumph: An Historical Memoir of the 66th Infantry Division in WW II* (Houston: Odyssey International, 1995), 164–65.

28. Sanders, *The Night Before Christmas,* 285–86

29. Ibid., 7.

30. The British Admiralty has not released its Board of Inquiry Report. The U.S. Navy declassified its Jackson Report (named for its senior author, Captain M.C. Jackson, USN) in 1953. Copy in file "SS Leopoldville, file RM 2400–Navy," National Archive, Washington, DC. See Secret Memorandum for Admiral Harold R. Stark, U.S. Navy, subject: Loss of SS Leopoldville, Serial No. 00448, dated 6 January, 1945, signed M.C. Jackson, Captain, USNR, 8 pages. As Jackson states, life-saving drills would have been effective. To prove his point, four days after the sinking of the *Léopoldville,* the *Empire Javelin* was torpedoed in mid-channel with a loss of only six lives!

31. In the character of Private Wenk, Heinrich Boll created a German version of our story's Red. In the novel *A Soldier's Story* (London: Seckar and Warburg, 1985), Wenk is stationed in 1944 in Normandy, where he discovers that his real enemies are boredom, corruption, and hunger; "army supplies have become a profitable racket for the German High Command."

32. B.H. Liddell Hart, *The German Generals Talk* (New York: William Morrow & Co., 1948), 239–40.

33. Larry Collins and Dominique Lapierre, *Is Paris Burning?* (New York: Simon & Schuster, 1965), 170–71, 196, 304. Bruce was later the ambassador to Germany and Great Britain. Also see Taki Theodoracopulos, "Putting on the Ritz," *National Review,* November 7, 1994, 80–82.

34. Interview with Jerzy Solak at his California home, February 9, 1996.

35. Margo Kurtz, *My Rival, The Sky* (New York: G.P. Putnam's Sons, 1945).

36. Letter, May 29, 1943, from Basic Training at Fort Francis E. Warren, and letter, August 22, 1943, from Cheyenne.

37. Letter, August 25, 1943, Cheyenne, and letter, November 22, 1943, from Armed Service Training Center, University of Wyoming.

38. Letter, December 8, 1943, and letter, December 13, 1943, both from Armed Services Training Center, University of Wyoming.

39. Institute of Marxism-Leninism, *Great Patriotic War of the Soviet Union* (Moscow: Progress, 1974), 369.

40. By 1942 the American economy had recovered from the Great Depression. WW II fiscal policies were instrumental in the overall restoration of full employment. See J.R. Vernon, "WW II Fiscal Policies and the End of the Great Depression," *Journal of Economic History* (December 1994): 850–69.

41. Dennis L. Breo, "June 6, 1944: Two Doctors Relive D-Day Dangers," *Journal of the American Medical Association,* June 8, 1994, 1799–1805; and Douglas Starr, "Again and Again, in WW II, Blood Made the Difference," Smithsonian (March 1995): 124–36.

42. Vannevar Bush, *Science: The Endless Frontier* (Washington, DC: National Science Foundation, 1945), 49. The availability of blood and plasma for transfusions was unheard of in other armies. See Starr, "Again & Again, in WW II, Blood Made the Difference."

43. Richard Abrams, "The U.S. Military and Higher Education: A Bried History," *Annals of the American Academy* (March 1989): 15–28.

44. Maurice Matloff, *Strategic Planning for Coalition Warfare, 1943–1944* (Washington, DC: Government Printing Office, 1959), 5.

Epilogue

Letter from France, May 8, 1945:

Dear Folks: Well, the war is over. Actually now and officially at 1201 tonight. Wish I could express to you by means of this letter just how I feel, but I'm afraid I won't be able to. We thought maybe it was over yesterday or last night, the French people were celebrating, but we couldn't get any news other than rumors until this afternoon when we got our radio in operation.

At present we are bivouacked in our pup tents on the grassy slope of a little hill in regular parade ground fashion. The radio is going within hearing range. Heard a V day program from the States by Bing Crosby and Bob Hope and other stars. Then heard a broadcast from in front of Buckingham Palace where a great crowd of people had gathered to pay homage to the King and Queen. It was very interesting because I have seen the Palace and the different monuments that the broadcaster described. It is a great day for England, a greater day for them than it is for us.

The thought just ran through my mind that I haven't written for a few days and you might be worried about me. Hope this letter comes through fast and I'll try to write to-morrow so that you will be sure of hearing from me. The European war is over and your little boy is still safe and sound. I know that is quite a load off your mind. I'm sure you have worried about the war more than I have as a whole.

In one of the broadcasts I heard tonight a portion of the Gettysburg Address was quoted, and it hit home making me sorta blue. I lost an awfully good buddy over here—one of the old Laramie gang (Wyoming basic training). I have several pictures of him at home, and I'll tell you as much of his story as I know when I get home. But that is part of war, suppose you just have to learn to take it like you learn to take the other things.

Well it's getting rather late, in about another hour or less the German surrender will be official. But I'm going to sleep because the candle is burning low and I'm tired.

Good-nite my family.

With all my love,

Red

Red's own candle did not go out for another two decades. After occupation duty in Austria, he joined the millions quickly demobilized by the government. With his honorable discharge in hand, Red returned to civilian life, visited his folks in California, married a Californian, finished college at the University of Missouri, returned to California, and fathered two daughters. Red died on February 18, 1966, and his family, by then Californians, buried him in the Oakland hills overlooking San Francisco Bay.

Rum travels well. What Red's comrades in Austria did not drink went underground in Linz until the town fathers surfaced it with a "for sale" sign. American military authorities, then stationed in West Germany, decided to buy. Offered in military Class VI stores as "Rommel's Rum," it became a collector's item. While I was traveling in Europe with my thirteen-year-old niece, Michele, a friend in Giessen, West Germany, Lieutenant Colonel Bill Haynes, presented me with a bottle. It now rests in a Javanese treasure box in my home in the Oakland hills overlooking San Francisco Bay.

Riding the waves of Pacific victory, the *Jeremiah O'Brien* finished the war afloat. On her last wartime voyage home she carried Australian war brides to the United States. GIs had scored again! In February 1946, excess to the needs of the day, she joined hundreds of her sister ships mothballed in a reserve fleet near San Francisco. In 1978, the National Liberty Ship Memorial, Inc., a California nonprofit corporation, decided to restore an original, unaltered Liberty ship. They chose the *O'Brien,* which they restored in 1979.

With much fanfare the *O'Brien* departed the safety of San Francisco Bay in 1994, steamed down the coast of Central America, through the Panama Canal and the Caribbean, and into the North Atlantic. Racing the clock to arrive in time, she, the only survivor of the five thousand ships that fought in the Normandy assault, went back for the fiftieth anniversary of D-Day. The *O'Brien* made it with time to spare, arriving in Portsmouth harbor by June 5, 1994, in time to rendezvous with other ships and cross to Normandy the next day. After the trip over to Normandy and with festivities completed, the *O'Brien* returned to its home anchorage in San Francisco Bay, within view of the Oakland hills.

Our robust trio of North American subjects—soldier, ship, and spirits—had met a quintet of nature's forces—sky, sand, snow, sea, and shore—under wartime conditions. They survived to tell their own tales, augmentation to the larger story of twentieth-century warfare.

As for the aftermath, at Germany's expense the allies compensated Poland for land it lost to the Soviet Union, divided what remained of German territory into four occupation zones, brought to trial war criminals, executed some, and began a period of denazification. And the North Atlantic people in general? Politically, democracy regained its place on Europe's western tip and began making inroads for social and economic democracy there and around the Atlantic basin in general. Dislodged from the role of colonial masters, the war-torn western European economies experienced a release of energy that led to a dramatic recovery. Unfortunately, the North Atlantic people had only two years of jittery peace before strife began again, the long-lasting Cold War, round three of this century's political war. But that is another story.

Suggested Readings

Adams, Michael C.C. *The Best War Ever: America and World War II* (Baltimore: John Hopkins University Press, 1994).

Adamthwaite, Anthony P. *The Making of the Second World War* (London: Allen & Unwin, 1977).

Albrecht, Donald, ed. *World War II & How Wartime Building Changed a Nation* (Cambridge, MA: MIT Press, 1995).

Allanbrook, Douglas. *See Naples* (Boston: Houghton Mifflin, 1995).

Ambrose, Stephen E. *Band of Brothers: E Company, 506th Regiment, 101 Airborne— From Normandy to Hitler's Eagle's Nest* (New York: Touchstone, 1992).

Anderson, Karen. *Wartime Women: Sex Roles, Family Relations, and The Status of Women During World War II* (Westport, CT: Greenwood Press, 1981).

Baer, George W. *One Hundred Years of Sea Power: The U.S. Navy, 1890–1990* (Stanford, CA: Stanford University Press, 1994).

Barnett, Correlli, ed. *Hitler's Generals* (London: Weidenfeld & Nicolson, 1989).

Barraclough, Geoffrey. *The Origins of Modern Germany* (Oxford: Blackwell, 1976).

Bartov, Omer. *Hitler's Army* (New York: Oxford University Press, 1991).

Beauvoir, Simone de, ed. *Quiet Moments in a War: The Letters of Jean-Paul Sartre to Simone de Beauvoir 1940–1963* (New York: Charles Scribner's Sons, 1993).

Beeby, Dean. *Cargo of Lies: The True Story of a Nazi Double Agent in Canada* (Toronto: University of Toronto Press, 1996).

Bekker, Cajus. *Luftwaffe War Diaries: The German Air Force in WW II* (Garden City, NY: Doubleday, 1968).

Bendiner, Elmer. *The Fall of Fortresses* (New York: Dorset Press, 1980).

Bergreen, Laurence. *As Thousands Cheer: The Life of Irving Berlin* (New York: Viking, 1990).

Berube, Allan. *Coming Out Under Fire: The History of Gay Men and Women in WW II* (New York: Free Press, 1990).

Biddle, Wayne. *Barons of the Sky* (New York: Simon & Schuster, 1991).

Blair, Clay. *Hitler's U-Boat War: The Hunters, 1939–1942* (New York: Random House, 1996).

Bland, Larry, and Sharon Stevens. *The Papers of George C. Marshall: The Right Man for the Job,* vol. III (Baltimore: Johns Hopkins University Press, 1981).

Blum, John Morton. *V Was for Victory: Politics and American Culture During World War II* (New York: Harcourt, Brace, Jovanovich, 1976).

Bogart, Stephen Humphrey. *Bogart: In Search of My Father* (New York: Dutton, 1995).

Boritt, Gabor, ed. *War Comes Again: Comparative Vistas on the Civil War and World War II* (New York: Oxford University Press, 1995).

Bournazel, Renata. *Rapallo: Ein Franzosisches Trauma* (Colonge: Markus, 1976).

Boyd, Carl. *The Extraordinary Envoy: General Hiroshi Oshima and Diplomacy in the Third Reich, 1934–39* (Washington, DC: University Press of America, 1980).

Bracher, Karl Dietrich. *Turning Points in Modern History: Essays on German and European History* (Cambridge, MA: Harvard University Press, 1995).

Brodie, Howard. *Drawing Fire: A Combat Artist at War* (Mountain View, CA: Portola Press, 1996).

Brooks, Thomas R. *The War North of Rome: June 1944–May 1996* (New York: Sarpedon, 1996).

Buderi, Robert. *The Invention That Changed the World: How a Small Group of Radar Pioneers Won the Second World War* (New York: Simon & Schuster, 1996).

Bullock, Alan. *Hitler: A Study in Tyranny* (New York: Harper & Row, 1962).

———. *Hitler and Stalin: Parallel Lives* (London: HarperCollins, 1991).

Bunker, John. *Heroes in Dungarees: The Story of the American Merchant Marine in WW II* (Annapolis, MD: Naval Institute Press, 1995).

Butterfield, Herbert. *Christianity, Diplomacy and War* (New York: Abington-Cokesbury, 1953).

Caldwell, Donald L. *JG26: Top Guns of the Luftwaffe* (New York: Ivy Books, 1991).

Campbell, D'Ann. *Women at War with America: Private Lives in a Patriotic Era* (Cambridge, MA: Harvard University Press, 1984).

Carnes, Mark C., ed. *Past Imperfect: History According to the Movies* (New York: Holt, 1995).

Chambers, John W., and David Culbert, eds. *World War II, Film, and History* (New York: Oxford University Press, 1996).

Childers, Thomas. *Wings of Morning: The Story of the Last American Shot Down Over Germany in World War II* (Reading, MA: Addison-Wesley, 1994).

Chuikov, Vasilii I. *The Battle of Stalingrad* (New York: Holt, Rinehart and Winston, 1964).

Cloud, Stanley, and Lynne Olson. *The Murrow Boys: Pioneers on the Front Line of Broadcast Journalism* (Boston: Houghton Mifflin, 1996).

Coleman, Penny. *Rosie the Riveter: Women Working on the Home Front in WW II* (New York: Crown Books, 1995).

Conquest, Robert. *Harvest of Sorrow: Soviet Collectivization and the Terror-Famine* (New York: Oxford University Press, 1986).

Cowdrey, Albert E. *Fighting for Life: American Military Medicine in WW II* (New York: Free Press, 1994).

Craig, Gordon A. *The Politics of the Prussian Army: 1640–1945* (New York: Oxford University Press, 1955).

Creveld, Martin Van. *Supplying War: Logistics from Wallenstein to Patton* (London: Cambridge University Press, 1977).

Crimp, R.L. *Diary of a Desert Rat* (London: Cooper, 1971).

Crook, D.M. *Fighter Pilot* (London: Cooper, 1941).

Cull, Nicholas John. *Selling War: The British Propaganda Campaign Against American Neutrality in WW II* (New York: Oxford University Press, 1995).

Davidson, Eugene. *The Unmaking of Adolf Hitler* (Columbia, MO: University of Missouri Press, 1996).

de Gaulle, Charles. *The War Memoirs of Charles de Gaulle: The Call to Honor; the Call for Unity; the Call for Salvation* (London: Collins, 1955, three volumes).

Dear, I.C.B., and M.R.D. Foot. *The Oxford Companion to World War II* (New York: Oxford University Press, 1995).

D'Este, Carlo. *Decision in Normandy* (New York: Dutton, 1983).

———. *Patton: A Genius for War* (New York: HarperCollins, 1995).

Detwiler, Donald, ed. *World War II German Military Studies,* 24 vols. (New York: Garland, 1979).

Djakov, Yuri, and Tatyana Bushuyevor. *The Red Army and the Wehrmacht* (Amherst, NY: Prometheus Books, 1994).

Doherty, Thomas. *Projections of War: Hollywood, American Culture, and World War II* (New York: Columbia University Press, 1993).

Donitz, Karl. *Memoirs: Ten Years and Twenty Days* (Cleveland: World Publishing Company, 1959).

Douglas, Keith. *Alamein to Zem Zem* (London: Faber, 1966).

Drez, Ronald J., ed. *Voices of D-Day* (Baton Rouge, LA: University of Louisiana Press, 1994).

Earle, Edward Mead. *Makers of Modern Strategy* (Princeton: Princeton University Press, 1941).

Edmonds, Robin. *The Big Three: Churchill, Roosevelt, and Stalin in Peace and War* (New York: Viking Penguin, 1991).

Eisenhower, Dwight D. *Crusade in Europe* (Garden City, NY: Doubleday, 1948).

Erenberg, Lewis, and Susan Hirsch, eds. *The War in American Culture: Society and Consciousness During WW II* (Chicago: University of Chicago Press, 1996).

Erickson, John. *The Road to Stalingrad* (New York: Harper & Row, 1975).

———. *The Road to Berlin* (Boulder, CO: Westview Press, 1983).

Feldman, Gerald D. *The Great Disorder: Politics, Economics, and Society in the German Inflation, 1914–1924* (New York: Oxford University Press, 1993).

Fermi, Laura. *Mussolini* (Chicago: University of Chicago Press, 1961).

Fest, Joachim C. *Hitler* (New York: Harcourt, Brace, Jovanovich, 1974).

Fraser, David. *Knight's Cross: A Life of Field Marshal Rommel* (New York: HarperCollins, 1993).

Friedrich, Otto. *Blood and Iron: From Bismark to Hitler, the Von Moltke's Family History Impact on German History* (New York: HarperCollins, 1995).

Fussell, Paul. *Wartime: Understanding and Behaviour in the Second World War* (New York: Oxford University Press, 1989).

Gannon, Michael. *Operation Drumbeat: The Dramatic True Story of Germany's First U-Boat Attacks Along the American Coast in WW II* (New York: HarperCollins, 1995).

Gardiner, Juliet. *Overpaid, Oversexed, and Over Here: The American GI in WW II Britain* (New York: Abbeville Press, 1995).

Gavin, James M. *On to Berlin: Battles of an Airborne Commander, 1943–1946* (New York: Viking, 1978).

Gehlen, Reinhard. *The Service: The Memoirs of General Reinhard Gehlen* (New York: World Publishing, 1972).

Gerschenkron, Alexander. *Bread and Democracy in Germany* (Berkeley: University of California Press, 1943).

Gilbert, Martin. *Churchill: A Life* (New York: Holt, 1991).

––––––. *The Second World War: A Complete History* (New York: Holt, 1994).

––––––. *The Day the War Ended: May 8, 1945—Victory in Europe* (New York: H. Holt, 1995).

Glantz, David M., and Jonathan M. House. *When Titans Clashed: How the Red Army Stopped Hitler* (Lawrence, KS: University Press of Kansas, 1995).

Gleason, Ian. *The Unknown Force: Black, Indian and Colored Soldiers Through Two World Wars* (Rivonia: Ashanti, 1994).

Goerlitz, Walter. *History of the German General Staff* (New York: Praeger, 1953).

Goodwin, Doris Kearns. *No Ordinary Time: Franklin and Eleanor Roosevelt— The Home Front in WW II* (New York: Simon & Schuster, 1994).

Gretton, Peter. *Convoy Escort Commander* (London: Cassell, 1964).

Grossman, Vasily. *Life and Fate: A Novel* (New York: Harper & Row, 1980).

Guderian, Heinz. *Panzer Leader* (New York: Dutton, 1952).

––––––. *Mit den Panzern in Ost und West* (Berlin: Volk und Reich, 1942).

Harlan, Louis R. *All at Sea: Coming of Age in WW II* (Champaign, IL: University of Illinois Press, 1996).

Hartmann, Ursula, and Manfred Jager. *German Fighter Ace Erich Hartmann: The Life Story of the World's Highest Scoring Fighter Ace* (Atglen. PA: Schiffer, 1992).

Haslam, Jonathan. *The Soviet Union and the Struggle for Collective Security in Europe, 1933–39* (New York: St. Martin's Press, 1984).

Hastings, Max. *Das Reich: Resistance and the March of the 2nd SS Panzer Division Through France* (London: M. Joseph, 1981).

––––––. *Bomber Command* (London: M. Joseph, 1987).

Hatcher, Patrick L. "On the Beach: Rommel's Rum," *California Monthly,* September 1994, 14–15.

Hawkins, Ira L., ed. *B-17s Over Berlin: Personal Stories from the 95th Bomber Group (H)* (Washington, DC: Brasseys, 1990).

Hays, Otis, Jr. *Home from Siberia: The Secret Odysseys of Interned American Airmen in WW II* (College Station, TX: Texas A&M University Press, 1991).

––––––. *The Alaska-Siberia Connection: The World War II Air Route* (College Station, TX: Texas A&M University Press, 1996).

Heckmann, Wolf. *Rommel's War in Africa* (Garden City, NY: Doubleday, 1981).

Heide, Robert, and John Gilman. *Home Front* (San Francisco: Chronicle Books, 1995).

Heldeking, Jurgen, and Christol Mauch, eds. *American Intelligence and the German Resistance to Hitler: A Documentary History* (Boulder, CO: Westview Press, 1996).

High Command of the Navy. *U-Boat Commander's Handbook (Geheim)* (Gettysburg, PA: Thomas Publications, 1989).

Hildebrand, Klaus. *The Foreign Policy of the Third Reich* (Berkeley: University of California Press, 1973).

Hillgruber, Andreas. *Germany and the Two World Wars* (Cambridge, MA: Harvard University Press, 1981).

Hodges, Andrew. *Alan Turning: The Enigma* (New York: Simon and Schuster, 1983).

Hodgson, Marion Stegman. *Winning My Wings: A Woman Airforce Service Pilot in WW II* (Annapolis, MD: Naval Institute Press, 1996).

Hoffmann, Peter. *Stauffenberg: A Family History, 1905–1944* (New York: Cambridge University Press, 1995).

Holborn, Hajo. *A History of Modern Germany: 1840–1945* (Princeton: Princeton University Press, 1969).

Holloway, David. *Stalin and the Bomb: The Soviet Union and Atomic Energy, 1939–1956* (New Haven, CT: Yale University Press, 1994).

Holmes, Blair, and Alan Keele, eds. *When Truth Was Treason: German Youth Against Hitler* (Champaign, IL: University of Illinois Press, 1995).

Horne, Alister, and David Montgomery. *Monty, The Lonely Leader, 1944–1945: A Biography of Field Marshal Bernard Law Montgomery* (New York: Pan Books, 1994).

Horowitz, Roger. "Oral History and the Story of America in WW II," *Journal of American History,* September 1995, 616–39.

Hough, Richard, and Dennis Richards. *The Battle of Britain: The Greatest Air Battle of WW II* (New York: Norton, 1989).

Howard, Michael. *War and the Liberal Conscience* (New Brunswick, NJ: Rutgers University Press, 1978).

———. *Strategic Deception in WW II* (New York: Norton, 1995).

Howe, George F. *U.S. Army in WW II: Mediterranean Theater of Operations* (Washington, DC: Government Printing Office, 1957).

Hughes, Thomas. *Overlord: Pete Quesada and the Triumph of Tactical Air Power in WW II* (New York: Free Press, 1995).

Huston, James A. *The Sinews of War: Army Logistics 1775–1953* (Washington, DC: Government Printing Office, 1966).

Hyland, William G. *The Song Is Ended: Songwriters and American Music, 1900–1950* (New York: Oxford University Press, 1995).

Institute of Marxism-Leninism. *Great Patriotic War of the Soviet Union* (Moscow: Progress, 1974).

Ippisch, Hanneke. *Sky: A True Story of Resistance During WW II* (New York: Simon & Schuster, 1996).

Jahn, Hubertus F. *Patriotic Culture in Russia During World War I* (Ithaca, NY: Cornell University Press, 1995).

Janeway, Eliot. *The Struggle for Survival: A Chronicle of Economic Mobilization in WW II* (New Haven, CT: Yale University Press, 1951).

Jarvie, Ian. *Hollywood's Overseas Campaign: The North Atlantic Movie Trade, 1920–1950* (New York: Cambridge University Press, 1992).

Johnson, James E. *Full Circle: The Story of Air Fighting* (London: Chatto & Windus, 1964).

Junket, Detlef. *Kampf um die Weltmacht: Die USA und das Dritte Reich, 1933–1945* (Düsseldorf: Droste, 1988).

Kaes, Anton, Martin, Jay, and Edward Dimendberg, eds. *The Weimar Republic Source Book* (Berkeley: University of California Press, 1994).

Kagan, Donald. *On the Origins of War and the Preservation of Peace* (New York: Anchor, 1994).

Keegan, John. *The Mask of Command* (New York: Penguin, 1987).

———. *The Second World War* (New York: Penguin, 1989).

———. *Churchill's Generals* (New York: Grove Weidenfeld, 1991).

———. *Battle for History: Re-fighting WW II* (New York: Vintage, 1996).

Kelshall, Gaylord T.M. *The U-Boat War in the Caribbean* (Annapolis, MD: Naval Institute Press, 1988).

Kemp, Peter. *Decision at Sea: The Convoy Escorts* (London: Dent, 1978).

Knappe, Siegfried, and Ted Brusaw. *Soldat: Reflections of a German Soldier, 1936–1949* (New York: Bantam, 1992).

Koppes, Clayton, and Gregory Black. *Hollywood Goes to War: How Politics, Profits and Propaganda Shaped World War II Movies* (Berkeley: University of California Press, 1990).

Kracauer, Siegfried. *The Mass Ornament: Weimar Essays* (Cambridge, MA: Harvard University Press, 1995).

Kreimeier, Klaus. *The UFA Story: A History of Germany's Greatest Film Company, 1918–1945* (New York: Hill & Wang, 1996).

Krull, Kathleen. *V Is for Victory: America Remembers World War II* (New York: Random House, 1995).

Kuhl, George C. *Wrong Place! Wrong Time! The 305 Bomber Group and the 2nd Schweinfurt Raid, October 14, 1943* (Atglen, PA: Schiffer, 1993).

Kurowski, Franz. *German Fighter Ace Hans-Joachim Marseille: The Life Story of the Star of Africa* (Atglen, PA: Schiffer, 1994).

Lamb, Hubert H. *Climate, History and the Modern World* (New York: Routledge, 1995).

———. K.S. Douglas and C. Loader. *A Meteorological Study of July to October 1588: The Spanish Armada Storms* (Norwich, UK: University of East Anglia, 1978).

———, and Fred Frydendahl. *Historic Storms of the North Sea, British Isles, and Northwest Europe* (New York: Cambridge University Press, 1991).

Lane, Frederic. *Ships for Victory: A History of Shipbuilding Under the U.S. Maritime Commission to World War II* (Baltimore: Johns Hopkins University Press, 1951).

Laurie, Clayton D. *The Propaganda Warriors: America's Crusade Against Nazi Germany* (Lawrence, KS: Kansas State University Press, 1996).

Leonov, Viktor. *Blood on the Shores: Soviet Seals in WW II* (Annapolis, MD: Naval Institute Press, 1993).

Lewin, Ronald. *Ultra Goes to War* (New York: McGraw-Hill, 1978).

Lewis, Norman, *Naples '44: An Intelligence Officer in the Italian Labyrinth* (New York: Pantheon, 1978).

Library of America. *Reporting World War II: 1938–1944* (New York: Library of America, 1995).

————. *Reporting World War II: 1944–1946* (New York: Library of America, 1995).

Lih, Lars, Oleg Naumov, and Oleg Khlevniuk, eds. *Stalin's Letters to Molotov, 1925–1936* (New Haven: Yale University Press, 1995).

Lindsay, Franklin. *Beacons in the Night: With the OSS and Tito's Partisans in Wartime Yugoslavia* (Stanford: Stanford University Press, 1993).

Lipfert, Helmut, and Werner Gerlig. *The War Diary of Hauptmann Helmut Lipfert: JG52 on the Russian Front 1943–1945* (Atglen, PA: Schiffer, 1993).

Masefield, John. *The Nine Day Wonder: Operation Dynamo (Dunkirk)* (London: W. Heinemann, 1941).

McDougall, Walter A. *France's Rhineland Diplomacy 1914–1924: The Last Bid for a Balance of Power in Europe* (Princeton: Princeton University Press, 1978).

————. *Promised Land, Crusader State: America's Encounter with the World Since 1776* (Boston: Houghton Mifflin, 1997).

McGuire, Phillip. *He, Too, Spoke for Democracy: Judge Hastie, WW II, and the Black Soldier* (New York: Greenwood Press, 1988).

————. *Taps for a Jim Crow Army: Letters from Black Soldiers in WW II* (Santa Barbara: ABC-Clio, 1983).

McNeill, William H. *The Pursuit of Power: Technology, Armed Force, and Society* (Chicago: University of Chicago Press, 1982).

————. *Europe's Steppe Frontier, 1500–1800: A Study of the Eastward Movement in Europe* (Chicago: University of Chicago Press, 1964).

Mellenthin, F.W. von. *Panzer Battles* (Norman, OK: University of Oklahoma Press, 1956).

Merkel, Peter H. *Political Violence Under the Swastika: 581 Early Nazis* (Princeton: Princeton University Press, 1975).

————. *The Making of a Stormtropper* (Princeton: Princeton University Press, 1980).

Middlebrook, Martin. *The Battle of Hamburg: Allied Bomber Forces Against a German City in 1943* (New York: Scribner, 1981).

Miller, Nathan. *War at Sea: A Naval History of WW II* (New York: Scribner, 1995).

Mommsen, Hans. *From Weimar to Auschwitz: Essays in German History* (Princeton: Princeton University Press, 1991).

Morison, Samuel Eliot. *The Two-Ocean War: A Short History of the US Navy in the Second World War* (Boston: Little, Brown, 1963).

Mullenheim-Rechberg, Burkard Baron von. *Battleship Bismark: A Survivor's Story* (Annapolis, MD: Naval Institute Press, 1990).

Neillands, Robin. *The Conquest of the Third Reich: D-Day to VE Day—A Soldier's History* (New York: New York University Press, 1994).

Nesaule, Agate. *A Woman in Amber: Healing the Trauma of War and Exile* (New York: Soho Press, 1995).

Neufeld, Michael J. *The Rocket and the Reich: Peenemunde and the Coming of the Ballistic Missile Era* (New York: Free Press, 1995).

Newton, Steven H. *Retreat from Leningrad: Army Group North, 1944–1945* (Atglen, PA: Schiffer, 1995).

Nolte, Carl, and Michael Emery. *From Dry Dock to D-Day: The Return Voyage of the SS Jeremiah O'Brien* (San Francisco: Chronicle Books, 1995).

O'Neill, William L. *A Democracy at War: America's Fight at Home and Abroad in World War II* (Cambridge, MA: Harvard University Press, 1995).

Overy, R.J. *War and Economy in the Third Reich* (New York: Oxford University Press, 1994).

Padfield, Peter. *Donitz, The Last Fuhrer* (London: Gollancz, 1984).

Payne, Stanley G. *A History of Fascism, 1914–45* (Madison: University of Wisconsin Press, 1995).

Petersen, Neal H, ed. *From Hitler's Doorstep: The Wartime Intelligence Reports of Allen Dulles, 1942–1945* (University Park, PA: Pennsylvania State University Press, 1996).

Phillips, C.E. Lucas. *The Greatest Raid of All* (Boston: Little, Brown, 1960).

Plievier, Theodor. *Stalingrad* (Vienna: Globus, 1946).

Poolman, Kenneth. *Allied Escort Carriers of WW II* (Annapolis, MD: Naval Institute Press, 1988).

Porch, Douglas. *The Conquest of the Sahara* (New York: Knopf, 1984).

Prien, Gunther, *Mein Weg Nach Scapa Flow* (Berlin: Im Deutschen, 1940).

Raach, R.C. *Stalin's Drive to the West, 1938–1945* (Stanford: Stanford University Press, 1995).

Raeder, Erich. *My Life* (Annapolis, MD: Naval Institute Press, 1960).

———. *Struggle for the Sea* (London: W. Kimber, 1959).

Rauss, Erhard, Hans von Griffenberg, and Waldemas Erfurth. *Fighting in Hell: The German Ordeal on the Eastern Front* (London: Stackpole, 1995).

Ray, John. *The Battle of Britain: New Perspectives* (London: Arms & Armour, 1994).

Reinhardt, Klaus. *Moscow: The Turning Point—The Failure of Hitler's Strategy in the Winter of 1941–42* (Oxford: Providence, 1992).

Rentschler, Eric. *The Ministry of Illusion: Nazi Cinema and Its Afterlife* (Cambridge, MA: Harvard University Press, 1996).

Reynolds, Michael. *The Devil's Adjutant: Jochen Peiper, Panzer Leader* (New York: Sarpedon, 1995).

Ritter, Gerhard. *The Sword and the Scepter: The Problem of Militarism in Germany,* Vol. 4 (Coral Gables, FL: University of Miami Press, 1973).

Roberts, Andrew. *Eminent Churchillians* (New York: Simon & Schuster, 1995).

Roeder, George H. *The Censored War: American Visual Experience During World War II* (New Haven, CT: Yale University Press, 1993).

Rohwer, Jurgen. *Axis Submarine Successes, 1939–1945* (Annapolis, MD: Naval Institute Press, 1983).

Rolin, Ron. *The Barbed-Wire College: Reeducating German POWS in the U.S. During WW II* (Princeton: Princeton University Press, 1995).

Rommel, Erwin. *Attacks* (Vienna, VA: Athena Press, 1979).

Rooney, Andy. *My War* (New York: Random House, 1995).

———. *Air Gunner* (New York: Farrar & Rinehart, 1944).

Ross, Alan. *Blindfold Games* (London: Collins Harvill, 1986).

Sajer, Guy. *The Forgotten Soldier* (New York: Harper & Row, 1971).

Sanders, Jacquin. *The Night Before Christmas* (New York: Putnam's & Sons, 1963).

Schaeffer, Heinz. *U-Boat 977* (London: William Kimber, 1953).

Schofield, Brian B. *The Russian Convoys* (London: B.T. Batsford, 1964).

Schulte-Sasse, Linda. *Entertaining the Third Reich: Illusion of Wholeness in Nazi Cinema* (Durham, NC: Duke University Press, 1996).

Seabury, Paul. *The Wilhelmstrasse: A Study of German Diplomats Under the Nazi Regime* (Berkeley: University of California Press, 1954).

Sereny, Gitta. *Albert Speer: His Battle with Truth* (New York: Knopf, 1995).

Seth, Ronald. *The Fiercest Battle* (London: Hutchinson, 1961).

Shtemenko, S.M. *The Soviet General Staff at War, 1941–1945* (Moscow: Progress, 1970).

Simpson, Gary L. *Tiger Ace: The Life of Panzer Commander Michael Wittmann* (Atglen, PA: Schiffer, 1994).

Skorzeny, Otto. *My Commando Operations: The Memoirs of Hitler's Most Daring Commando* (Atglen, PA: Schiffer, 1995).

Smith, Kevin. *Conflict over Convoys: Anglo-American Logistics Diplomacy in the Second World War* (New York: Cambridge University Press, 1996).

Solak, Boleslaw Jan. *Joga Stonca: Wspomnienia Pilota I Podroznika* (Warsaw: Pruszkow, 1994).

Soviet War Correspondents. *Sevastopol: November 1941–July 1942* (London: Hutchinson, 1943).

Spahr, William J. *Zhukov: The Rise and Fall of a Great Captain* (Novato, CA: Presidio Press, 1993).

Speier, Hans. *German White-Collar Workers and the Rise of Hitler* (New Haven, CT: Yale University Press, 1986).

Spender, Stephen. *Letters to Christopher: Spender's Letters to Isherwood, 1929–1939,* ed. Lee Bartlett (Santa Barabara, CA: Black Sparrow Press, 1980).

Standley, William H., and Arthua A. Ageton. *Admiral Ambassador to Russia* (Chicago: H. Regnery, 1955).

Stenbuck, Jack, ed. *Typewriter Battalion: Dramatic Frontline Dispatches from WW II* (New York: William Morrow, 1995).

Stites, Richard, ed. *Culture and Entertainment in Wartime Russia* (Bloomington, IN: Indiana University Press, 1994).

Strahan, Jerry E. *Andrew Jackson Higgins and the Boats that Won WW II* (Baton Rouge, LA: University of Louisiana Press, 1994).

Studnitz, Hans-Georg von. *While Berlin Burns: The Diary of Hans-Georg von Studnitz* (London: Weindenfeld & Nicolson, 1964).

Syrett, David. *The Defeat of the German U-Boats: The Battle of the Atlantic* (Columbia, SC: University of South Carolina Press, 1994).

Taylor, A.J.P. *The Origins of the Second World War* (New York: Atheneum, 1962).

Thompson, Robert Smith. *Pledge to Destiny: Charles de Gaulle and the Rise of the Free French* (New York: McGraw-Hill, 1974).

Tournier, Michel. *The Wind Spirit: An Autobiography* (Boston: Beacon Press, 1988).

———. *The Ogre* (Baltimore: John Hopkins University Press, 1996).

Trachtenberg, Marc. *Reparation in World Politics: France and European Economic Diplomacy, 1916–1923* (New York: Columbia University Press, 1980).

Trevor-Roper, H.R. *The Last Days of Hitler* (New York: Macmillan, 1947).

———. *Hitler's War Directives* (London: Sidgwick & Jackson, 1964).

Tutle, William M. Jr., *Daddy's Gone to War: The Second World War in the Lives of America's Children* (New York: Oxford University Press, 1993).

U.S. War Department, *Handbook on German Military Forces* (Baton Rouge, LA: University of Louisiana Press, 1990).

Vaculik, Serge. *Air Commando* (New York: Dutton, 1954).

Vatter, Harold G. *The U.S. Economy in WW II* (New York: Columbia University Press, 1985).

Verges, Marianne. *On Silver Wings: The Women Airforce Service Pilots of WW II* (New York: Random House, 1991).

Virden, Jenel. *Good-Bye, Piccadilly: British War Brides in America* (Champaign, IL: University of Illinois Press, 1996).

Voinovich, Vladimir. *The Life and Extraordinary Adventures of Private Ivan Chonkin* (New York: Farrar, Straus & Giroux, 1977).

Volkogonov, Dmitri. *Stalin: Triumph and Tragedy* (New York: Grove Weidenfeld, 1991).

Voyetekhov, Boris. *The Last Days of Sevastopol* (New York: Knopf, 1943).

Warlimont, Walter. *Inside Hitler's Headquarters* (London: Weidenfeld & Nicolson, 1964).

Waters, John M., Jr. *Bloody Winter* (Annapolis, MD: Naval Institute Press, 1984).

Watson, Lyall. *Heaven's Breath: A Natural History of the Wind* (New York: Morrow, 1984).

Watt, Donald Cameron. *How War Came: The Immediate Origin of the Second World War, 1938–1939* (New York: Pantheon, 1989).

Webster, David K. *Parachute Infantry: An American Paratrooper's Memoirs of D-Day and the Fall of the Third Reich* (Baton Rouge, LA: University of Louisiana Press, 1994).

Weinberg, Gerhard L. *A World at Arms: A Global History of World War II* (New York: Cambridge University Press, 1994).

———. *Germany, Hitler, and World War II* (New York: Cambridge University Press, 1995).

Welchman, Gordon. *The Hut Six Story: Breaking the Enigma Codes* (New York: McGraw-Hill, 1982).

Wharton, Edith. *In Morocco* (Hopewell, NJ: Ecco Press, 1919).

Wieder, Joachim and Heinrilch Graf Von Einsiedel. *Stalingrad: Memories and Reassessments* (London: Arms & Armour, 1993).

Williams, Charles. *The Last Great Frenchman: A Life of General de Gaulle* (London: Little, Brown, 1993).

Willoughby, Malcolm F. *Rum War at Sea* (Washington, DC: Government Printing Office, 1964).

Wilt, Alan F. *War from the Top: German and British Military Decision Making During WW II* (Bloomington, IN: Indiana University Press, 1990).

Winston, Keith. *V-Mail: Letters of a WW II Combat Medic* (Chapel Hill, NC: University of North Carolina Press, 1985).

Winter, Jay. *The Experience of World War I* (New York: Oxford University Press, 1989).

————. *Sites of Memory, Sites of Mourning: The Great War in European Cultural History* (New York: Cambridge University Press, 1995).

Wollenberg, Charles. *Marinship at War: Shipbuilding and Social Change in Wartime Sausalito* (Berkeley: Western Heritage Press, 1990).

Wright, Gordon. *The Ordeal of Total War: 1939–1945* (New York: Harper & Row, 1968).

Zhukov, Georgi K. *Marshal Zhukov's Greatest Battles* (New York: Harper & Row, 1969).

————. *The Memoirs of Marshal Zhukov* (London: Cape, 1971).

Ziemke, Earl F. *Stalingrad to Berlin: The German Defeat in the East* (Washington, DC: Office of the Chief of Military History, 1968).

Index

Patrick Lloyd Hatcher is a native-born Virginian. Coming from a military family, he spent the first three years of his life on the island of Corregidor in the Philippines. He graduated from Thomas Jefferson's alma mater in colonial Williamsburg, the College of William and Mary, crossed the Mississippi (which Jefferson bought) and settled in California. He earned a Master's degree in American History at the University of Missouri and a Ph.D. in Business and Economic History from the University of California, Berkeley. Dr. Hatcher has taught at various colleges in the Bay Area and in 1988 was elected University of California, Berkeley Instructor of the Year.

When not teaching, Dr. Hatcher resides in northern California near the Russian River, not far from where Russian fur traders used to bargain. Among other activities, he has been a commentator on Channel 4 News (KRON), the San Francisco NBC affiliate. An avid traveler, Dr. Hatcher has led numerous tours abroad. He is the author of two previous books, *The Suicide of an Elite: American Internationalists and Vietnam* (Stanford, 1988) and *Economic Earthquakes: Converting Defense Cuts to Economic Opportunities* (Berkeley, 1994).